Praise for
The Giving Way to Happiness

"With expertise, passion, and captivating real-life stories that keep you at the edge of your seat, Jenny Santi reminds us of the life-changing power of giving—it is essential to our well-being as individuals, families, and communities. *The Giving Way to Happiness* is an important book for people of every generation who want to be fully alive in the world."

—TARA STILES,
FOUNDER AND CEO OF STRALA YOGA

"This is an inspirational book, which addresses both philosophical and practical questions. Santi's perceptive account is uplifting and insightful. The book is packed with heartwarming stories, fascinating research, personal revelations, useful tips, and timely advice. *The Giving Way to Happiness* explores the very real connection between helping others and helping ourselves."

—ILIAN MIHOV,
DEAN, INSEAD

"An enlightening read, filled with open, honest glimpses into the lives of inspirational personalities from different walks of life . . . This book is a friendly, approachable yet sharply written, narrative packed with ideas you'll want to immediately start applying to your life."

—MALVINDER MOHAN SINGH,
EXECUTIVE CHAIRMAN OF FORTIS HEALTHCARE LTD.

"*The Giving Way to Happiness* will change the way you approach giving, shifting the focus from charity to empathy, from a one-way transfer to a mutually beneficial act, from guilt and obligation to pleasure and happiness. Jenny Santi, through her well-researched, eloquent, and insightful book, teaches us how we can help ourselves by helping others."

—CARL LIEDERMAN,
FORMER CEO OF ONE YOUNG WORLD,
AND FOUNDER AND CEO OF LIEDERSHIP

"As Jenny Santi so eloquently shows, to give is not just better than to receive; to give *is* to receive. The people in this book are from all walks of life—a dolphin captor who comes to regret his work, the grieving mother of a 9/11 victim, a Bangladeshi economist doubtful that what he's teaching really matters, an entrepreneur struggling with ALS, and many others—but they share a passion for giving that changes them in profound ways. Their stories are a testament to the fact that when we give of ourselves, we not only improve the lives of others, but we find genuine happiness and deeper meaning in our own."

—Brandt Goldstein,
visiting associate professor at New York Law School
and author of *Storming the Court*

"A wonderful book for a new generation of individuals who not only want to make a difference but also want to live exciting, fulfilling, and happy lives. Packed with inspiring stories of people from different walks of life and with lessons directly applicable to your own. Just pick it up and you'll be hooked!"

—Katherine Lorenz,
president of the Cynthia and George Mitchell Foundation

"Given the growing inequity on our planet, what is the solution? Santi shows us that a culture of giving can change the world around us while fulfilling each of our lives at the deepest level. Impressive, inspiring, and full of wisdom!"

—Shiv Khemka,
vice chairman of SUN Group

"Jenny Santi has succeeded in crafting a compelling blend of moving stories, powerful insights, and practical advice on how each of us can find 'the giving way to happiness.' This book demonstrates that each of us can feel the impact and spiritual rewards of giving if we choose to make the journey. Her efforts and personal experiences will be an inspiration to many."

—Alex Charlton,
president of Cavendish Global

"Authentic, candid, and insightful, *The Giving Way to Happiness* masterfully interweaves touching and often surprising stories into the analysis of how people live lives full of meaning, purpose, and happiness. This is an important book that sends a wonderful message that is so simple at its core but that is unfortunately too often overlooked—that the act of giving creates a multiplier effect, adding something to the life of those in need but also intrinsically rewarding the giver too, making him or her happier as well. Altruistic or not—the effect is positive. Santi's book is filled with lessons you'll want to immediately start applying to your life."

—Boris FJ Collardi,
CEO of Julius Baer

"This book presents a groundbreaking new perspective on happiness. Through her exciting career as a philanthropy advisor to some of the world's most generous individuals, Jenny Santi offers us a view into the principles that have made them not only successful but truly happy."

—Jayesh Parekh,
cofounder of Sony Entertainment Television
and managing partner of Jungle Ventures

"In a very readable and compelling way, Jenny Santi weaves together science and strategy that will inspire anyone who is looking to build more strategic purpose into philanthropy, gain insights into volunteering, or better understand their purpose. A must-read!"

—John R. Hart,
vice chairman of New York Private Bank & Trust

The
Giving
Way *to*
Happiness

JEREMY P. TARCHER/PENGUIN

an imprint of Penguin Random House

New York

The
Giving
Way *to*
Happiness

❊

Stories and Science Behind
the Life-Changing Power of Giving

JENNY SANTI

JEREMY P. TARCHER/PENGUIN
An imprint of Penguin Random House LLC
375 Hudson Street
New York, New York 10014

Most Tarcher/Penguin books are available at special quantity discounts for bulk
purchase for sales promotions, premiums, fund-raising, and educational needs.
Special books or book excerpts also can be created to fit specific needs. For
details, write: SpecialMarkets@penguinrandomhouse.com.

Library of Congress Cataloging-in-Publication Data

Santi, Jenny.
The giving way to happiness: stories and science behind the life-changing
power of giving / Jenny Santi ; foreword by Deepak Chopra.
pages cm
Includes bibliographical references and index.
ISBN 978-0-399-17549-7 (Hardcover)
978-0-399-18377-5 (Export)
1. Happiness.   2. Generosity.   3. Self-actualization (Psychology)   I. Title.
BF575.H27S3436   2015
179'.9—dc23

Printed in the United States of America
1   3   5   7   9   10   8   6   4   2

Book design by Ellen Cipriano

To Mama

CONTENTS

FOREWORD

Clues to the Mystery of Giving

If you ask people why they give, the readiest answers offer clues to the mystery. God wants me to. I feel better about myself. Others need, and I have. I want to share. It's only right. A hazy halo encircles these good-hearted answers, and if we bring it into focus, the following seems true: Giving takes you out of yourself. You expand beyond your limitations. The founder of CharityFocus, a volunteer-run organization that has delivered millions of dollars of web-related services to the nonprofit world for free, declares that "it's impossible to create a better world without inner change that results from selfless service." Others might argue that inner change precedes selfless service, but no matter. *Selfless* means that you have been taken to a place outside yourself.

The more you give, the more you will receive, because you will keep the abundance of the universe circulating in your life. In fact, anything that is of value in life only multiplies when it is given. That which doesn't multiply through giving is neither worth giving nor worth receiving. If through the act of giving you feel you have lost something, then the gift is not truly given and will not result in increase. If you give grudgingly, there is no energy behind that giving.

When giving results in an experience of love, joy, peace, community, charity, caring, and self-worth, the process of expansion has begun. Some visionaries foresee an economy based entirely on giving. That would be the ideal way to heal the excesses of unfettered capitalism (and many other woes), but the basis for universal giving can only be expansion beyond our present sense of self. Merely turning the tables, expecting to be rewarded for how lavishly you give, won't work. Expansion of the self brings a direct experience of love and joy. You get a glimpse of ecstasy.

The mystery of giving is revealed only when you crave the ecstasy that has been glimpsed. Then a realization hits you with full force: I must give myself away. Without realizing it, you have been trying to do that all your life. In giving yourself away you open a conduit for the kind of happiness that no one can ever steal from you. Someone once said that permanent joy results when you can give away your last penny. Actually, the penny is only a symbol. Permanent happiness results when you no longer have a personal stake in the world.

When you see through the constant needs of I, me, and mine, no more needs will remain, and then every breath is bliss giving itself to bliss. That's the rhythm of life. I'm sure you've felt it. It came over you the last time you truly gave yourself away. Stand there and all the money in the world wouldn't buy a ticket back. You would wish to be there forever.

Deepak Chopra
2014

PREFACE

The Most Satisfying Thing You'll Ever Do
Confessions on What Giving Does to the Giver

Seven years ago, I stumbled into the unusual career of advising extraordinarily wealthy people on their charitable activities. Straight out of business school, I was hired by one of the world's largest private banks to be part of their team of in-house philanthropy advisors, and I relocated from New York City to Singapore. It was a dream job for many, including me. To this day, almost every day, I get random requests from people wanting to hear how I landed a position that they perceive to be about "telling rich people how to give away their money." (The job definitely had aspects of that, but as with any corporate job, it was not nearly as glamorous as people would imagine.)

My job exposed me to an extraordinary world where the clients I met were hundreds of times richer than Madonna. My clients had made enough money—hundreds of millions, even billions—to give in a significant way, often through a formal family foundation or a charitable trust. Week after week, I met with them privately, listening to the stories of what moved them to do what they do, probing deeply to understand their values and motivations so that I could guide them toward the most appropriate and natural course of action.

Reflecting on the stories my clients told me in those meetings over the years, I realize that most of these tales were yet unheard, except by me, because it was my job to listen to them. In those meetings set in skyscraper penthouses, five-star-hotel lobbies, and wood-paneled offices, my clients told me how their own acts of giving were transforming their lives and bringing them fulfillment in a way that was different from—and sometimes greater than—what they got from material wealth. I saw many of them cry, but only happy tears.

Through my work as a philanthropy advisor, I also had a chance to meet and speak privately with so many men and women from the social sector—social entrepreneurs, nonprofit professionals, young students, and volunteers from different walks of life. Not everyone had a lot of money to give away. Many were giving their time, their talents, and a big part of their lives to something that mattered deeply to them, and again I was struck by what I observed. Every time they spoke about their work—regardless of how grim the issues they were addressing, whether it was cancer, global warming, or domestic abuse—they beamed with purpose, and radiated with something that I can only call joy.

Yet outside those private settings, it seems that the world is all too hesitant to embrace the idea that by giving, we indeed receive. We are quick to pass judgment on companies that do good when they reap financial benefits in doing so; we label people as smug when they emerge from a volunteer trip brimming with smiles; we lambast founders of foundations named after themselves. Some generous givers, such as the multi-Grammy-winning singer Michael Bolton, whose namesake charity benefits abused women and children, tell me that they simply do not want to derive any joy from their charitable work. They say it is their duty, and that's it. Just as the philosopher Immanuel Kant considered acts motivated by sympathy as not praiseworthy (because they make the do-gooder feel better), it seems we have convinced ourselves that giving should be a sacrifice, an act of moral responsibility that renders itself null when we derive any joy from it. But why?

And so in public settings, the same people I meet talk about something else, something we have all heard before. In their speeches, media interviews, and public forums, they talk about their beneficiaries: the kids whose lives they have transformed for the better, the patients they have cured, the blind to whom they have given sight, the schools they have rebuilt from rubble.

These days, we are approaching a tipping point in terms of giving—or philanthropy, a word I try to avoid using because it sends images of Bill Gates writing billion-dollar checks to save the world, excluding the rest of us who can't afford to do the same. (In the same way, Christy Turlington Burns told me, "I want to be described as an advocate, an activist, or as a servant of other people, not as a 'philanthropist,' because to me, that word sort of creates a disparity between those who can give versus those who need to be given to; it doesn't feel comfortable to me and yet I know that's just a perception.")

There is a growing body of media articles, books, programs, and conferences that focus on giving, philanthropy, fund-raising, social entrepreneurship, and impact investing. They provide insights on various aspects of doing effective giving, such as how to set up a formal foundation, how to succeed in fund-raising, how to measure the effectiveness of a project, and so forth. But almost nothing out there focuses on the origin of the philanthropic impulse: the heart.

I believe that givers start giving because they are moved by a cause, but they endure because giving brings them happiness and fulfillment. As Bill Clinton said, "When I was president, Make-A-Wish brought forty-seven young people to see me, either in the White House or during my visits to communities where the children lived. Those kids did a lot more for me than I did for them."[1] The work I have done with notable individuals, wealthy donors, and various people from different walks of life over the past seven years has given me a glimpse of this and taught me that there is much more to uncover about the transformative effects of giving upon the self.

Many mystics, historians, and religious figures have alluded to this in the past. Aristotle coined the concept of eudaimonia, a state in which an individual experiences happiness from the successful performance of his or her moral duties.

Winston Churchill said: "We make a living by what we get, but we make a life by what we give."

Or in the simple, beautiful words of an old Chinese proverb: "If you want happiness for an hour, take a nap. If you want happiness for a day, go fishing. If you want happiness for a year, inherit a fortune. If you want happiness for a lifetime, help somebody."

Modern science sheds new light on this phenomenon. More than twenty years ago, Allan Luks brought forward the concept of the "helper's high," resulting from studies showing that groups who had helped through time and/or money experienced a "euphoria" similar to that of those who had completed a physical challenge such as a race. Other sources have proven that giving activates the same brain regions that are activated by cocaine use. I am not suggesting that drug use take the place of donations, but it seems that both activate the ventral striatum region, the pleasure part of the brain; furthermore, at least two of the nonprofit professionals I have met in the course of writing this book have described the thrill they get from their work as similar to getting high on a drug.

A 2008 study by Professor Elizabeth Dunn of the University of British Columbia found that spending money on others promotes happiness more than spending money on oneself. In an experiment, participants were given an envelope containing either five dollars or twenty dollars, which they were asked to spend by the end of the day. Participants who were instructed to spend the money on a gift for someone else or for a charitable donation reported greater happiness than those who were instructed to spend the money on themselves. The study concluded that policy interventions that encourage people to invest income in others rather than in themselves may be worthwhile in the service of translating increased national wealth into increased national happiness.

My own journey is an example. It was no accident that I chose a career in the philanthropy sector. Growing up in Manila, the Philippines, as I was chauffeured to an exclusive school every day, I would look out a car window upon which beggars knocked, asking for food and loose change. It was always in the back of my mind that I had to do something about it, although I did not know how. When I was in business school, I knew I would not be happy with myself if I chose to work in finance, traditional management consulting, or in a consumer goods company coming up with marketing strategies for soap. I craved to do something that made a difference, although

I knew that I was not exactly the type of person who could happily move to Africa and live in a hut.

My twenties were some of the most difficult years in my life. I had a string of bad relationships, including one with a physically abusive man. My mom was diagnosed with cancer, and my parents' thirty-year marriage collapsed and tore my family apart. But through all this, my career, first as a teacher and then as a philanthropy advisor, always kept me happy. As a teacher I woke up every day looking forward to being in the classroom, knowing that I was being of service to my students. When I became a philanthropy advisor, day after day I met with inspiring people working hard to make a difference, and their concern for something bigger than them made me realize that there is more to life than worrying about my own problems. I found strength in them and in their stories.

On one particularly miserable day, in the wake of the painful ending to an important relationship, I decided to do something good for the world instead of the usual day out with girlfriends for retail therapy and the blow-by-blow analysis of what the guy had done wrong. Being an animal lover, I volunteered for a day at Noah's Ark Natural Animal Sanctuary, a haven for seven hundred dogs, three hundred cats, and dozens of reptiles, horses, rabbits, and other creatures who have been abandoned by their owners. What the animals got from me was a few morsels of food and perhaps some affection. But what I got from them was a deep sense of hope, meaning, and strength greater than I had thought possible. And one Christmas Eve, not too long ago in New York City, when I found myself with no set plans for the occasion, I volunteered to feed the homeless at a soup kitchen run by the Church of the Holy Apostles. I look back at that day as one of the most meaningful I've ever had. These experiences reminded me of the times when my mother would spend her birthday in an orphanage, in the company of children who, she said, brought her more joy than any present could.

Every day I see people trying to fill their time with something meaningful—what TV show to watch, what restaurant to indulge in, which mall to spend the whole day in. I see young people trying to find some pastime to entertain them, and old people worried about what to do during their retirement. And yet countless people have, since the dawn of history, alluded to a completely different pathway to happiness, fulfilment, and meaning in life. There is something else out there. We hear throughout history, philosophy, and literature the same themes regarding giving, which you'll read about in the stories and science that fill the pages of this book:

Giving is the most satisfying thing you'll ever do.

It's the source of true happiness, the meaning of life, the source of the greatest emotional and psychological returns.

It's the best way to recover from the worst tragedies, even from the grief of losing a loved one.

It's a greater pleasure than the creation of wealth, the most direct route to happiness, which neither money nor career success can provide.

Giving is what liberates the soul. What brings families closer together. What combats the blues. What fills the gap. What provides a feeling of security. What provides a sense of empowerment and accomplishment. What can heal. What allows us to experience a deep connection with others. What gives inner peace. What brings great meaning, fulfillment, and happiness.

The answer lies in giving.

So why don't more of us give? Every day a charity appeal says, "If only we all gave a dollar . . . if only everyone just gave the time they could, it would help millions of people." But that doesn't work.

Why not? Perhaps it is because we have not heard enough stories of how happy it can make us—stories from people we admire; from people we dream of meeting; from people whose businesses we follow, whose songs we listen to, whose movies we watch. I have had the privilege of meeting many of these people through my work—some of them are celebrities, some are well recognized for the good they have done in the world, and some are incredibly wealthy and successful in business. I'd heard their stories of how giving their time, resources, and talents to the causes they care about has brought them happiness and fulfillment far greater than they had ever imagined. It occurred to me that these stories must be told, as they hold the power to inspire others to do the same.

The Making of This Book

One of the first things people ask me when they hear what my book is about is, "How did you get all those people involved?" But the real question for me, which ultimately led me to the idea of this

book, was, "What am I going to do with all these people I have had
the privilege to meet?"

Tom Freston, cofounder of MTV and one of the inspiring givers
featured here, told me during our interview, "In the world of philanthropy, one door opens up ten." Looking back, I know exactly what
he means. In the social sector, people are so passionate about what
they do, and when they meet someone who has the burning desire to
make something happen, they have the proclivity to enable that person to fulfill his or her dream. My dream was to create a shift in
consciousness about giving, from something that we perceive to be
drudgery and a grinding moral obligation, to something that we want
to do because it gives us fulfillment, meaning, and happiness in life.

Having worked as a philanthropy advisor, I am fortunate
enough to have met a number of high-profile personalities, and I
asked three of them (in a carefully worded, scrupulously polite, and
formal e-mail that I hoped masked my quivering self-consciousness)
if they would be willing to take a chance on me and express their
views in a book that I intended to write about the joy of giving.

I started with communications entrepreneur Mo Ibrahim, because I find his fascinating personal story to be such a powerful
example and because I knew my project would benefit from both his
clout and his wisdom. David Foster also came immediately to mind
because of his stellar reputation in the music industry and his "street
cred" as a generally good human being. Rounding out my top three:
Deepak Chopra. (Because he's *Deepak Chopra*. Need I say more?)

I made a mental list of all the reasons they could possibly say no:
*I don't want to appear smug and talk about how giving brought me joy.
The questions you ask are very personal. How self-serving it is to talk
about what my charitable work has done for me!* But to my surprise,

all three gladly said yes. Next, I approached a team of researchers at the University of British Columbia, and they were all too willing to share with me their latest studies on the links between giving and happiness. Day by day, my project was growing.

Although I started with my trusted contacts, I had to branch out further. I am neither a celebrity nor an ultra high–net worth individual, and contacting these people was an exercise in resourcefulness. I dug out all the business cards I had collected over the years and created an Excel spreadsheet of the people I would contact and how. One by one, I approached big-ticket donors and celebrities, always with a formal letter, asking them if they would like to join the ranks of the people who had already expressed a willingness to share their stories on the transformative power of giving upon the self. It was not my intention to write a book about celebrity giving, but I knew that if someone like Goldie Hawn was happy to share her story about finding joy in giving, it would be easier to get others to follow suit. Day by day, the "confirmed" list on my spreadsheet grew, and although the life of a writer is solitary and isolating, I had a strong sense that I was surrounded by like-minded people believing in what I was doing.

Sometime around the fifth month, as if by magic, people started suggesting names of others I should be featuring in the book, instead of me making the request. In many cases, I was simply in the right place at the right time, as though the universe was conspiring to help me make this project happen. There were lots of days when I "just so happened" to be sitting beside exactly the person I needed. And to my surprise, even people who I've been told are obsessively private agreed to be interviewed. One of them was Ray Chambers ("the greatest philanthropist no one has ever heard of"), who prefers to work behind the scenes and is said to have paid people a lot of money to keep his name out of the press.

I was touched when Ray said of this project, "What really appeals to me about your pursuit is how it could lead to the aggregation of hundreds of millions of people feeling that way, recognizing what giving can do for the self. And then, can we dare to hope, that with the spreading of that knowledge, we begin to see a shift." I tell him that is precisely what I hope to achieve.

Of course, there were also mountains to climb, red tape to cut, and thousands of hours flying back and forth between Singapore, New York, Geneva, Zurich, Los Angeles, San Francisco, Washington, D.C., Bangkok, London, and the Philippines. (So far I've logged 391,266 miles—and counting—on this project alone.) I had to work around my interviewees' schedules: the Oscars, the Cannes Film Festival, the World Economic Forum, New York Fashion Week, and someone having to spend the day getting a star on the Hollywood Walk of Fame.

But looking back, I would not have it any other way!

I cannot adequately express my gratitude to all the people who've generously devoted time, energy, and resources to this project. We share the hope that you, Dear Reader, will be inspired to look at your own time, energy, and resources in a new light and that you will experience in a whole new way the transformative power of giving.

Jenny Santi
Singapore
2014

Of Drugs and Donations

Activating the pleasure part of the brain

The Science Behind
the Transformative Power of Giving

The morning of December 26, 2004, Czech model Petra Nemcova, then age twenty-five, and her fiancé, photographer Simon Atlee, thirty-three, were vacationing in the resort town of Khao Lak, Thailand. They had met two years earlier on a photo shoot, and were living out a fairy-tale long-distance romance. Petra lived in New York, while Simon lived in London, but they were always traveling around the world—Portugal, Miami, Cape Town, Chile, Vermont, wherever their jobs took them. Petra planned the vacation in Thailand as a special surprise for Simon, who had never been there. They had spent the first few days on a scuba diving cruise, sleeping under the stars. "It was just so, so beautiful. Simon was so happy. It's just strange how, in the split of a second, everything can change so much."

That morning, one of the strongest earthquakes in recorded

history took place, triggering a series of devastating tsunamis along the coasts of the Indian Ocean. Petra and Simon were in their bungalow when the first wave hit. "I heard people screaming, and people running away. Everyone was so frantic," she says. "It was just so . . . surrealistic." Then the water flooded their bungalow and pulled them outside in seconds. "Simon was screaming, 'Petra, Petra, what's going on?'" All the windows in the bungalow broke, and Petra was swept into a current of debris. "The power of the water was bringing all the fallen trees, all the broken buildings, and all the wood. It was such a strong current, you couldn't do anything. You just had to go with it."

Petra didn't know that after that moment, she would never see the love of her life again. "He again screamed, 'Petra, Petra.' It was the last time I saw him." The tsunami left a trail of destruction in fourteen countries and killed more than 230,000 people—including Simon.

Petra soon realized that her pelvis was broken, which disabled her legs and left her with only the use of her arms. "I was just screaming from the top of my lungs. The power of the water was pushing my hip and breaking it and breaking it and breaking it," she says. She moved toward a partially submerged palm tree and clung to it. She watched people sweeping by her, many of them children. They were calling for help, but she could do nothing. "I couldn't move my legs, I couldn't do anything. I so wish I could have helped," she says. "After half an hour, you didn't hear the children anymore. You didn't hear the people anymore."

Then the water levels began to drop, but that also increased her pain, because the water had been cushioning her broken pelvis. She struggled to find support for her lower body in the tree's branches, and passed out. She worried about the scale of the disaster, and wondered if she would ever be found. "You don't know if you stayed there for a few hours, for days. You have no idea," she says.

She clung to that tree for the next eight hours. Finally, two Thai men saw her and came to help. "I didn't have anything on me; the water had taken everything," says Petra, whose bathing suit had been ripped off by the raging torrent. "They tried to cover me, but that was the last thing you think about. The man asked if I can catch his neck so he can carry me on his back, but the pain was so strong I couldn't move. He brought me some juice, and then they went away. I didn't know if they were going to come back. I was thinking, if night would come, what was I going to do? The water would be too cold. But after a while one of the men came again with a few Thai people and a few Swedish people. All of them were risking their lives—they could be swept away; something could fall on them. But everyone forgot themselves for others. It was so amazing to see all these people doing incredible things. It was so beautiful."[1]

The next day Petra was transferred by helicopter to a hospital. Her pelvis was so badly fractured near her spine that doctors said it was a miracle she wasn't paralyzed; she had also lost half of her blood from internal injuries that included a hematoma on her kidney. She spent the next few weeks recovering in a hospital in Thailand, and in her parents' home in the Czech Republic.

But as soon as she recovered from her injuries, she returned to Thailand to see how she could help.

WE LEARN EARLY ON that it is better to give than to receive. We are taught to give and it feels good to help someone in need. But is there a deeper current to giving? What drives people such as Petra Nemcova to go back to the scene of devastation and help others (and eventually set up a foundation to help disaster victims) when it would have been far easier to stay in the comfort of her home and never return to Thailand? While it is gratifying to know that someone is benefiting from our help, there are times when we can't help asking ourselves, *Why am I doing this?*

For centuries philosophers and sociologists have speculated about the reasons for giving. "For it is in giving that we receive," said Saint Francis of Assisi. "The sole meaning of life is to serve humanity," said Leo Tolstoy. "We make a living by what we get; we make a life by what we give," said Winston Churchill. Or, in the words of the Chinese adage: "If you want happiness for an hour, take a nap. If you want happiness for a day, go fishing. If you want happiness for a year, inherit a fortune. If you want happiness for a lifetime, help somebody."

The wisdom of folklore, fables, and literature describes the same phenomenon. In Charles Dickens's classic tale *A Christmas Carol*, the central character, Ebenezer Scrooge, starts out as a misanthropist—a hater of everything and everyone, the exact opposite of a philanthropist. "Bah, humbug!" he is known to say. He is, as Dickens describes, "Hard and sharp as flint, from which no steel had ever struck out generous fire; secret, and self-contained, and solitary as an oyster. The cold within him froze his old features, nipped his pointed nose, shriveled his cheek, stiffened his gait; made his eyes red, his thin lips blue; and spoke out shrewdly in his grating voice. A frosty rime was on his head, and on his eyebrows, and his wiry chin. He carried his own low temperature always about with him."

But by the end of the story, he awakens on Christmas Day a happy man. Scrooge says: "I am as light as a feather, I am as happy as an angel, I am as merry as a school-boy. I am as giddy as a drunken man." What brought about this change? A series of dreams that prompted in him the desire to be generous to others.

While philosophers and saints wax poetic, and intuition and pop psychology suggest that helping others leads to happiness, is there any science and hard data that back up the idea that giving is good for the giver?

The resounding answer is yes. Today, scientific research has provided compelling data to support the anecdotal evidence: Giving is a powerful pathway to personal growth and lasting happiness. There exists a growing body of scientific literature pointing to the link between happiness and giving. Helping others may just be the best-kept secret to living a life that is not only happier but also healthier, wealthier, more productive, and meaningful. Although you may have heard that it is better to give than to receive, you may not believe it. Well, now scientific studies show that it's true.

Survival of the Kindest

At the University of California, Berkeley, researchers are challenging long-held beliefs that human beings are hardwired to be selfish. There is a growing body of evidence that shows we are evolving to become more compassionate and collaborative in our quest to survive and thrive. "Because of our very vulnerable offspring, the fundamental task for human survival and gene replication is to take care of others," says Dacher Keltner, codirector of UC Berkeley's Greater Good Science Center. "Human beings have survived as a species because we have evolved the capacities to care for those in need and to cooperate." Does this oppose Charles Darwin's "survival of the fittest" competition model, in which every man has to look after himself? Not so, it seems. In *The Descent of Man*, Darwin talks about benevolence ninety-nine times, concluding that love, sympathy, and cooperation also exist in the natural world, like the way a pelican might provide fish for a blind pelican in their flock. "As Darwin long ago surmised, sympathy is our strongest instinct," says Keltner.

Our Brains Are Hardwired to Serve

"You gotta see this!" Dr. Jorge Moll wrote in an e-mail. Moll and Jordan Grafman, neuroscientists at the National Institutes of Health, had been scanning the brains of volunteers as they were asked to think about a scenario involving either donating a sum of money to charity or keeping it for themselves. As Grafman read the e-mail, Moll came bursting in. The scientists stared at each other. Grafman was thinking, "Whoa—wait a minute!"

Grafman led one of two studies in the mid-2000s that examined where in the brain the impulse to give originates, thereby shedding light on why it feels so good to help others. Both studies asked people to make donations to charities and looked at the resulting brain activity using functional magnetic resonance imaging (fMRI), which creates images of the brain's activity by detecting physical changes such as blood flow resulting from the activity of neurons.

The researchers also tied the results of these imaging experiments to the subjects' everyday behaviors by asking them about their involvement in charitable work, or about their general capacity for altruism.

Grafman was more interested in what happened when subjects donated or opposed donation at a cost to themselves. The study involved nineteen people, each of whom had the potential to walk away with a pot of $128. They also were given a separate pool of funds, which they could choose to distribute to a variety of charities linked to controversial issues, such as abortion, euthanasia, nuclear power, war, and the death penalty. A computer presented each charity to the subjects in a series and gave them the option to donate, to oppose donation, or to receive a payoff, adding money to the pot. Sometimes, the decision to donate or oppose was costly, calling for subjects to take money out of the pot. They gave an average of $51 from the pot and pocketed the rest.

It turned out that a similar pattern of brain activity was seen when subjects chose either to donate or to take a payoff. In either case, an area of the brain toward the forehead, known as the anterior prefrontal cortex, lit up. When Dr. Grafman and his team asked subjects to rate their charitable involvement in everyday life, he found that those with the highest ratings also had the highest level of activity in the prefrontal cortex.

The results demonstrated that when the volunteers placed the interests of others before their own, the generosity activated a primitive part of the brain that usually lights up in response to food or sex. Donating affects two brain "reward" systems working together: the midbrain VTA (ventral tegmental area)-striatum mesolimbic network, which also is stimulated by food, sex, drugs, and money;

and the subgenual area, which is stimulated when humans see babies and romantic partners.

What is so startling about Grafman and Moll's 2006 study? In 1989, economist James Andreoni introduced the concept of "warm glow giving," which attempts to explain why people give to charity. If our brains have evolved to maximize our own survival, why are we motivated to help others despite incurring personal costs? It's an ongoing question that baffles neuroscientists and evolutionists. The economist's answer is that people engage in "impure altruism": Instead of being motivated solely by an interest in the welfare of the recipients of their largesse, "warm glow givers" receive utility from the act of giving. "Utility" is an important concept used by economists to measure the usefulness a consumer obtains from any object or circumstance (for example, how much one enjoys a movie, or the sense of security one gets from buying a dead bolt). In the simplest sense, economists consider utility to be revealed in people's willingness to pay different amounts for different goods.

The utility in the case of giving is the warm glow—the positive emotional feeling people get from helping others. Moll says that their 2006 study "strongly supports the existence of 'warm glow' at a biological level. It helps convince people that doing good can make them feel good; altruism therefore doesn't need to be only sacrifice." Their experiment provided the first evidence that the "joy of giving" has a biological basis in the brain—surprisingly, one that is shared with selfish longings and rewards. Altruism, the experiment suggests, is not a superior moral faculty that suppresses basic selfish urges; rather, it is hardwired in the brain and pleasurable.

As the telecommunications magnate John Caudwell puts it, "My message to those who have not yet found philanthropy is that

they may well find that it becomes a drug that gives far more pleasure than the creation of wealth."

THE IDEA OF ALTRUISM behaving like a miracle drug has been
around for at least two decades. The euphoric feeling we experience
when he help others is what researchers call the "helper's high," a
term first introduced twenty years ago by volunteerism and wellness expert Allan Luks to explain the powerful physical sensation
associated with helping others.

Luks looked at the physical effects of giving experienced by
more than 1,700 women who volunteered regularly.[2] The studies
demonstrated that a full 50 percent of helpers reported feeling
"high" when they helped others, while 43 percent felt stronger and
more energetic. An astonishing 13 percent even experienced fewer
aches and pains.

As Harvard cardiologist Herbert Benson puts it, helping others
is a door through which one can go to forget oneself and experience
our natural hardwired physical sensation. As the runner's high happens when a runner's endorphin levels rise; the helper's high happens
when people perform good deeds for others. In other words, the
helper's high is a classic example of nature's built-in reward system
for those who help others.[3]

Over the years more and more studies have pointed toward the
same idea, that helping another person not only benefits the receiver
directly, but it also has positive effects on the person doing the helping. But is this true when the act of helping is required and not
voluntary?

A 2007 study by economist Bill Harbaugh and psychologist

Ulrich Mayr, both from the University of Oregon, explored the differences in brain activity when donations were voluntary or mandatory. They gave each subject one hundred dollars and told them that nobody would know how much of it they chose to keep or give away, not even the researchers who enlisted them in the experiment and scanned their brains. Payoffs were recorded on a portable memory drive that the subjects took to a lab assistant, who then paid the subjects in cash and mailed donations to charity without knowing who had given what.

The brain responses were measured by an fMRI as a series of transactions occurred. Sometimes the subjects had to choose whether to donate some of their cash to a local food bank. Sometimes a tax was levied that sent their money to the food bank without their approval. Sometimes they received extra money, and sometimes the food bank received money without any of it coming from them.

Sure enough, when the typical subject chose to donate to the food bank, he was rewarded with that "warm glow." The areas of the brain that release the pleasure chemical dopamine unexpectedly lit up (the caudate, nucleus accumbens, and insula)—the same areas that respond when you eat a dessert or receive money.

Surprisingly, when the subject was forced to pay a tax to the food bank, these pleasure centers were also activated—albeit not as much. Consistent with pure altruism, the experiment found that even mandatory, taxlike transfers to a charity elicit neural activity in areas linked to reward processing. Even when it was mandatory for subjects to donate, the pleasurable response persisted, though it wasn't as strong as when people got to choose whether or not to donate.[4]

Are Children Happier When They Give Than When They Receive?

The studies discussed so far prove that we feel pleasure when we help others. Is this true just for adults, or are we born with this peculiarity? Psychologists from the University of British Columbia, led by Professor Elizabeth Dunn, conducted research on the relationship between giving and happiness in young children.

Dunn and her colleagues examined and rated videotaped expressions of twenty-three toddlers who were engaged in games of giving. The toddlers were to receive Goldfish cracker "treats" and were at liberty to give them away without sacrificing personal cost. Each child interacted with puppets who were "cracker monsters" and who loved to eat treats. Puppets "ate" the treats placed in their bowls and made eating noises. The children were to believe that the puppets actually ate and enjoyed the treats.

Children were then introduced to a monkey puppet. They were encouraged to pet and play with the monkey and were told that the monkey loved crackers too. The children would learn about limited resources and were told, "You and Monkey don't have treats." The toddlers then watched as the experimenters introduced eight new treats and placed them in the children's bowls, while they were told there were none available for Monkey. The experimenters then brought out a "found" ninth treat and gave it to the puppet. A tenth treat was then handed to the toddlers, who were asked to give it to the puppet. They were then asked to give one a treat from their own bowl.

Surprisingly, the toddlers did not display any aversion to giving. They actually exhibited happier expressions when giving treats to the puppet then when receiving treats themselves.

The joy of helping others, says researcher Lara Aknin, is an inherent part of human nature. "You can construe prosocial[5] behavior broadly to include giving time volunteering, giving money to causes, or giving other resources. All of these correlate to happiness."[6] Dunn and her colleagues concluded that even babies are innately sociable and enjoy helping others. Children are happier when they give than when they receive.

But what about when we give to ourselves?

The Starbucks Experiment

Money can buy happiness if . . .

When we think of money, we often think about what we can buy for ourselves. Dr. Dunn, together with Michael Norton, a professor of business administration at Harvard Business School, led an experiment in which one morning, "money fell from the sky" for some students in Vancouver, Canada.

The students were given an envelope containing five dollars or twenty dollars, and were randomly assigned to spend the money either on themselves or on someone else. Each student was also asked to rate his or her happiness. Norton has called this the Starbucks Experiment. When students were asked to buy things for themselves, they reported spending the money on things such as coffee, food, makeup, and jewelry. When students were asked to spend money on others, they bought gifts such as coffee or toys for a sibling, or gave the money to charity.

In the evening, the research team called the students back and asked them to describe their happiness. Those who spent money on others or gave it to a charity were significantly happier. In fact, students who had spent their money on themselves had not changed their mood since the morning, whereas those who spent their money on others were happier.

Dunn and Norton also explored the possibility that this human phenomenon is limited to a culture of excess like Canada. They looked to see if spending on others led to happiness in Uganda. Canada and Uganda differ in almost every way imaginable, from history and religion to climate and culture, but most important, the two countries lie at opposite ends of the spectrum in terms of per capita income. Canada falls in the top 15 percent of the world's wealthiest countries; Uganda, in the bottom 15 percent. "You can imagine that if you're in a wealthy country and you spend your money on somebody else, it will make you happy, because your basic needs are already being met and your life is pretty good overall. We really did wonder, if we went to a very poor country, whether it would still be the case that giving could lead to more happiness than spending on yourself, even when you're worried about your very own basic needs," says Norton.

When faced with the same experiment, individuals in the two countries recalled very different kinds of spending experiences. In Canada, there were very few instances of people spending on others for serious need. Most recalled spending money on birthday presents and things of that nature. In Uganda, however, many of the things that people recalled spending money on were actually to help someone with a medical problem or to help someone in serious need. According to Dunn and Norton, a young woman in Canada who had been asked to think about a time she spent money on someone else wrote: "I went with my sister to buy a birthday present for my mom. We went to an accessory store in a mall to buy her a purple scarf. It was about $15 or so from Aldo Accessories."

Faced with the same set of instructions, a young woman in Uganda recalled: "On Sunday, I was walking and met a longtime friend whose son is sick with malaria—the father had no money at the time, they left their home, she decided to visit a nearby clinic. I then ended up giving her 10,000 [shillings] for medical bills and transport."

Nevertheless, overall in both cultures, spending money on other people was linked to happiness. "Even when people are in need themselves, giving still provides more happiness than spending more on yourself," says Norton.

"What we see again, though, is that the specific way that you spend on other people isn't nearly as important as the fact that you spend on other people in order to make yourself happy, which is really quite important. So you don't have to do amazing things with your money to make yourself happy," he adds.[7] "If you buy something you really like a lot, you might feel a little bit happy. But then, that's it. No one else is going to benefit from that purchase. But when you give, not only are you making somebody else happy, you're also making yourself happy. And there you have two people happy instead of just one. When you hear stories from people who spent their lives giving, that's often the feeling that they express: that not only do they feel that they made an impact on other people, but they're actually improving their own lives as well. All of us can do this. We just don't take as much advantage of it as we could and should."

The findings were consistent with those in a study conducted in Singapore by Professor David Chan, of Singapore Management University: Giving and well-being are strongly linked, and people who volunteer or donate are more likely to be satisfied and happy with their lives. The study found that among people who volunteered and/or donated, two-thirds (66 percent) were satisfied and happy with their lives; that is, they had high levels of subjective well-being. In contrast, among non-givers, less than half (45 percent) had high subjective well-being.[8] The study also found that:

- A higher proportion of those who had served twelve or more volunteer hours in the previous twelve months had high subjective well-being compared with those who had served less (71 percent versus 63 percent).
- A higher proportion of those who had given one hundred dollars or more in the previous twelve months had high subjective well-being compared with those who had given less (72 percent versus 59).
- The pattern of findings remained after taking income status into account.

Explaining the results, Chan says: "The findings for this first national study in Singapore on giving and the giver's well-being are consistent with research from elsewhere which showed that giving and well-being can influence each other. Happy people are more likely to give, but people who give also tend to become happier. This is because the act of giving not only benefits the recipient but also leads to positive outcomes for the giver. When you give, you derive a sense of personal meaning from helping others. You also become more grateful for your own life conditions as you appreciate the situation of those who are less fortunate. The outcomes can also be indirect. For example, when helping others, your interactions with the recipients and other givers produce positive social relationships and a sense of community."

Researchers have classified the benefits of engaging in a philanthropic act into two broad groups: public benefit and personal benefit. Public benefit is the result of the activities that individuals, philanthropists, and nonprofit organizations pursue for the benefit of others. It takes various forms, such as improved education, delivery of food and health services to the destitute, increased employment opportunities for the less fortunate, accessibility of art to all, etc. Private benefit of philanthropy is the reward experienced by the donor, the volunteer, the activist, or the philanthropist. This can be a matter of feeling better about oneself, a sense of achievement, recognition, or acknowledgment by society; access to powerful politicians; invitations to high-level events; etc. The vast majority of empirical research to date has found that private benefits are the primary motive for giving. In general, the motivation for being charitable ranges widely between selflessness and self-interest. Researcher K. H. Erskine summarized a comprehensive list of seven reasons why people give: altruism, appreciation, competition, devotion, guilt, self-interest, and tradition.[9]

Long Live the Volunteer

Imagine you are on your annual weeklong beach vacation. Your work stress level has been at an all-time high, and you are still very anxious and tired. Your doctor has told you that you need to get some rest to reduce your stress. You are on your third day of sitting on an uncomfortable sun chair, covered in sunscreen, and you are on page three of a stress-reduction self-help book your partner insists that you read, when suddenly you hear a call for help. You look out to the ocean and see someone waving his arms, and suddenly he starts to sink below the surface. Despite not having a torpedo rescue buoy and red and yellow beach attire, you instinctively morph into a heroic lifeguard, hurdle over sunbathers, throw yourself into the ocean, pull the half-drowned swimmer out, and perform mouth-to-mouth resuscitation on someone you realize hasn't brushed his teeth after eating chicken curry.

After witnessing your heroism, the beachgoers erupt in applause and tears. Benefiting from your fearless courage, the swimmer coughs in your face and regains consciousness. You feel good about yourself for your brave actions. But what are the other benefits to you? You are exhausted and self-conscious, with all eyes on you. As you wipe the sand from your lips, all you can think about is that everyone is looking at your not-so-beach-ready body. You ask yourself, What's in it for me?

Ask some doctors and they will tell you: a lot.

Science can now explain that jumping in and saving the swimmer did more to reduce your stress than a full day sunning yourself and getting foot massages while sipping piña coladas. How is that possible? Well, it turns out that when we help someone, our body triggers the release of healthy chemicals. Good deeds release "do-good" chemicals that do good things to our bodies. Helping can reduce your stress levels. Your heart may beat with a healthier rhythm. You may also get a boost to your immune system. In fact, some studies suggest that helping people on a regular basis may help us live longer.

When we face anxiety, stress hormones such as cortisol are released and our heart and breathing rates increase. Helping others acts like an antidote. In order to help us overcome any apprehension at the thought of helping someone, our brains release a "do-good" hormone called oxytocin.[10] Think of it as the bonding, compassion, or, as some scientists call it, "cuddle" hormone: the hormone that helps prepare mothers for bonding with their babies, which is the same one that is released during sex.

When our compassion circuits are turned on, our angry circuits cannot be activated. Both circuits can't be on at the same time. When oxytocin circuits are turned on, any negative feelings are pushed to the side so we can enjoy these "it's all good" moments. In other words, oxytocin drives away our anxiety, reduces our apprehension, and prepares us to help a stranger.

To help someone you don't know, you have to overcome the natural impulse to avoid risk. Every time you help a stranger, you are reaching out a little, and that can make you feel vulnerable. The theory is that to overcome those fears, your body releases oxytocin, which helps you buffer stress while increasing social trust and tranquility. This "compassion hormone," it turns out, is very good for your body. "You are limiting exposure to stress hormones like cortisol," says Dr. Stephanie Brown, who is now associate professor of preventive medicine at Stony Brook School of Medicine, in New York.

But wouldn't we be better off if we just let others help us out, without giving anything in return?

A 2003 study by a team of researchers led by Brown indicates that we wouldn't. She and her colleagues analyzed data for 423 older married couples in the Detroit area who had responded to a 1988 survey on lifestyles. They combed local obituaries for the next five years to see which individuals who had participated in the survey had died. The goal was to correlate the deaths with social behavior in the individuals based on their survey responses.

The study measured instrumental support and emotional support, and two dimensions: giving and receiving. Giving support was determined by asking whether respondents had helped others outside the family with shopping, housework, child care, or other tasks. Receiving support was measured a bit differently: Respondents were asked whether they "could count on" others, including family members, to help if they needed it. Emotional support was measured only for spouses: Respondents were asked if they felt loved and if their spouse listened to them, and vice versa.

Surprisingly, Brown and her team found that people who helped others were less likely to die in that period than people who only received help. They found that giving social support reduced the odds of mortality by more than 40 percent, while receiving social support increased the odds of mortality by 30 percent during the five years following the survey. The effect of social contact, by contrast, was only a 19 percent reduction in mortality. Similarly, giving emotional support to a spouse was also associated with a 30 percent reduction in mortality after controlling for other factors, while receiving emotional support did not significantly alter mortality.

Of course, these results are all just correlations. For a true experimental study, groups would have to be randomly assigned to giving or receiving conditions—indeed, it's difficult to conceive of an ethical experiment to duplicate Brown's results, which is why we must sometimes rely on correlational data. In any case, this study does offer compelling evidence that philosophical statements like "It is better to give than to receive" aren't just empty declarations.[11]

Another study conducted by Brown, in 2009, reinforces this idea. Results of this national longitudinal study of 3,376 elderly married individuals showed that spending at least fourteen hours per week providing care to a spouse predicted decreased mortality for the caregiver, independent of behavioral and cognitive limitations of the care-receiving spouse, and of other demographic and health variables. These findings run counterintuitive to the generally held notion that caregivers face health risks due to providing help. Indeed, under some circumstances, caregivers may actually benefit from providing care.[12]

It was way back in the 1950s that scientists discovered (albeit unintentionally) the link between helping others and stress reduction and longevity. A team of psychologists from Cornell University surveyed married women with children. They investigated all levels of their potential stressors: number of children, education, social class, work status, etc. The assumption? The highest stress levels would be found in the women with more children, who would also die earlier. But surprisingly, they found that the number one factor in reducing stress was helping others. They found that 52 percent of the housewives who did not perform volunteer work had experienced a major illness, compared with 36 percent of those who did volunteer.[13]

The first study to intentionally examine the effect of motives of volunteers on their subsequent mortality was conducted in 2011 by a team led by Sara Konrath, of the University of Michigan.[14] Respondents who volunteered were found to be at lower risk for mortality four years later, especially those who volunteered more regularly and frequently. The study showed that volunteers live longer than non-volunteers—but this is true only if they volunteer for specific reasons.

What reasons?

There are a multitude of reasons to volunteer, but they can basically be classified into two types: self-focus and other-focus. Self-focus refers to motives that explicitly consider some personal reward, such as improving one's mood or self-esteem, escaping one's problems, learning a new skill, or even getting a promotion or enhancing one's social connections. These are all legitimate reasons to volunteer that are not good or bad in themselves. Other-focus refers to a genuine concern for something beyond oneself.

In 2005, researcher Omri Gilliath and his colleagues found that college undergraduates who volunteer because they have compassion for needy people (i.e., other-focus) indeed derive the most interpersonal benefits from volunteering: They are less lonely and have fewer interpersonal problems. Researcher Sarah Konrath's 2011 study likewise found that volunteers live longer than non-volunteers—but only if they volunteer for other-oriented reasons.

Researchers from the University of British Columbia's Faculty of Education and the Department of Psychology were curious to see how volunteering might impact physical health, particularly among adolescents. The researchers found that just one hour of volunteering per week improved the health of adolescents.[15] For the study, researchers split 106 tenth-grade students from an inner-city Vancouver high school into two groups—one that volunteered regularly for ten weeks and one that was wait-listed for volunteer activities. The researchers measured the students' body mass index (BMI), inflammation, and cholesterol levels before and after the study. They also assessed the students' self-esteem, mental health, mood, and empathy.

The group of volunteer students spent one hour per week working with elementary school children in after-school programs in their neighborhood. After ten weeks they had lower levels of inflammation and cholesterol and lower BMIs than the students who were wait-listed.

"The volunteers who reported the greatest increases in empathy, altruistic behavior, and mental health were the ones who also saw the greatest improvements in their cardiovascular health," says Hannah Schreier, now a postdoctoral fellow at the Icahn School of Medicine at Mount Sinai, in New York. "It was encouraging to see how a social intervention to support members of the community also improved the health of adolescents."

The same is true for older adults. Research from Carnegie Mellon University shows that volunteering for at least two hundred hours per year (four hours a week) dramatically lowers blood pressure in older adults. High blood pressure, or hypertension, triggers a chain reaction in adults that often leads to morbidity due to cardiovascular conditions. "Every day, we are learning more about how negative lifestyle factors like poor diet and lack of exercise increase hypertension risk," says Rodlescia S. Sneed, a Ph.D. candidate in psychology at Carnegie Mellon's Dietrich College of Humanities and Social Sciences. "We wanted to determine if a positive lifestyle factor like volunteer work could actually reduce disease risk. And, the results give older adults an example of something that they can actively do to remain healthy and age successfully." For the study, Sneed and her team studied 1,164 adults between the ages of fifty-one and ninety-one from across the U.S. The participants were interviewed twice, in 2006 and 2010, and all had normal blood pressure levels at the first interview. Volunteerism, various social and psychological factors, and blood pressure were measured each time.

The results showed that when evaluated four years later, those who reported at least two hundred hours of volunteer work during the initial interview were 40 percent less likely to develop hypertension than those who did not volunteer. The specific type of volunteer activity was not a factor—only the amount of time spent volunteering led to increased protection from hypertension.

"As people get older, social transitions like retirement, bereavement, and the departure of children from the home often leave older adults with fewer natural opportunities for social interaction," Sneed says. "Participating in volunteer activities may provide older adults with social connections that they might not have otherwise. There is strong evidence that having good social connections promotes healthy aging and reduces risk for a number of negative health outcomes."

. . .

JUST AS A HEROIC firefighter races into a burning building, there are times when we volunteer without any expectations. Our brains sometimes just follow the Nike adage: When help is required, we "Just do it." And when we do it, it feels good. And apparently, it also makes us live a little longer.

Why should volunteering have such positive effects? One such explanation is that volunteering is a social activity that enhances one's social resources, which in turn improves one's health. But above and beyond the usual hedonistic social activities, such as partying with friends, volunteering together contributes to a sense of shared purpose that engenders a certain camaraderie.[16]

Fortunately, a large portion of us do volunteer. In a national survey of 4,582 American adults, four out of ten reported volunteering an average of two hours per week. Even more striking is that 68 percent of volunteers agreed that volunteering "has made me feel physically healthier." In fact, the survey indicated that volunteers have less trouble sleeping, have lower stress levels, and have better personal relationships. Finally, an incredible 96 percent said volunteering "makes people happier."[17] People are starting to subscribe to the "helping others antidote." "If you could create a pill with the same results as indicated by the survey of American volunteers," says writer Stephen Post, "it would be a best seller overnight."[18]

IT TURNS OUT THAT we don't even need to take a pill. Take a bit of time and imagine yourself volunteering to help someone.

Did you feel anything? Don't feel bad if you didn't, because your brain's mesolimbic system actually just did. Even thinking or imagining helping someone releases chemicals that make this system light up. The mesolimbic system is widely believed to be the source of feelings related to reward and desire and acts as the pathway to the soothing hormone dopamine and the antidepression hormone serotonin. When we give, imagine giving, or watch someone give, our mesolimbic system releases chemicals that dominate our other stress hormones.[19] In one related study, students who watched a film of Mother Teresa working with the poor displayed significant increases in protective antibodies associated with improved immunity.[20]

Interestingly, our brain is structured to distinguish between happiness derived from the Mother Teresa–like pursuit of noble principles and hedonistic happiness that is based on a life of pleasure. Researchers Steven Cole and Barbara Fredrickson examined these two types of happiness by looking at the overall health and depression of a collection of adults. They took blood samples and ran a series of tests to look for patterns associated with something called the "conserved transcriptional response to adversity," or CTRA. A high CTRA produces symptoms similar to those of a person subjected to chronic stress, threat, or trauma, which are associated with cardiovascular disease. What Cole and Fredrickson discovered was that those people who reported high levels of happiness from living a purposeful life had a low CTRA and a corresponding better immune response profile. In contrast, those with high levels of hedonic happiness had a high CTRA profile. Therefore, happiness derived from leading a life with purpose produced healthier benefits.[21] Even on a cellular level, it is better for you to do good for others than for yourself.

Giving Time Gives You Time

Don't have enough time? Giving is a way to gain more time.

Those who volunteer their time feel like they have more of it. Cassie Mogilner and coresearchers Zoë Chance and Michael Norton suggest that volunteering our limited time may actually increase our sense of unhurried leisure. When we give, our sense of time expands. The researchers conducted a set of four experiments that revealed that when it comes to easing the pressures of time, volunteering will beat wasting time watching TV or making time for yourself, and even beats receiving a windfall of time.

In one experiment, 218 college students were assigned one of two five-minute tasks that had them either giving or wasting time. Giving time involved spending five minutes writing an encouraging note to a sick child. In a survey after the assignment, those who gave their time reported feeling like they had more time than those in the other. Giving away time boosts one's sense of personal competence and efficiency. This in turn stretches out time in our mind. Giving time makes people more willing to commit to future engagements despite their busy schedules.

In another study, giving time involved spending fifteen minutes helping an at-risk high school student with a homework essay assignment. In the wasting time group, subjects were given mundane and routine meaningless tasks. For instance, they were asked to circle the letter *E* in Latin text. Gaining a windfall of free time happened

when subjects were offered the option of leaving the lab fifteen minutes early to spend time on themselves. The results revealed that
those who had spent the time helping someone else actually reported
feeling that they had more time than those who spent it on themselves or wasted it. Objectively, all participants have less time because
they gave some of it away, yet subjectively, the ones who gave time
felt they had more time.

The results suggest this effect occurs because spending time on
others makes one feel more effective, capable, and competent. When
more happens in a particular period of time, then that period of
time is perceived to be longer. This feeling of having spent time in
a very effective way makes you feel like you've accomplished a lot
and therefore that you can accomplish a lot in the future. (It sure
explains how the typical CEO of any big multinational also happens to sit on a dizzying number of charity boards.)

In another experiment, participants were not only asked to measure how much time they thought they had, but they were also
given an opportunity to commit their future time. Those who spent
time helping someone were more committed to do more in the
future than those who were allowed to leave fifteen minutes early.
The experiment suggests that spending time on other people relaxes
a person's perceived time constraints.[22]

Healing the Wounded Healer

Sometimes when you face a problem, those closest to you can offer
support and love, but they are not able to provide understanding.
The best person to help someone with a problem is someone who

has been there herself. It is the notion of having "walked in another person's shoes."

Whether one is fighting an addiction or dealing with a debilitating disease, people connect more with someone who has been through similar situations. In one study, people with multiple sclerosis were trained to provide support over the telephone for fifteen minutes a month to a fellow person with multiple sclerosis. The helpers proved to be more self-confident, had better self-esteem, and displayed less depression. In a similar study, people with chronic pain who counseled those with similar conditions experienced a drop in their own symptoms of pain—and depression. In a study of alcoholics going through the Alcoholics Anonymous program, those who helped others were nearly twice as likely to stay sober a year later, and their levels of depression were lower, too.[23] Experts call this the "wounded healer" principle. Helping has a tremendous benefit for those who need it, and for the helpers themselves.

This is perhaps what makes Petra Nemcova the model of giving. Barely a year after the tsunami, and still recovering from her physical and emotional wounds, she set up the Happy Hearts Fund with the vision of rebuilding schools and the lives of young victims of natural disasters, transforming her grief into a life raft of inner strength, a new passion for life, and a completely changed outlook. As she told me one winter morning in 2013, by giving, "you can heal faster emotionally, but also physically. You can have an impact on many lives and you can bring joy to the lives of others. There's a selfish element in it, really. When we make someone happy, we become even happier."

There was no fMRI machine around to measure her brain activity, but Nemcova was the picture of pure happiness—skin glowing, eyes twinkling, nose crinkling as she smiled. "If you decide yourself that you will help in some way, you will benefit the most because it will create amazing joy. Those who are not doing anything are missing out on a very profound joy."

The Pursuit of Purpose

What are we here for?

Many persons have a wrong idea of what constitutes
true happiness. It is not attained through self-gratification
but through fidelity to a worthy purpose.

—HELEN KELLER

"Stop!" yelled four-year-old Joshua Williams, as he sat in a booster seat in the backseat of his mother's car on the way to church one sunny day in Miami Beach, Florida. Joshua's grandmother had just given him a twenty-dollar bill as a present, and he was busy imagining all the different ways he could spend his money. At that moment on the way to church, he knew exactly how.

A homeless man on the street was holding a sign reading HELP ME, and little Joshua urged his mother to stop driving so that he could help the man. "It's my money; I want to help him, Mom," Joshua said, and promptly handed the man the twenty-dollar bill.

Barely a year after that incident, Joshua Williams became quite possibly the world's youngest foundation president, leading the Joshua's Heart Foundation, which he named himself. Why the name? "Because I felt like I was putting my heart into my mission," he says. At the age of five, when our biggest missions involve climbing ladders and trees, hopping on one foot, buttoning our own shirts, and lacing our own shoes, Joshua was already leading a band of volunteers who hand out food to the needy. It wasn't always easy, especially in the beginning, as he was trying to enlist support for his plan to feed the hungry. He first asked for help from his aunt. "But she didn't do anything. So I fired her," Joshua says. Eventually he asked his mother, but sadly she was too busy to be of much help. After prodding her daily for months, he finally made progress and together they began to give away food and other items to people in need. Around that time, Joshua thought he should start a company that would feed the world's hungry. One of his aunts rose to the challenge and pointed them in the direction of starting a nonprofit foundation. Soon afterward, the Joshua's Heart Foundation was born.

As I meet the philanthro-prodigy, now twelve and a veteran in his work, the first thing I notice is his hair: gloriously big, very curly, and he rocks it. The hair renders him iconic—think Albert Einstein's frizz, Elvis Presley's pompadour, the Beatles' mop tops, and other coifs that have defined the greatest icons. In a way he already is one, at least in the state of Florida, where he has received more than forty awards for his humanitarian work. His influence extends beyond his home state: In 2010, a flag was flown over the United States Capitol at the request of the Honorable Ileana Ros-Lehtinen, member of Congress, in honor of Joshua's mission to end hunger. He also received the President's Volunteer Service Award and has his profile on the White House website, among those of other champions of change at least four times his age. These experiences have clearly given him a lot of confidence. I meet him one afternoon soon after he gets home from Ransom Everglades School, in Miami, and as I spend the first five minutes carefully explaining what I do and asking if he has any questions, he simply shrugs and replies, "No."

"I believe that giving your time and money is happiness because through time you will see who you are helping and the impact you had. This leads to happiness. Everything that I do when I help people makes me happy. Every moment is inspirational. 'Cause when you help others, it leads to happiness." He laughs, throwing his head back. "If you're lonely, you're with a lot of people now, so you're not lonely anymore. If you're depressed, then you're now happy because you're helping people and you know that you're doing the right thing. So technically, helping people leads to the cure of a lot of things."

He has an ambitious expansion plan. "I want my foundation to become a worldwide organization. I want to help more people and make people aware that hunger is not only in the United States, but worldwide. In the next five years, I see my foundation as a national foundation, and then in the next ten, fifteen years, I see my foundation as an international organization. Two of the places that I really want to help are Africa and Asia.

"Basically whenever I help people from my distributions, I have a good feeling in my heart. You know that you're doing the right thing—and you're happy! It's that simple." I ask him how this has changed his life, and he says, "I was four and a half when I started, so it wasn't much of a difference that I could really tell, but I just know that it's better. You see everything in a different way. I have been able to have more experiences and talk to people about different subjects. I am more aware of my surroundings and what is happening in the world."

Joshua enjoys public speaking and attended his first global conference at the age of nine. "I speak to youths and adults alike about hunger, making a difference and giving back. I didn't think I would be traveling and speaking at such a young age," he says.

Once, a reporter asked him what the title of his book would be, if he were ever to write one. "*What Is Your Purpose?*" Joshua replied. Being around him, I realize why he phrased his book title as a question. Joshua's single-mindedness about his own reason for living challenges people to discover their own, and even in his baby voice, he is a sage when he gives advice: "Basically, just always go with it. Go do your passion and your mission in life." Gazing at me with his big brown eyes through black-rimmed glasses, he says, "I believe that everyone has a purpose in life and that it is their choice to follow it. If you do so, it will be a great achievement. My purpose in life is to help those in need. If I didn't do this I would have no purpose." And then he excuses himself, saying he needs to get back to his homework.

Joshua's Heart Foundation has two primary goals: to "stomp out world hunger" and to "break the cycle of poverty." The foundation hosts quarterly food distributions and healthy cooking demonstrations around South Florida, and provides weekly food distribution as well as food in backpacks on the weekends for children who otherwise would have no food. To date, people in need have received 450,000 pounds of food through the foundation.

The Science of Purpose

In 2012, Gallup reported that the happiness level of Americans was at a four-year high—as was the number of best-selling books with the word *happiness* in the title. Gallup also reported that nearly 60 percent of Americans felt happy, without a lot of stress or worry. But in this modern era in which people claim to be happy, psychotherapists around the world often hear complaints such as "My life has no meaning" and "What is my purpose?" These statements signal the lack of and search for meaning in life that has become so apparent in today's society. According to the Centers for Disease Control, about four out of ten Americans have not discovered a satisfying life purpose. Nearly half of Americans feel neutral or do not have a strong sense of what makes their lives meaningful.

But what is purpose? Theories in social psychology, cognitive neuroscience, evolutionary theory, and economics provide evidence that support the different aspects and descriptions of purpose, its underlying mechanisms, and the consequences of finding—or not finding—it.

First, it is important not to confuse seeking happiness with finding your purpose. Happiness is what you experience in the daily flow of life—the highs and lows that are situational. They will fluctuate. Purpose is deeper. It leads us to the answers to the abiding questions: *Who am I? What am I doing here? Where am I going?* It is an underlying sense of peace and fulfillment that transcends everyday highs and lows, disappointments and successes, loves and losses. "When you're living in accordance with your life's purpose," says Steve Taylor, senior lecturer in psychology at Leeds Beckett University, in the U.K., "you view all of the above as part of what you encounter along the road. They don't distract you from that larger vision, your ideal, which is like a magnet steadily pulling you toward it."[1]

Neither is purpose synonymous with "goals." Goals are more precise and focus on a specific endpoint. Purpose is broader: It is "a central, self-organizing life aim that organizes and stimulates goals, manages behaviors, and provides a sense of meaning," according to scientists Patrick E. McKnight and Todd B. Kashdan.[2] And while purpose directs life goals, motivates daily decisions, and offers direction just as a compass guides a navigator, following that compass is optional.

How do we recognize our purpose? Everyone feels a pull toward some defining purpose to their lives, no matter how far back it may have been pushed along the way. Most of us have within ourselves at least a tinge of awareness of our life's unique purpose. It often feels like a leaning, an inclination that pulls at us. Sometimes it is right in front of our eyes but we don't allow ourselves to see it, like when you're hunting for your missing keys and then discover that they've been right in front of you the whole time. But when we embrace it, it feels very natural. As Joshua Williams said at a tender young age, "The path to your purpose might be hard and rough or it might be easy and smooth. What I do seems natural and right to me. My purpose in life is to help those in need. Helping people in any way I can, knowing that I was able to help someone who needed help, and seeing the smiles on the faces of the people I help are what bring me the most happiness."

The Pluses of Purpose

*I believe we're all put on this planet for a purpose, and we all have
a different purpose. . . . When you connect with that love and that
compassion, that's when everything unfolds.*

—ELLEN DEGENERES

*Our prime purpose in this life is to help others. And if you can't help
them, at least don't hurt them.*

—DALAI LAMA

"It is the very pursuit of happiness," said Austrian neurologist and
psychiatrist Viktor Frankl, "that thwarts happiness." Other scientists agree that the single-minded pursuit of happiness (versus the
search for meaning, and the recognition of the responsibility for
something greater than the self) is, ironically, leaving people less
happy, and they caution against this approach. Living in accord with
one's purpose, however, offers a self-sustaining source of meaning
and happiness. Scientists agree that it is mood enhancing to engage
in activities that are congruent with one's purpose. In much of
the research in this area, the implication is clear that meaning in life
contributes to a happier life. Dr. Martin Seligman, director of the
Positive Psychology Center at the University of Pennsylvania, whose
research concentrates on what makes people feel happy and fulfilled, concluded that happiness has three dimensions that can be
cultivated: the Pleasant Life, the Good Life, and the Meaningful
Life. The Pleasant Life is realized when we fill our lives with the

sensual pleasures, such as good food, good sex, and nice things. The pursuit of pleasure, research determined, has hardly any contribution to lasting fulfillment. The Good Life is achieved through discovering our signature strengths and using them to obtain gratification. The Meaningful Life goes one step beyond this, and happens when we use our unique strengths in service of something larger than ourselves. "To live all three lives is to lead a full life," says Seligman. His theory reconciles two conflicting views of human happiness: the individualistic approach, which emphasizes that we should take care of ourselves and nurture our own strengths; and the altruistic approach, which emphasizes sacrifice to achieve a greater purpose—moving beyond simply seeking good feelings to pursuing a better life.

For people like Joshua Williams, the attainment of happiness is not the goal of life. Rather, when they find their purpose, happiness comes naturally.

And so do other good things. This is not the stuff of esoteric New Age self-help books that speak of things abstruse and metaphysical like being "connected to the Source." There is now a critical mass of empirical evidence and a convergence of expert opinions that having purpose and meaning in life is important for mental and physical health and well-being. High levels of meaning in life predict low levels of psychological distress and high levels of happiness and self-esteem, and the relationship between meaning in life and psychological well-being is substantial.[3] For example, scientists Sheryl Zika and Kerry Chamberlain found that meaning in life was the most consistent predictor of psychological well-being among college students. In fact, it has been shown to relate positively to psychological well-being at almost every stage of the life span, from adolescence to late adulthood.[4] Meaning in life has been found to be an essential part of the folk concept of a "good life."[5] Research has also shown that having purpose and meaning in life increases overall life satisfaction, enhances resilience and self-esteem, and decreases the chances of depression. People with more meaningful lives are more emotionally stable[6] and demonstrate less neuroticism, anxiety, and depression than individuals with less meaningful lives.

On top of all that, people who live with a purpose are more consistent in their behavior, their purpose serving as the motivating force to overcome obstacles, seek alternative means, and maintain focus on their goals, in spite of changing environmental conditions. People who have meaning in their lives, in the form of a clearly defined purpose, rate their satisfaction with life higher even when they are feeling down than those who do not have a clearly defined purpose.

"When you have a sense of purpose, you never get up in the morning wondering what you're going to do with yourself. When you're 'in purpose'—that is, engaged with and working toward your purpose—life becomes easier, less complicated and stressful. You become more mono-focused, like an arrow flying toward its target, and your mind feels somehow taut and strong, with less space for negativity to seep in," says Steve Taylor.[7] People who awaken to their life purpose radiate a calm inner strength, inspiration, power, and success in whatever they do with their lives. Purposeful activities often require exercising character strengths, such as courage and justice, that result in challenges against other people or established norms. Living in accord with a purpose increases people's endurance during mentally, physically, and emotionally challenging activities. Nowhere is this more evident than in the life of Viktor Frankl.

Finding Meaning in Life Even Amid
the Most Desperate Circumstances

In Vienna in 1930, a young Austrian high school counselor by the name of Viktor Frankl noted that at least one out of five students who sought counseling exhibited "enduring weariness of life and thoughts of suicide,"[8] and that the incidence of actual suicide increased considerably in the days immediately preceding and following the distribution of report cards. In the same year, Frankl organized the first special campaign for student counseling, paying particular attention to the critical period of the school year's end. The campaign proved to be a great success. For the first time in many years, 1931 recorded no student suicides in Vienna.

Born in Vienna in 1905, Viktor Frankl was the son of hardworking Jewish middle-class parents. His father was director of the Social Affairs Ministry; his mother, a housewife. Even as a child, Frankl showed an early interest in people and their motivations. While in high school, he began to study psychology and corresponded with Sigmund Freud. After the success of the suicide prevention program, Frankl rose quickly through the ranks despite his young age. He became a doctor of neurology and psychiatry, and coined the term *logotherapy*, a new school of psychology for which he would become famous, centered on the idea that man is driven by a will to establish meaning in his life. By 1937, he had opened a private practice in both psychiatry and neurology.

But Frankl's life changed dramatically the following year. Hitler and his troops invaded Austria, and Frankl was forced to close his practice. The Nazis revoked his medical license, and he was only allowed to treat Jewish patients out of his parents' home. He managed to get a visa that would have allowed him to immigrate to the United States. But he was unwilling to leave his elderly parents behind, so he let it expire. That decision ensured that he, like so many of his fellow Jews, would be deported to the Nazi death camps.

In 1942, Frankl was arrested, along with his new bride, his parents, and his brother. He spent three years in concentration camps, including Auschwitz, and lost every member of his family to those camps, except a sister who had immigrated to Australia. He also lost the manuscript he had been working on for years.

The Price of Not Having a Purpose

Following his liberation from Auschwitz, Frankl published his seminal work, *Man's Search for Meaning*, which has sold millions of copies worldwide and is often included in lists of the most influential books of all time. Frankl returned to Vienna in the wake of the Holocaust, starting his life over again.

As a concentration camp inmate himself, Frankl observed the lives of the other inmates from the objective perspective of a psychiatrist. The camps became the proving ground for Frankl's theories on what makes people not only survive but find meaning in life even amid the most desperate circumstances. He noted that the people most likely to survive the most painful and dehumanizing situations were not those who were physically strong, but those who felt they had a goal or purpose. "Life is never made unbearable by circumstances, but only by lack of meaning and purpose," he said.

"Being human always points, and is directed, to something or someone, other than oneself—be it a meaning to fulfill or another human being to encounter. The more one forgets himself—by giving himself to a cause to serve or another person to love—the more human he is."[9]

Frankl's experience as a concentration camp inmate taught him that the most powerful motivating and driving force in humans is not pleasure, as Freud believed, but meaning. This is the premise behind Frankl's signature contribution to the field of clinical psychology—logotherapy, an approach meant to help people overcome depression and achieve well-being by finding their unique meaning in life. Frankl emphasized that life's meaning is unique to each individual, noting that "meaning must be found and cannot be given." Man can obtain meaning in life in one of three ways: by engaging in fulfilling deeds; through relationships with another person or persons; or in his attitude toward the unavoidable suffering in life—that is, finding meaning even in the midst of pain. "We who lived in concentration camps can remember the men who walked through the huts comforting others, giving away their last piece of bread," he said.

While people have found meaning amid extreme circumstances, the irony is that even people who have comfortable lives and are stable in their work or relationships can feel hollow and unfulfilled, and describe feeling "off track" or "out of sync" in some way despite their conventionally successful lives. People who experience a clear inclination toward their purpose but don't pursue or fulfill it remain unfulfilled and dissatisfied. Their lives are filled with loneliness and despair, and they become vulnerable to boredom, anxiety, and depression. Those with addictive personalities become vulnerable to substance abuse. They wonder whether they've chosen the wrong career, the wrong life partner, or ultimately the wrong path. Because their true inner selves know that they are not living their life purpose, they feel a chronic, lingering dissatisfaction and an absence of inner peace.

Frankl coined the phrase "Sunday neurosis" to refer to the dejection that is felt at the end of the workweek when a person realizes just how empty and meaningless his life is. This existential vacuum may lead him to all sorts of excesses such as neurotic anxiety, avoidance, bingeing on food and drink, overworking, and overspending. In the short term, these excesses can compensate for the vacuum, but in the longer term they prevent action from being taken and meaning from being found. For Frankl, depression can result when the chasm between what a person is and what he ought to be becomes so vast. Depression is a person's way of telling himself that something is seriously wrong and needs working through and changing. Unless this can be achieved, there will continue to be a mismatch between his lived experience and his desired experience, between the meaninglessness of everyday life and the innate drive to find meaning.

Many other scientists agree that a lack of meaning is predictive of depression and disengagement,[10] substance abuse and addiction,[11] and the prevalence of depression, feelings of emptiness, and suicide.[12] Caregivers who support their loved ones through grave illnesses, disability, and old age may either find meaning in their work or compromise their health and well-being in the process. Those who recognize these efforts as part of their purpose find joy, while those who are motivated by obligation, coercion, or guilt do not.[13]

From Russia with Love

The sole meaning of life is to serve humanity.

—LEO TOLSTOY

In the dead of winter, the temperatures in the Russian industrial town of Nizhniy Novgorod are so biting that exposed hair will be covered in frost in mere minutes. Commonly known as a breeding ground for criminals, this town in the heart of Russia was no place for a young girl of eleven to be outdoors for up to twelve hours a day. Yet this was the scene of Natalia Vodianova's first job: selling fruit outside in conditions so harsh that most of us would never leave the house. "I would come home and scream in pain as my fingers and my toes were literally defrosting," Natalia has said. With barely enough time to rest and recover, she would be back outside selling apples the next day.

Natalia's first role in life was defined well before she had so much as a memory. When she was just a toddler, her father joined the Russian army, disappearing without a trace. By age six, Natalia was left to look after her younger half sister, Oksana, who had cerebral palsy and severe autism. She says that her mother, Larisa, "worked nearly twenty-four hours a day," but her three jobs washing floors at Natalia's school, working nights in a car factory, and selling fruit on the streets were not enough to feed the family. Barely old enough to babysit, much less work, Natalia would be so exhausted by the time she got to school that she could hardly focus, and often missed school entirely. "I remember once finding a ruble on the street—at a time when the average salary was perhaps twenty-five rubles a month," Natalia says. The little coin in her hand is worth a mere $0.03 today. For Natalia, though, the find was worth a lot more. "I grabbed it with a feeling of euphoria, ran back to my mother, and was allowed to go shopping for food with it. It was a wonderful feeling to be able to do that for my family.

"I had this weird knowledge that, one day, things would be good," says Natalia. By the time she was fifteen, and already with five years of experience selling fruit, things became slightly better. Her fruit stand business was doing well, she loved her circle of friends, and she enjoyed going out. She also began to notice that men were looking at her. "Really looking at me," she says. She started going out with a boy who attended the local modeling school, and who soon convinced her to try it out herself. The boyfriend paid the entrance fee because she could not afford it. He also vehemently objected to her tweezing away her naturally thick eyebrows—at a time when all the other girls had plucked theirs to oblivion. Armed with determination and a pair of bushy brows, she soon had a modeling gig at a local show, where the fifty dollars she earned was more than she could hope to make selling fruit for a month.

Her newfound modeling career picked her up like a rescue helicopter out of poverty. Within two years, she was living in Paris and quickly becoming one of the most renowned faces in the modeling industry. Fast-forward to 2014, and the former fruit vendor is now ranked third on the Forbes list of highest-paid models, with an estimated income of $8.6 million, headlining campaigns with Guerlain, Calvin Klein, and many other fashion and beauty giants. Natalia's status has become so iconic in the world of fashion that she has joined the ranks of Twiggy, Iman, Naomi, Christy, Gisele, and the other one-name supermodels before her.

Before she even turned twenty years old, Natalia could check off every marker of societal success: a high-profile modeling career, living in one of the most desirable cities in the world, married (to now ex-husband Justin Portman), and on the cusp of becoming a mother to her firstborn, Lucas. The days of finding money on the streets and worrying about where dinner would come from were over. But somewhere in the crevices of her heart, Natalia ached for something more. Her hometown may have been more than two thousand miles away, but it was never far from her mind.

"I had this lovely husband, a beautiful baby boy, and even though I was very young, I just didn't see the meaning in my life," Natalia tells me as she sits comfortably in her Paris home. I scan her face for signs of her turbulent history, but there are no traces. Her makeup-free face has a marked innocence that makes her seem much younger than her thirty-one years. She pauses for a few seconds before adding, "I was feeling like I had no identity anymore."

Her identity had been tied to a harsher reality—and it had morphed into something unrecognizable, almost overnight. Here was a woman who was used to clawing and toiling just to make it through the day. And suddenly she was being coveted by the likes of Marc Jacobs and Stella McCartney, jet-setting to New York, and seeing her own face on the cover of *Vogue* as she passed newsstands on any normal day. The 180-degree turn her life had taken left Natalia "confused and a little depressed," she says. "Even though I enjoyed it tremendously, I felt there was something else I should be doing with my life."

"Why am I here?" She remembers herself asking one of the great questions of life. "It's a difficult question to ask. I'm trying to do my best to justify my existence and for taking this space and air and the resources of this wonderful planet, and why I'm here. I believe the answer to this question is something you discover every single day of your life, through your actions." She wondered, "Why do I have all these gifts?"

The answer came to her in the wake of the 2004 Beslan school siege, a tragedy that riddled a school with bullet holes visible to this day, took the lives of 186 children, and left hundreds deeply traumatized in Natalia's home country. During a visit to the Beslan site, she surveyed the damage caused by the three-day siege. "Unfortunately, something positive doesn't always come from a good place," she says. Desperate to do something, Natalia became intent on giving the surviving children their childhood back with "play, the most therapeutic way to feel normal again for these kids." She recalls her own childhood and missing out on the simplest things, such as running around freely, and she remembers having "not one place to go" to take her sister for a break, to just be a kid. "In our childhood, we build our identity, we build who we are. It's not something you can just throw away or forget; it really is part of you," she says.

Within a month of the Beslan siege, Natalia raised $350,000, and her Naked Heart Foundation was born. Decades younger than so many philanthropists, who typically feel the compulsion to give back at the end of their careers, Natalia was only twenty-two—and just beginning to taste success in an industry she knew was fickle— when she started directing her energy into the charity. In doing so, she found a greater purpose for her life: a grounding dynamic to her meteoric rise in the hypercompetitive modeling world.

Now she channels her time and energy to bring joy back into the lives of children. Over the past nine years, the Naked Heart Foundation has built playgrounds across Russia. The one hundredth was constructed in Natalia's hometown in 2013. Her efforts have affected thousands of lives, but the reward has gone back to her.

"I am a woman of opposites; I am as weak as I am strong. I am a survivor; that's my identity," Natalia says. "I used to fight for my own personal survival and for my immediate family. We all have our own purpose in life and I feel very strongly that I have a bigger purpose than giving to just my immediate family and friends. Today I fight for thousands of people, and that gives you a very different purpose in life, a bigger purpose. And I have found, completely, an endless source of love."

A moment later, Natalia apologizes. "I'm sorry; it was very, very deep."

"The Most Exciting and Thrilling Ride of My Life"

We must have a theme, a goal, a purpose in our lives. If you don't know where you're aiming, you don't have a goal. My goal is to live my life in such a way that when I die, someone can say, she cared.

—MARY KAY ASH

In giving their time, their talents, or their entire lives to a cause, people of various ages and walks of life—from sunny Miami Beach to bitterly cold Nizhniy Novgorod—are finding the answer to the ultimate question, *What is my purpose?* As I take the elevator to Academy Award–winning actress Goldie Hawn's Manhattan penthouse, I hear another story that validates this truth.

Goldie Hawn is standing next to me in the elevator leading up to her apartment when she closes her eyes, takes a deep breath, and asks, "What is that? There's something in here that smells so good!"

At about four minutes past four p.m. on a windy day in January, Goldie had swung through the revolving doors into her building lobby. Before I could fix my hair and powder my nose, which had turned red from the cold, she walked straight up to me, apologizing for being three minutes late. Although I knew exactly whom I was expecting to meet, I was startled when one of Hollywood's most enduring stars turned up, wearing oversize sunglasses and a large furry hood covering most of her face and that famous blond hair. I had handed her a bouquet of spray roses and eucalyptus, and thanked her for meeting me.

"It's the flowers," I say now. She stares at the bouquet but is not convinced. She sniffs the elevator air, twitching her nose like a bloodhound, and leans close. "It's you! You smell so good!" It turns out I am wearing the same perfume she wore years ago, and I am flattered to hear this from a woman who once taught people to smell their way into inner peace and happiness by wearing jasmine and lavender oils every day.

"The joy that I get from bringing happiness to people is something that I've experienced all my life," she says, as we sit across from each other on low sofas in her living room after having been greeted by two men who make her laugh: Kurt Russell, her partner of thirty years; and, in the form of a portrait in her hallway, an Indian nobleman, the maharajah of Mysore. Her apartment displays her fascination with all people, places, and things spiritual, and although the sweeping views of Central Park and the Hudson River give it a certain majesty, the place is conducive to intimacy. Across from us is a statue of a Buddha in lotus pose, and a Chinese opium bed topped with huge pillows covered in Indian silk. Listening to Goldie's soothing voice, I feel like I am at a meditation retreat.

"I was a very compassionate and empathetic child. I could feel other people's joy and also their pain. I went to a school where there were handicapped and cerebral palsy–afflicted students, and I remember feeling deeply for them. I befriended them, and it made me feel good to do so. I didn't want them to feel so alone."

The compassionate spirit followed her through her years as a young adult. "When I was in my twenties, I used to put on a hat while in a convertible. The hat would flap and it would look funny, and I wore it because I would look at my rearview mirror and I could see people behind me laughing," she says, a smile lighting up her face. "They didn't know who it was that had the hat on, but I enjoyed being a part and parcel in making someone feel better." Even acting, she says, was being in service through her God-given talent to make people laugh and feel better. "I just felt that I was in the right place by making other people happy," she says.

By the time she was in her fifties, Goldie's compassionate and empathetic nature found an even greater calling. Noticing the alarming jump in stress, violence, and depression among children, and thinking about the "unthinkable reality that children aren't happy," she began to advocate for the importance of social and emotional learning for young people, and the Hawn Foundation was born. "I was concerned about the well-being of our youth. We live in stressful times and our children are suffering the alarming symptoms of this, from aggression and bullying to depression and attention deficit disorder. I wanted children to gain better tools to deal with their emotions and stress today so that they can learn better and be happier. So I set up the foundation to give children these tools to navigate through their life."

The Hawn Foundation teaches the technique of mindful awareness to children from kindergarten to seventh grade. A study by the University of British Columbia indicates that children who participate in the program increase significantly in the areas of optimism and positive emotions, while decreasing in aggression. In addition to setting up her foundation, Goldie wrote a meditation manual, the *New York Times* best seller *10 Mindful Minutes*, aimed at parents and teachers in hopes that they will encourage children to practice the basics of yoga and meditation.

"This makes me happy. I feel that I'm contributing, that I'm learning." Goldie, who has proven to be one of cinema's most significant and well-loved stars, began her acting career in the 1960s, and made her name by playing the ever-smiling blonde. "I've grown beyond and around that world of show business. I'm not talking to people in show business today—I've been doing that for thirty-five, forty years. I'm now speaking to neuroscientists and educators, people who I've met who are giving back to the world. Wealthy people, people who've made millions and billions of dollars, are focusing on how they can help the world become a better place. This makes me happy, because you meet like-minded people who want to connect to other like-minded people and how vital it is to give back." This is a departure from her nine years spent in therapy, feeling depressed and anxious as she coped with panic attacks caused by her early success in Hollywood. She has since been called "the perfect model for happiness" and "the most deliriously contented person alive." (It is no wonder she is also a supporter of Operation Smile, which offers reconstructive surgery to youngsters in less-developed countries.) "I'm generally known as a happy person, but years ago I suffered from panic and anxiety. I've learned to manage the fear and pain," she says.

I ask Goldie whether her philanthropic work makes her feel fulfilled, and she replies, "Creating my MindUP program for schools was one of the most challenging things I have ever done. My dream was to help children regulate emotions, eliminate bullying, and live happier healthier lives. There is no question that it took a lot of work and tenacity and the love of children. However, after twelve years and changing over five hundred thousand children's lives, it has definitely been the most exciting and thrilling ride of my life."

"How is the happiness you get out of your charitable work different from the happiness you get from your career?" I ask.

"It's quite different. One is self-centered, and there are lots of happy things that can happen to us that way. You know, you can get enough money to buy a new house; you can buy new shoes. These are all fleeting aspects of happiness. They don't last. They're like ripples on the water. They come and go. As long as the money is there, you're happy and you're okay. But when you're really working toward making a difference, you get a deeper, deeper level of satisfaction, because it's not for you. It's for something bigger than just you, and the people that you meet along the way are your soul mates. They fortify you. They thrill you. They make you happy. And when you get into it, you realize that you'll attract people who are doing things aligned with your vision. Your connection to them also brings you lasting joy.

"Look, winning an award is wonderful," she continues, "but I like to think that those things help us get to a place where we can give back."

Goldie is convinced that those who are looking for happiness will find it in giving. "That has been researched time and time again. It really brings people out into the light from darkness. It's a very important aspect to continue to exercise in our lives—how you give back, how you think about humanity, how you consider yourself of value. You can go and be of help; you are engaged in the world. This helps people become happier. Giving back is as good for you as it is for those you are helping, because giving gives you purpose. When you have a purpose-driven life, you're a happier person. You're engaged. You're alive."

In the end, she has no words to describe the sense of happiness and fulfillment she gets from giving. "The Dalai Lama says, 'You can't explain the taste of a tangerine; you have to experience it.' It's the same thing here, upon giving back. It's very difficult to explain to others. You could say, 'Oh, it feels so wonderful to give back.' But it's bigger than that."

Goldie Hawn is an Academy Award–winning actress, producer, director, best-selling author, and children's advocate. The Hawn Foundation seeks to provide children with the tools to succeed and experience true happiness. Working with leading neuroscientists, educators, and researchers, the Hawn Foundation developed the evidence-based MindUP program, a collection of social, emotional, and attention-enhancing self-regulatory skills and strategies for cultivating well-being, emotional balance, and resilience.

The Path to Purpose

So how do you find this purpose?

- Sometimes it is evident in childhood and confirmed by life experiences in older age. "It has been clear to me since my earliest childhood memories that my reason for being was to help others," says billionaire industrialist Jon Huntsman, Sr. *The Chronicle of Philanthropy* listed the Huntsman family's donations to past charitable causes or foundations at $1.2 billion. His later experiences confirmed his childhood inklings: "As my sweet mother took her last breath in my arms and succumbed to the cancer she could no longer fight, I realized that our humanitarian focus must center on cancer. I saw with clarity the vision that the Huntsman fortune is a means to cure cancer and that my purpose on earth is to facilitate the research which will illuminate its mysteries."

- Sometimes the path to purpose is triggered by unanticipated, random events—such as receiving a cabbage. This is what Katie Stagliano, of Summerville, South Carolina, discovered. Katie is the founder of Katie's Krops, a not-for-profit organization with the mission to start and maintain vegetable gardens of all sizes and donate the harvest to help feed people in need, as well as to assist and inspire others to do the same. The idea for Katie's Krops began one day in 2008 when Katie, who was then a third-grader, brought home a tiny cabbage seedling, which she tended and cared for until it grew to an amazing forty pounds. Knowing her cabbage was special, she donated it to a local soup kitchen, where she served her cabbage to 275 guests. Katie decided that day to start a vegetable garden and donate the harvest to those in need. Within five years, she managed to create a sustainable solution to hunger from the ground up. She has donated thousands of pounds of healthy food to people in need, and there are more than fifty Katie's Krops gardens growing in twenty-two states across the country. Katie became the youngest recipient ever of the Clinton Global Citizen Award for Leadership in Civil Society. "I believe that my purpose in life is to work toward ending hunger and inspire others to follow their heart, regardless of their age," says Katie. "I believe that everything happens for a reason. Although we may not always know the reason at the time, there is a higher purpose. When I received my cabbage I had no idea the true reason. The true reason I was given my cabbage seedling is so I could learn how I, at only nine years old, could help end hunger one vegetable garden at a time."

Sometimes finding your purpose happens by conscious intent. "Seek, and you shall find," as the proverb goes. Consider what you hope others will say about you when they describe you, or what you would want to be written in your obituary. What legacy do you want to leave? You will be known for something. What do you want it to be? What would you like to do for others? Service for something beyond themselves is always a common thread in those who've found their purpose. Once you have an inkling, take a moment to write down your own special purpose. It doesn't have to be perfect—just write it down. You can hone it as you go. The simple act of writing things down greatly increases the likelihood of your words turning into action.

From Career to Calling

Recipes for super happiness from those who
"gave it all up" and made it cool to be good

*The two most important days in your life are the day you are born
and the day you find out why.*

—MARK TWAIN

On the sweltering morning of April 20, 2010, while crewmen were drilling at the Macondo Prospect oil field in the Gulf of Mexico, about forty miles southeast of the Louisiana coast, the Deepwater Horizon oil rig caught fire and exploded, killing eleven workers. The resulting fire could not be extinguished. Two days later, the oil rig sank, leaving the well gushing at the seabed and causing the largest environmental disaster in the history of the United States. On the surrounding beaches, evidence of the catastrophe appeared. Dozens of sea turtles—animals that are on the endangered species list—were found dead. Weathered oil floated across the ocean surface until reaching estuaries and washing ashore in Alabama, Louisiana, Mississippi, and Florida's panhandle, as the explosion caused the leakage of nearly five million barrels of oil into the sea.

Barely a month after the disaster, the then-thirty-year-old environmentalist Philippe Cousteau, a tanned, athletic, surfer-blond social entrepreneur who has been called the "eco-friendly heartthrob" and who could have easily made a living based upon his looks, dived into the toxic soup of the Gulf of Mexico to investigate the extent of the damage on sea life brought about by the oil spill. Philippe, who grew up wanting to be a firefighter, was shocked and appalled at what he found: massive globs of oil and chemicals, and plumes of orange particles floating twenty-five feet below the surface, threatening the gulf's fragile ecosystem. The dive, which gave him an underwater view of the worst oil spill in U.S. history, was one of the most terrible experiences of his life. "It was a nightmare, a nightmare."

To change the world is Philippe's dream, and indeed there are days that seem like fantasies straight out of the adventures of his childhood hero Indiana Jones. As he fights to make the world a better place, his expeditions have brought him to the shark-infested waters of Australia, to the highlands of Papua New Guinea, and to war-torn Sarajevo, Bosnia, where he has provided humanitarian aid. The home page of his website, philippecousteau.com, features a dramatic, awe-inspiring photo of his bearded face (no need to shave to meet the polar bears) wearing snow goggles that reflect an image of what appears to be the sun rising over the Arctic.

I have seen him on at least two of those days that make young idealists want to live a life just like his. Once was in Mexico's Riviera Maya, a stretch of coastline dotted with exclusive resorts. He was delivering a keynote address to a group of about two hundred wealthy Latin Americans seated by the poolside of a six-star hotel, at a philanthropy event I had helped organize. The sun had just set, and the amethyst waters of the Caribbean blended seamlessly into the night sky. Philippe spoke passionately about the impact humans are making on the world's oceans, the sound of crashing waves punctuating his slow, deliberate sentences and drowning out the clinking of wineglasses and cutlery around us. A year later, I met him once again in New York City, in a corporate boardroom high above Park Avenue, inspiring a group of young heirs and heiresses to make a difference.

But beyond the few days per year spent in fancy resorts and speaking to Park Avenue royalty, Philippe's chosen career has exposed him to many risks and struggles, whether outdoors exploring extreme science, or indoors running a nonprofit. Philippe was present for the filming of the documentary *Ocean's Deadliest* on the Australian coast, during which the beloved Steve Irwin, a.k.a. the Crocodile Hunter, was stabbed in the heart with a stingray's barb. For an hour and a half, Philippe helped administer CPR, but Irwin died on the way to the hospital, leaving behind a young widow and a little girl. It was a scene all too familiar to Philippe, whose own father, explorer Philippe Cousteau Sr., died in a seaplane crash six months before he was born. During the recent financial crisis, Philippe took a nearly 100 percent pay cut to avoid having to fire anybody from his charity, EarthEcho International, and constantly faces the tough task of fund-raising for ocean exploration. "The national budget for space exploration is one thousand times bigger," he points out.

"Running a nonprofit, overseeing investment funds, launching a few businesses, writing books, public speaking, and all that kind of stuff—they're really hard to do. But if I hadn't done the work of trying to help people and the environment, I'd be miserable," he says, emphasizing the last word as he furrows his brows in dread of what could have been. "I don't think I would do anything differently than I have."

The Unexpected Joys of Bearing the Burden

One day in 1993, Jill Robinson, the young wife of a British expatriate, traveled from Hong Kong to the Chinese province of Guangdong to join a sightseeing tour. Jill had been an animal lover all her life, shunning dolls as a child and playing with teddy bears instead. A journalist told her about the tour, which included a visit to a bear farm. The journalist alerted Jill to the horrible cruelty she had seen in the farm, and Jill, knowing very little about the issue, wanted to see it for herself. Shortly after moving to Hong Kong, Jill had grown alarmed at the extent of animal cruelty that she saw in the region, felt compelled to assist local vets, and worked for the International Fund for Animal Welfare.

At first, the outing seemed to Jill like a jolly one in which the farmers led them around a pit with about twenty bears and encouraged the tourists to feed the animals with apples attached to a fishing line. But Jill knew she had not joined the trip to have fun, and that the farm they were visiting was a bear bile farm. Bile, a digestive juice stored in the gall bladder, is prized in traditional Chinese medicine, even though there are at least fifty-four different effective herbal and synthetic alternatives to it.

So as the group was led to the adjacent bile shop, which sold all manner of bile-enriched elixirs promising to lower fevers, protect the liver, improve eyesight, break down gallstones, and even increase sex drive and cure hangovers, Jill abandoned the group and sneaked into a dark basement.

"I saw shadows of cages inside, and I could hear the bears' vocalizations." Suddenly, she realized that the tour group had seen a version that was so sanitized, it could not be further from the truth. The closer she got, the more frantic the bears became. "I realized that my presence was causing them anxiety that something horrible was going to happen. When I got close to the cages, I could see exactly why they were afraid."

She saw bears rammed into cages so small, their crushed bodies had grown into the bars. Some were even wearing full-metal jackets to restrict their movements. She saw severely emaciated bears with scars running the length of their bodies, their teeth worn down to their gums from gnawing at their cages. Most of the bears were missing paws from being caught in the wild in leg-hold traps. All of them were out of their heads with fear.

Decades later, she has become the world's leading expert on the cruel bear bile industry. Still haunted by her first brush with bile farms, she tells me her story with her voice trembling and eyes welling up.

More than ten thousand endangered Asiatic black bears are kept in bile farms in China, and around twenty-four hundred in Vietnam. The bears are often called "moon bears," after the crescent white patch found on their chests. The farmers confine the bears in crush cages so small they are unable to turn around or stand on all fours. Bears develop infections, hernias, and tumors from thrice-daily "milkings" that are facilitated by surgically implanting catheters into their gall bladders and forcing them to lie permanently on their backs. Some bears are put into cages as cubs, and stay there in constant pain for their entire life span of thirty years. When they run out of bile, they are killed for their meat, fur, paws, and organs, while others die from infections.

Now fifty-four, Jill has spent nearly all her adult life in defense of animals, and is now the founder and CEO of Animals Asia Foundation, a role that regularly exposes her to some of the most gruesome scenes imaginable. She recalls how in her youth, she forced herself to look at a picture of a monkey on which surgery for experimental reasons was being conducted—while it was still alive. "I remember this raw shock, like a bolt of lightning going through my body." Recently, while on a trip to investigate the dog meat trade in Korea, a dog slaughterer threw entrails at her. "It wasn't pleasant," she says, with her British dry sense of humor intact. "I must have seen hundreds or thousands of dogs in these horrible, horrible hellhole markets being slaughtered in front of our eyes. We've actually begged—*begged* the traders to kill the dogs quickly when they had blood and snot streaming from in their noses and their mouths, just screaming in agony. I was just screaming at the traders, saying, 'Please, please, kill them!' You can't rescue everyone." She wipes a tear and brushes her bangs away from her face. "I can't say that I haven't wished terrible things on the people who do this.

"Going to these bear farms, going to these markets kills you," Jill continues. "It just takes a little piece of you every single time. With every bear that dies here, it's like losing your favorite dog." It's not just depressing, but dangerous too. Her life is at risk, and there is twenty-four-hour security at the animal rehabilitation center she operates because she is fighting people's cruel livelihoods. (Another animal welfare activist, Dian Fossey, was famously murdered in 1985, presumably by those who saw her as an obstacle to the touristic and financial exploitation of the gorillas she saved.) Jill hasn't had a weekend off since 2003, and as a result, her marriage ended. Jill doesn't even stop for a meal until late at night.

"Has it been worth it?" I ask, implying that there must have been trade-offs when she chose this path versus a safer, saner corporate job.

"Sorry, Jenny, I'm not quite sure what you mean by that," says Jill, wrinkling her forehead and running her fingers through her slightly disheveled blond hair. "I just love what I do; I love every day, really. It's knackering and I don't enjoy looking like this, that's for sure, but I do love what I do. I'm not being a martyr; I love it."

When You're Looking for a Calling, Not Just a Job

Finish this sentence:
The most rewarding thing about working at a nonprofit is
_____.
   Let us know!

In July 2014, on the very same day that I was writing this chapter, the *Stanford Social Innovation Review*, a magazine covering best strategies for nonprofits, foundations, and socially responsible businesses, posted the above statement on the popular career networking site LinkedIn. A contact of mine, Sean,[1] who has had a remarkable career in social finance and social entrepreneurship, immediately posted the following reply:

The most rewarding thing about working at a nonprofit is becoming a manic depressive. You either feel ecstatic or want to slash your wrists. Prozac, anyone?

In the 1980s, the movie *Wall Street* summed up the business community's ethos as "Greed is good." Three decades later, an alternative zeitgeist is emerging: "Giving is good." For a new generation of socially conscious individuals, a lucrative career on Wall Street is no longer enough. We have entered an era in which it is "cool" to give, and nowadays there seems to be a consensus that it is less cool to be a banker and way cooler to be a social innovator. More and more people all over the world are driven by their desire for meaning and purpose, and graduates who used to take their talent to Wall Street are looking seriously at applying their energy, smarts, business savvy, and entrepreneurial DNA to the nonprofit sector instead. Passionate about social causes, brimming with new ideas for problem solving, and equipped with digital tools and networks, people want to work in the social sector, believing they will find great happiness and fulfillment in doing so.

Even for-profit corporations know they can attract talent by calling attention to their socially oriented activities. As former New York City mayor Michael Bloomberg said in his Giving Pledge to commit the majority of his assets to charity: "One of the senior managers at my company, Bloomberg L.P., recently told me that part of his new hires recruiting pitch is to ask, 'What other company can you work for where the owner gives nearly all the profits to charity?' Nothing has ever made me prouder of my company than that one story."

The expectation of meaningful work and work-life integration is firmly entrenched in the minds of millennials and Generation Y members. One might argue that they want jobs, internships, and volunteer opportunities in the social sector simply because being able to weave the story of building huts in rural Ningbo, China, into a job interview or MBA admissions essay gets them closer to their coveted spot at JPMorgan Chase or Harvard, but I believe the desire is sincere. There is not a week that goes by that I do not hear from an acquaintance—or at times, a totally random person—asking for advice on how to get started in the social sector, or how to switch from a for-profit to a nonprofit career.

Twenty-one years ago, at top business school INSEAD, two MBA students, Philippe Dongier and Katie Smith Milway, sent a school-wide e-mail asking if anyone was interested in cultivating coursework for careers related to nonprofits. Overnight, 126 students, staff, and faculty responded—a number equal to 50 percent of the newly arrived class. With seed funding from the school, Dongier and Smith founded INDEVOR, INSEAD's social enterprise club.

Across the Atlantic, John Whitehead, the former managing partner of Goldman Sachs and the board chair for several nonprofits, approached the dean of Harvard Business School with a similar idea. He asked how HBS could apply its distinctive competencies to help improve management within the social sector. From this, the Social Enterprise Initiative was born.

INSEAD and Harvard aren't the only schools where students have shown great interest in the social sector. Across all the top MBA programs, students have been increasingly interested in the topic in recent years, as the data from the Bridgespan Group shows:

Courses in philanthropy and social entrepreneurship are among

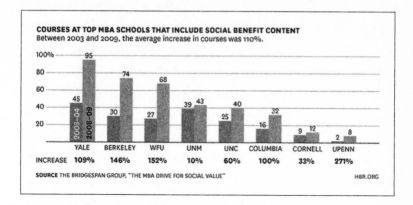

COURSES AT TOP MBA SCHOOLS THAT INCLUDE SOCIAL BENEFIT CONTENT
Between 2003 and 2009, the average increase in courses was 110%.

	YALE	BERKELEY	WFU	UNM	UNC	COLUMBIA	CORNELL	UPENN
INCREASE	109%	146%	152%	10%	60%	100%	33%	271%

SOURCE THE BRIDGESPAN GROUP, "THE MBA DRIVE FOR SOCIAL VALUE"   HBR.ORG

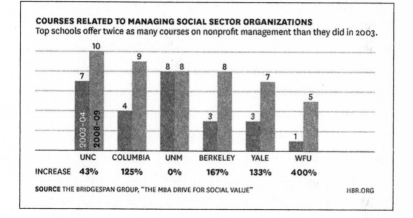

COURSES RELATED TO MANAGING SOCIAL SECTOR ORGANIZATIONS
Top schools offer twice as many courses on nonprofit management than they did in 2003.

	UNC	COLUMBIA	UNM	BERKELEY	YALE	WFU
INCREASE	43%	125%	0%	167%	133%	400%

SOURCE THE BRIDGESPAN GROUP, "THE MBA DRIVE FOR SOCIAL VALUE"   HBR.ORG

the most popular at colleges and universities, and the interest shows
no sign of letting up, whether the economy is in expansion, in reces-
sion, or just gliding along. In fact, thirty-six of the world's business schools now offer philanthropy-related courses. Professors at
those schools say the topic appeals to business students because
many may wish to eventually serve on the boards of nonprofits or
become philanthropists themselves. Some schools, including Stanford, Columbia Business School, and Boston University's Questrom

School of Business, teach entire courses focused solely on the topic, while others weave philanthropy into the curriculum of social enterprise courses. A growing number of MBA graduates want to work for NGOs or firms that say they have a social purpose. Young, energetic talent is entering the sector as volunteers, donors, employees, board members, and consultants.

Net Impact, a student club started by a group of thirteen graduate business students in the early 1990s to convene young people interested in using business skills in support of various social and environmental causes, has now ballooned to more than fifty thousand student and professional leaders from more than three hundred volunteer-led chapters across the globe. "There really has been an explosion in interest in curricular offerings in social impact," says Kat Rosqueta, founding executive director of the Center for High Impact Philanthropy at the University of Pennsylvania. "There has for a long time been interest among students, but clearly the faculty and administration have now taken notice. It simply became very difficult to ignore the clear hunger and demand among young people."

I asked Tom Freston, cofounder of MTV, whether this phenomenon was evident back in the 1960s. "No, no! I never knew anybody in the social sector," he insists. "It seemed there were some people who worked in these fields, but you never really saw them. It wasn't that common. Ten years ago, if you got out of a good school you'd work in Wall Street; thirty years ago you'd have worked in journalism." When Tom himself stepped into the humanitarian realm, he discovered a new class of people he describes as "magnetic."

"When I became the board chair of the ONE Campaign, I found that there's a whole subculture of young, creative people. They're not driven by the kind of motivations that you would find in the private sector," he says, recalling someone who has been in the company for six years and never once asked for a raise. "But they were just as exciting, just as interesting, just as creative. To me, it was a whole other tribe of people. That's something I didn't expect, and I found it thoroughly enjoyable."

According to Campus Compact, a coalition of American universities and colleges promoting civic engagement, there are approximately one hundred courses offered across the U.S. on the topic, with the largest program being run by the Pay It Forward Foundation. The federally funded, Ohio-based program offers courses on thirty-three college campuses, and allocates a chunk of money to each class for students to donate to local nonprofits.

For Babies and Baby Boomers Too . . .

"My daughter Grace, who is in fourth grade, attends a very issue-oriented school. It's very progressive, and social justice is a big focus of the curriculum, and that's one of the reasons we chose it," says Christy Turlington Burns, founder of Every Mother Counts. "She's a very compassionate, nurturing person, and I think that's partly because of the way that they're teaching social justice in school. She hasn't found her voice or her specific cause yet, like 'I want to save the turtles' or 'I want to be a vegetarian,' but I know in time she will." Indeed, more and more kindergartens and primary and secondary schools are integrating social issues into their curricula.

At the other end of the spectrum—retirement—more and more older people are discovering a new life purpose. "Encore careers" in the social sector are on the rise, and people are engaging in projects that they realize are more in sync with their inner selves but that have, until now, lingered in the back of their minds.

At an age when many women are slowing down and spending their days playing bridge, Hilde Schwab cofounded the Schwab Foundation for Social Entrepreneurship with her husband, Klaus. She says about her work, "This makes me feel very good; I think it's fantastic!" In the middle of our meeting in her office in Geneva, she proudly hands me a professionally formatted, spiral-bound document along with a few other brochures. The documents detail the stories of various social entrepreneurs whom her foundation has elected and supported along the way, from a South African woman providing employment to juvenile ex-offenders, to volunteer networks making a first response to natural disasters. "There are many, many other stories. I have a whole book full of profiles," Hilde says, patting the book proudly. "I think sometimes these people are really genius—they find ways to improve things. I read the profiles even of the people I haven't met yet, but I'm involved in the selection process of these people and I get such a lot out of it. This energy, this inventiveness of the people. This has added value to my life and I feel energized about this. I think it's just absolutely fantastic! I can't imagine being happy with just leaning back and enjoying my life. I think maybe something would be missing."

NUMEROUS WEBSITES that cater to people who are interested in nonprofit careers have emerged. The nonprofit job site Idealist has more than one million registered users. Many other websites, such as Opportunity Knocks and Common Good, focusing exclusively on social sector jobs have mushroomed. Most of these jobs don't pay very well, but that doesn't deter everybody.

In September 2013, the career networking site LinkedIn added a feature that allows its members to say whether they want to volunteer or serve on the board of a nonprofit. It posted about a thousand listings seeking volunteers. In just eight months, one million members raised their virtual hands.[2] Clearly, there were more people looking for ways to volunteer than there were spots. Hard to believe, but that is true for much of the nonprofit world.

Arthur C. Brooks, president of a public policy think tank in Washington, D.C., says, "When I taught graduate students, I noticed that [those] who pursued nonprofit careers were some of my happiest graduates. They made less money than many of their classmates, but were no less certain that they were earning their success. They defined that success in nonmonetary terms and delighted in it."[3] But the reality, as my LinkedIn contact Sean freely expressed, is that working in a nonprofit can sometimes be pleasurable only if tempered with a healthy dose of Prozac. The reality is that it takes a very special kind of person to be able to endure the unique set of challenges that people who have truly committed their entire lives to the social sector are willing to go through.

Bill Drayton recognized this back in the 1980s. A former McKinsey & Company management consultant, he is responsible for the rise of the phrase "social entrepreneur" and has earned the distinction of being one of Harvard's one hundred most influential alumni. Today, "social entrepreneurship" is often used to refer to the act of doing business with a positive social impact, or how nonprofits can operate for-profit ventures to maintain self-sufficiency. But

Drayton's original concept of a social entrepreneur was simply some-one who had come up with an innovative solution to a social problem and was obsessed with spreading that solution. As David Bornstein describes them in his book *How to Change the World: Social Entrepreneurs and the Power of New Ideas*, social entrepreneurs are "transformative forces: people with new ideas to address major problems who are relentless in the pursuit of their visions, people who simply will not take 'no' for an answer, who will not give up until they have spread their ideas as far as they possibly can." These visionaries—who are possessed by their ideas, ambitious and persistent in tackling major social issues, unwilling and unable to quit, and absolutely willing to commit their lives to changing the direction of their field—are one in a million. There simply aren't that many of us who are willing to "give it all up" in the name of a cause that we believe in, and Drayton recognized that. In response, he started searching the world for these social entrepreneurs, and in 1980 he built a nonprofit organization called Ashoka, which provides them with a living stipend for about three years, allowing them to quit their jobs and focus full-time on building their institutions and spreading their ideas. The stipends are not investments in projects, but investments in people while they are "shaky and lonely and a little help means the world," as Drayton once said. Ashoka has since become the largest network of social entrepreneurs worldwide, with nearly three thousand members in seventy countries.

Bornstein says of his interactions with social entrepreneurs, "I assumed that the social entrepreneurs would be motivated by altruism. But social entrepreneurs are not selfless. If anything, they are self-more in the sense that they heed their instincts, follow their desires, and aggressively pursue their ambitions. And the rewards are ample."

Groupon founder Eric Lefkofsky, who signed the Giving Pledge, names these people as an inspiration. Initiated by Warren Buffett and Bill and Melinda Gates, the Giving Pledge is a commitment by the world's wealthiest individuals and families to dedicate the majority of their wealth to philanthropy.

In Lefkofsky's pledge he said, "For those of us that are fortunate enough to be asked to sign the Giving Pledge, the commitment is easy to make. We have so much more than we could ever possibly use or need, that giving is relatively painless. But for the people who are tirelessly devoted to a particular cause, devoted to making the world a better place—giving is hard. When you're barely able to pay the bills, every dollar matters. When you're working around the clock and raising a family, every minute counts. Yet, remarkably, people still find a way to give. . . . It's this spirit that has always inspired me and my wife, Liz, to give."

Activism: Taking It to the Extreme

IF YOU'RE NOT OUTRAGED, YOU'RE NOT PAYING ATTENTION. It's the unofficial bumper sticker of die-hard activists all around the world. Whether they are campaigning against war, nuclear proliferation, or animal testing; or pushing for ambitious changes in health care, gay rights, or the environment, activists are dissatisfied with the drift of the times, are furious at the misdeeds of their enemies, and perceive those wrongs to be so grievous that the only response can be action—and the more attention it gets, the better.

In 2013, the Peruvian actor and environmental activist (and Johnny Depp look-alike) Richard Torres took tree hugging to a new level by marrying a tree in Buenos Aires, Argentina. Torres, who in the previous year had been arrested for staging a nude protest against the removal of trees in a park in Peru, walked down the aisle wearing a white suit, while the tree wore a tie around its trunk. During the ceremony, which was officiated by an Argentinian artist, Torres took an oath and even kissed the tree to "consummate" the marriage. The wedding was part of Torres's larger attempt to spread environmental awareness across Latin America. He declared, "My marriage will be eternal and I will make love with all the trees. Hugging them, I will feel their energy."

Galvanized by their desire to make love, not war, other activists brandish homemade placards, march on the streets, and harangue politicians. The most zealous ones erupt in fistfights outside courthouses, get arrested for civil disobedience, and land in jail, like the environmental activist Ric O'Barry, a former dolphin trainer who was the subject of the Academy Award–winning documentary *The Cove* (see full story, page 80).

They go through the emotions of anger, stress, burnout, disillusionment, sadness, grief, and despair. They are sometimes overwhelmed by the magnitude of their ambitions, and by the sense that they oppose a culture that does not care much for them. And at the end of the day, whatever activists do, however long they stay out in the freezing cold or the scorching heat, wearing ridiculous costumes or, like Torres, in the nude, most of them have only a slim chance of ever making a difference. Torres's tree-marrying stunt has probably had a negligible positive effect on the environment. (But so do most other projects by environmental organizations that address issues so intractable that change can be palpable only in the very long term.)

In 2003, researchers Alice Mills and Jeremy Smith studied how people find happiness by calling for change.[4] Over the course of the year, they interviewed eleven activists with diverse backgrounds—Greens, Marxists, feminists, Christians, Buddhists, and nonaligned and community activists figured in the sample, with personal histories in antiwar, environmental, and community-based campaigns. Three had strong international connections with the left in Chile, South Africa, and South Korea, as well as being involved in Australian movements. Some were approaching middle age and were seasoned, and others were older, with track records that were decades long. The researchers asked them how they got involved, what motivated them, whether they were looking to get something personal out of their involvement, and whether their active commitment nurtured their happiness, or possibly hindered it.

As one activist interviewed in the study said:

> The realist in you looks at how much shit you're trying to push uphill, how much power the people you've got are battling and how they can use that. . . . Sometimes however . . . how very few people either understand or want to understand, or couldn't give a rat's (couldn't care—author) so when, when you look at it in that perspective you may as well slice your throat because you really, you're battling enormous odds, especially in this country.

Some activists are blinded and deafened by their anger, and the failure of ordinary existence to conform to their utopian ideals becomes a nagging source of pain. Others have a persistent sense of missed opportunities in life. I am haunted by the account of Scott Baker,[5] who works in marine conservation in Berkeley, California. "I don't have a family because I can't afford it," he told me.

Katherine, a thirtysomething member of a left-wing political party who has been an activist since entering college, says she enjoys her commitment amid the twists and turns through which it has taken her. Nonetheless, she has worried about what might have been for her and has adjusted the course of her life accordingly by giving more space to her personal priorities. Here meaningfulness and happiness are in potential conflict. She says, "I don't want to get to fifty or sixty and think, 'The party stole my life because I didn't do the things I wanted to do.' I certainly don't want to put myself in the situation where I've sacrificed so much that I'm going to be resentful."

Richard Rockefeller, who was chairman of Doctors Without Borders (Médecins Sans Frontières [MSF]) from 1989 to 2010, said, "There are people who burn themselves out in a cause including in MSF, and all kinds of causes. The environmentalists are sometimes the worst. It is very depressing. They're not making themselves happier, fighting harder and harder and banging their heads against the same enemies."

So why bother?

In 2009, Malte Klar, a practicing psychologist in Germany, and Tim Kasser, a professor at Knox College in Illinois, asked 344 college students a battery of questions to gauge how central political activism was to their lives, how committed they were to it, and how often they were likely to engage in activism. Klar and Kasser then asked them a set of questions meant to assess, using various measures, how happy they were: how fulfilled, how optimistic, how empowered, and how connected to those around them.

The scientists found a clear link between political activism and a person's sense of well-being. On most of the measures, activism did seem to correlate with happier, more optimistic, more social scores. When they ran the study for a second time, this time with 359 self-identified student activists and an identically sized control group, they got similar results. But while these studies showed correlation, they didn't show causation. It is very possible that happier, more optimistic, more cheerful, and more social people are the ones who become activists in the first place. But can activism actually make a person happier?

To answer this question, Kasser and Klar ran a third study, in which they got their subjects to think like activists, then measured how it affected their short-term happiness. They gave subjects a survey about the food in the college dining hall. Some were given questions that primed them to think about what Kasser and Klar call the "ethical-political aspects" of the food, and were encouraged to write to the management of the college cafeteria to ask them to source local or fair trade products. The other group was given suggestions that focused on apolitical, "hedonic and self-oriented" aspects such as the variety and taste of the food, and subjects were encouraged to write to the management to ask for tastier food.

When the students were assessed on their well-being, the group who had involved themselves in the political debate were far and away the strongest on the "vitality" scale: They felt more alive and enriched than those who merely complained about the menu. "What we found," says Kasser, "was that the activist felt significantly more vital and alive and energized than did the nonactivist group." The activist-students didn't necessarily care about food ethics, but just taking action made them feel better. And while sending a memo to the cafeteria management is hardly the most arduous action, it nevertheless had a significant impact on those doing it. The study showed that even a very small engagement with political activism can boost one's sense of vitality. "Activists live a happier and more fulfilling life than the average person," says Klar.

The researchers admit that although it is in some ways remarkable that a relatively brief and subtle manipulation had any effect whatsoever on well-being, it must be noted that these results were somewhat weak and limited to a single measure of well-being. Nonetheless, this evidence for the potential causal role of activism in people's well-being is consistent with preexisting research. A 2001 study by the psychologists Holly Hart, Dan McAdams, Barton Hirsch, and Jack Bauer found that activism was strongly correlated with a quality called generativity, a sense of responsibility for others. And generativity, several studies have found, is in turn correlated with happiness.

According to the notable community organizer Saul Alinsky, the draw of activism isn't just the chance to fix what is wrong, but something far more romantic. Being an activist allows people to feel alive, he writes, in ways that they were previously unaware of. In his 1971 book *Rules for Radicals: A Pragmatic Primer for Realistic Radicals*, Alinsky encourages aspiring organizers to play on that yearning and sense of excitement in recruiting volunteers. "People hunger for drama and adventure, for a breath of life in a dreary, drab existence. Political activism could meet that hunger." As for happiness, he says, "The pursuit of happiness is never-ending. Happiness lies in the pursuit."

In Mills and Smith's study, an interviewee named Keiko talks about a "glorious" memory of an antiwar demo she was involved in. "On a peak like that—with something like that, it's just totally, you just hack in it. It's all the good emotions that you can think of." Her choice to be an activist is, for her, a modest sacrifice, as she remains a working professional and not involved full time. Activism, for her, fulfills the greater human need, and weds her to the intimate connections that she is comfortable with. This sense of happiness and camaraderie fostered through intense shared experiences is one of the commonly voiced themes in the study. Activists form a deep and concentrated connection with other trusted, like-minded activists. They speak about connecting energetically with networks and throwing themselves into activity. As one subject says, "I really like the sense of community, of people who you don't have to explain yourself to . . . you're allowed to be yourself . . . without having to feel that you have to protect yourself, or a sense of being guarded."

The act of throwing themselves in links their emotions to the intense relations with others that they experience in the movements. Many back away only for a short time to contemplate the lessons of their experiences and to recuperate. Together, they understand themselves to be different from the rest of the world, going through stress, disillusionment, and despair—and also euphoria.

But does activism produce happiness simply because activists get to hang out with other people whose company they enjoy? Or does it differ appreciably from other apolitical yet social activities, such as going to church or playing in a softball league? One of the subjects in Mills and Smith's study offers a novel turn to the topic. Jose, a Chilean Australian in his late thirties, says:

> Political activism is as much the source of unhappiness . . . as of
> happiness, in that if I don't achieve in an area where I think I
> could be having an impact or doing something useful, that can
> be as much a source, or even a greater source of unhappiness,

immeasurably greater source of unhappiness than not watching
a video, losing a soccer match, or any of the things that I get
happiness out of. . . . So . . . politics is a source, is the fountain,
of both in a certain sense.

The idea that political activism makes people happier actually
has roots that go all the way back to Aristotelian times. In his book
Politics, which Aristotle wrote circa 350 BC, he argues that to
achieve eudaimonia (usually translated as "happiness"), all men
must embrace their responsibility in the political system, thereby
protecting the interests of their personal lives, social class, and community, as well as instilling virtue in oneself through civil servitude
and leadership.

Mohandas Karamchand Gandhi, the preeminent leader of
Indian nationalism in British-ruled India, described himself to have
submitted "cheerfully" to the consequences of his activism. He led
the country to independence and inspired movements for civil
rights and freedom across the world by employing nonviolent civil
disobedience. Gandhi traveled throughout India, often speaking to
crowds of more than one hundred thousand Indians. Although he
was constantly shadowed by the police, it was not until 1922 that
he was arrested and charged with sedition for three articles he wrote
in his magazine, *Young India*. In his statement during his trial at
Ahmadabad, where Gandhi pleaded guilty, he said, "I am here
to . . . submit cheerfully to the highest penalty that can be inflicted
upon me for what in law is a deliberate crime and what appears to
me to be the highest duty of a citizen."

After his statement before the court, Gandhi was sentenced to
six years' imprisonment and thanked the judge for his courtesy. He

was imprisoned again in 1930, 1933, and 1942, when he went on a hunger strike as part of his campaign of civil disobedience. He eventually collaborated with the English to gain independence for India, which was proclaimed twenty-five years later. He has said, "Happiness is when what you think, what you say, and what you do are in harmony."

"The power of political activism," says Kasser, "is that it manages to provide so many of the requirements for human happiness. It gives people a sense of efficacy and a conviction that they are changing their world. It provides an often rich social network. Because political causes are freely chosen, activism enhances a person's sense of their own independence. And it gives a sense of self-transcendence, of being a part of something larger than your own individual concerns." All these things, Kasser says, have been shown to make us happier. It's not just a life of self-denying dedication to a larger cause but a pursuit with immediate and enduring psychic rewards.

How to Do It

If you are intent on finding happiness in being an activist, there are three things to keep in mind:

1. Autonomy and freedom—Do not engage in activism because somebody is making you do it. Make it your choice.
2. Connectedness—Find a cause that you truly feel connected to.

3. Competence—Make sure you are competent in the specific role that you choose. Note too that "high-risk activism" (in which activists run the risk of being arrested or injured) doesn't correlate with higher levels of well-being.

"If you know of a cause that feels truly important to you, get informed, get organized, and get active," Klar says. "Activism might not only change your well-being for the better, but also for the world."

As Ayn Rand writes in *Atlas Shrugged*, "Happiness is a state of non-contradictory joy—a joy without penalty or guilt, a joy that does not clash with any of your values and does not work for your own destruction, not the joy of escaping from your mind, but of using your mind's fullest power, not the joy of faking reality, but of achieving values that are real, not the joy of a drunkard, but of a producer."

A Lifetime of Once-in-a-Lifetime Experiences

The celebrated activist Ric O'Barry, seventy-six, is not someone whom many people would describe as "happy." In 2009, a team of documentary filmmakers featured his work in *The Cove*, a film that was met with a standing ovation at the Sundance Film Festival when it opened in Utah, and eventually won an Academy Award. Ever since, interviews and photos of Ric have been circulating in the media, often depicting him with a morose expression, his sullen eyes darkened by the brim of the beat-up khaki hat that he perennially wears. Even his own website describes him as someone who "carries with him a loneliness, the weight of a martyr."

But if I were to assess him in view of what Ayn Rand said, then I have to say that Ric is one of the happiest people I have ever met.

"I've had a lifetime of once-in-a-lifetime experiences," says Ric, his brown eyes widening with laughter. The faded brown shades of his T-shirt and matching hat look misplaced against the cheerful, melon-colored space that he calls his office. Behind him is a wicker daybed with giant pillows covered in bright pink-and-green-striped fabric, and a window with palm-tree-printed curtains shading him from the Florida sun. All around the office are photos of young and old Ric hugging, kissing, feeding, and otherwise just hanging out with his most beloved creatures—dolphins.

"Excuse me." Ric stops himself mid-sentence while talking about how he got started, and disappears. "I had to let the cat out," he says, grinning.

In the 1960s, the underwater-loving Ric was working as a commercial deep-sea diver and scuba instructor when he was hired to be a diver and trainer for the Miami Seaquarium. It was a dream job for him. "It amused me that they should pay me for doing what was so much fun," he says. Part of his job was to capture dolphins, and because of his passion for what he did, he became among the most experienced dolphin hunters in the world. So good, in fact, that he reckons that one of the first marine mammal protection laws in the U.S. was aimed directly at him and his team. South Carolina state legislation passed a law against "netting, trapping, harpooning, lassoing, or molesting genus *Delphinus* or genus *Tursiops* in the waters of Beaufort County," one of the places where he hunted. But Ric was oblivious. "I thought the people criticizing us were weirdos," he says with a shrug.

At the Seaquarium, Ric became the trainer for the five dolphins that starred in the hit television series *Flipper*, about a bottlenose dolphin with an extraordinary degree of intelligence and understanding of human behavior. Flipper was the companion animal of a wholesome American family—essentially an aquatic Lassie—who in many ways started the fascination with dolphins that continues today. Ric made Flipper jump through hoops, bite cigarettes in two, walk on his tail, play basketball, and even free someone trapped in a car in the bottom of the "sea." Thanks to the popularity of the show, thousands of Flipper lunch boxes, coloring books, jigsaw puzzles, and all sorts of merchandise were sold, and kids all around the world dreamed of having their own pet dolphin, or at least swimming with one. Working for Hollywood, Ric had it made. "There was a lot of money in it, and I had three Porsches and a Jaguar."

For ten years Ric carried on with his job, staying underwater with the dolphins so much that his hair turned green from the copper sulfate in the water, and becoming known as the "dolphin man" at the Seaquarium. "They are social creatures—far more than I— so I stayed with them just to keep them company." In his memoir, *Behind the Dolphin Smile*, he writes, "I ate with the dolphins, I slept with them, I read the *Flipper* scripts while they frolicked all around me. When they were hungry, I fed them. When there was a new trick to learn, I taught them. And when they had to be moved, I perched on the edge of the box they were in, keeping them wet and reassuring them that all was well." He even sampled the fish that they were fed, taking some home to make sure it was fresh. "We were very close, my dolphins and I."

And so when Kathy the dolphin got sick a few years after the *Flipper* series wrapped, Ric rushed back to the Seaquarium to be by her side. He had just returned from a trip to India, where, unsure of what to do after the show was over, he contemplated his next steps. Back in the tank in Miami, he saw Kathy floating listlessly in the water, her entire body covered in big, ugly black blisters. Devastated, Ric leapt into the water, clothes and all. "She came over and into my arms. I held her for a moment and felt the life go out of her. Her tail flukes stopped, and she was dead." Kathy's body sank to the bottom of the tank.

Ric made a 180-degree turn and on that very day began what has become a forty-three-year crusade against the very industry that he had popularized for more than a decade. By sheer coincidence, more than twenty million Americans were celebrating the first-ever Earth Day during the same week when Kathy died. Earth Day didn't mean much to Ric back then, but the beginnings of the public outcry for environmental reform seemed to legitimize what he was about to do. Immediately after Kathy died, Ric flew to the island of Bimini, in the Bahamas, where he knew that Charlie Brown, a beautiful, sociable young dolphin he had caught off Miami years before, had been confined in a small and dreary pen. "I was on a pilgrimage to try to undo at least in part some of the mess I had made of things," he says.

His plan was to commit an act of "civil disobedience," Rosa Parks–style. In 1955, her refusal to give up her bus seat for a white man in Alabama led to nationwide efforts to end the systematic segregation of public facilities, and Ric hoped that by letting Charlie Brown escape, he could thereafter call attention to the absurd law permitting dolphins to be captured and sent to amusement parks all over the world. "Yes, she was breaking the law, but she was drawing and bringing attention to a very bad law," says Ric, who is quiet and introverted by nature. His plan required that he sneak into private property, dive underwater to cut down a fence, and set Charlie Brown free. For full effect, he had to turn himself in, get himself incarcerated in Nassau's filthy and notorious Fox Hill Prison, and get out of his introverted shell to make a public statement and defend himself with a lot of noise.

"Had I not known about Rosa Parks, I might not have done some of the things I've done." Unfortunately, his first step in trying to free all the dolphins in captivity did not completely work. The wire cage that he was cutting collapsed and pinned him to the sea-floor, nearly drowning him. To make matters worse, Charlie Brown simply kept swimming around the prison he had known for years, and refused to be freed, for reasons Ric would understand only later (dolphins in captivity have to be "untrained").

But land in jail, create a noisy scene, and attract attention he did, and his plan succeeded in sparking awareness about dolphin captivity. The next morning, half a dozen journalists were camped out in front of the jailhouse, leading to a cover story in the *Miami Herald* and, later on, in *Life* magazine. Because of the nationwide media attention, he began to receive dozens of letters every day.

"I never planned on being an activist," he says, explaining that he was only responding to those stamped letters that would arrive in his mailbox. "Someone has an emergency and was looking for help, and I would go and help them. One thing leads to the next." While supporting himself as a stuntman, he lived hand-to-mouth and put practically all his resources into his movement to stop dol-phin exploitation around the world. "I was motivated by guilt, because I helped create this industry that led to all of these captures. I realized I was trying to make amends."

These days, a bicycle has replaced Ric's fancy sports cars, and instead of stamped letters he gets hundreds of e-mails every day. "If there's a dolphin in trouble anywhere in the world, I will be contacted. Sometimes, it's a woman in Australia who wants me to interpret a dolphin dream she had last night, or it could be the mayor of Seoul, Korea, asking me to come and help them free the dolphins that he confiscated." Over the years, he has never questioned his life's purpose. "If somebody's really struggling with that question of purpose, they're on the right track. My advice is, keep looking. You'll find it."

I think about all the articles that depict Ric as a mournful, troubled soul and ask if it has been worth it.

"Oh, gosh, I kinda wish I had my old life back," he jokes. "This is hard. I spend most of my time going to faraway places. When you ask me where is home, I'm sort of . . . *Where is that?* I'm out on the dolphin trail; that's really my home," says Ric, whose wife and eight-year-old daughter live in Denmark. Just the week before, he was in Toronto publicly challenging a marine park owner about the educational value of captive dolphins, and the next day he is off to Japan, where he has been a leading figure in the fight to end the annual ritual slaughter of thousands of dolphins off the coast of Taiji. It was his work in Japan that gave him a measure of fame, when documentarists featured him as the central character in *The Cove*, which tackles the issues of overfishing, dolphins in captivity, illegal whaling, and the dolphin slaughter in Japan.

"Japanese government officials view dolphins as pests to be eradicated in huge numbers, to preserve the oceans' fish for themselves,"

Ric explains. And so in Taiji, and various other parts of Japan, fishermen drive entire schools of dolphins into a hidden cove, trapping them with nets. Once they are hemmed in, the fishermen slash the dolphins' throats with knives or stab them with spears. "The water turns red with dolphin blood, and the air fills with their screams," Ric says. The carnage continues for six months year after year, generally between September and April, and is in a way perpetuated by members of the international aquarium community, who "obtain a few show-quality dolphins for use in captive dolphin shows and swim-with programs. By paying huge prices for live dolphins, the aquarium industry basically subsidizes the slaughter," he says. The film's success created legions of activists for dolphin issues, mercury contamination, and the protection of marine life.

Now in his fourth decade as an activist, Ric says that he is "over the guilt thing. . . . Today, it's just like breathing. I don't think about it. I just do it. I realized that if I didn't have my experiences with the *Flipper* TV show, and working at the Miami Seaquarium, I wouldn't be talking to you about saving the dolphins. I understand that now. That's what I did before, and I had to do that to get to this place." Today he is rejoicing over the new law just passed banning the captivity of dolphins in India. The law is particularly important given the size of the country, where there are so many requests to open multimillion-dollar dolphinariums. All of those dolphins would have come from Taiji. He knows, however, that his victory may be short-lived. "In the Solomon Islands, there was a law banning the capture and export of dolphins; then the new government came in and threw that law out."

I ask him how he copes with the difficulties of his life's mission, a question that he describes as "a tricky one." He pauses and says he gets out on the water as often as he can, whether he may be in Biscayne Bay, the Bahamas, or Jeju Island, "just to remind myself why I do this. I need to see the dolphins in the wild." The day before the interview, he decided to relax while working, so when a team of journalists approached him for an interview he invited them to come out to Biscayne Bay on their paddleboards and join him in the water. Most of the time, he simply tries to pace himself.

"I'm pretty good at that, actually," he says in retrospect. "I just came from Canada and there were a thousand people there at the demonstration, and there's a lot of media there," he continues, waving his arms in the air to re-create the sense of commotion. "When I show up in front of these people, every one of them wanted to talk to me. Everyone wanted their picture taken, and they have a story I have to listen to about dolphins, and I get invited to dinner and to stay at people's houses. If I actually went there and have dinner with them, to them it's a relaxing time, but to me, it's another interview. So I don't go to dinner, and I don't stay at their house; I have to be alone. I go back to the hotel and spend time alone a lot. I become very, very reclusive when I'm not actually doing the work, and that's the only way I can keep from being burned out. If you're thinking about the issues and you're talking about the issues constantly, that's how you get burned out."

But amid all the challenges, Ric never saw what he did as a sacrifice. "No. I still don't. I mean, success is really living your life in your own way, and I'm doing that. This is what I choose to do and I do it. Success is not about money—that's something else. I feel much better about myself. I could walk out of this room right now and go to the Bahamas or the Caribbean and open up my dolphin therapy program and be making five or ten million dollars a year if

I wanted to, but I wouldn't be able to sleep at night. Instead, I go to Taiji, Japan, where I can't sleep at night," he says, letting out a big laugh. "Either way, this is what I choose to do and I'm totally okay with it. We have several billion people on the planet, and most of them get up in the morning hoping they don't bump into something on their way to work. They do their mindless job, they come home, watch television, they get up the next day, and they do it all over again. Most people are sound asleep." But the life he leads, he says, is "like a roller coaster ride, going a hundred miles per hour," and the lowest part of the ride is not seeing his family as often as he would like. Fortunately his wife, Helene, who has also worked in dolphin rescue, has been very supportive.

"What really motivates me now is seeing some results. That keeps me going. It's very fulfilling." Last year, only eight hundred dolphins were killed in Japan, which is less than half the number that Ric had observed in previous years. Many Japanese people have also stopped buying dolphin meat upon learning that it is contaminated with mercury.

Before we say good-bye, I confess to Ric that I delayed watching *The Cove* for years, fearing that it would show graphic dolphin massacre scenes and fill me with spite for humanity.

"I only watched it the other day, before I met you," I sheepishly admit.

And then he confesses that he hasn't really seen the movie either. "I've seen parts of it. I don't see the same thing the audience might see, because I see between the lines. I see a life before me, and I see marriages and divorces and births and deaths and courthouses and jail cells. I see so many things that nobody else sees. It's so hard for me to watch it."

As he reflects, I tell him about the various studies I've come across linking a purposeful life with a happy life, and ask him if he agrees with them at all.

"I'm much happier. I don't know how to put that in words." He pauses, and his expression is not quite the chirpy, smiley, bright-eyed vision of happiness that we have come to expect, but something more profound. "I know what it is, but I want to know how to word that. What I used to do is to capture dolphins and train them; today I'm doing the exact opposite. I'm untraining them and I'm putting them back in the ocean. That is, like, instant karma. I thought I was gonna have to come back many, many lifetimes to straighten out that mess I created, but I'm gonna do it all in one lifetime.

"I just put one foot in front of me and I just keep going," he continues. "If I thought about it, I would probably quit, because trying to stop this multibillion-dollar industry is kind of like going down to the seashore with a bucket and trying to stop the tide from coming in. It's not always about winning; it's really about showing up. That's what I do; that's what I've been doing since Earth Day in 1970."

Ric O'Barry's Dolphin Project is a campaign under the nonprofit Earth Island Institute's International Marine Mammal Project. The Dolphin Project aims to stop dolphin slaughter and exploitation around the world. This work has been chronicled in films such as *A Fall From Freedom* and the Oscar-winning documentary *The Cove*, and the Animal Planet miniseries *Blood Dolphins*. Campaigns for dolphin protection are currently under way in a variety of locations around the globe, including the Solomon Islands, Indonesia, Egypt, and Singapore.

How to Deal with Burnout

It's supposed to feel good . . . but it doesn't anymore!

Deep in France's Dordogne region lies Plum Village, a quiet monastic community started by one of the most respected Zen masters in the world, Thich Nhat Hanh. In the village, run mostly by monks and nuns, laypeople are welcome to enter and join the Buddhist practice. When I met a monk from the village, I asked him what types of people go there. I imagined stressed-out bankers, disillusioned hippies, and heartbroken women re-creating the *Eat, Pray, Love* experience. "All that," he said, nodding. But something else that he said truly surprised me. "Every year, among the thousands of people who go to Plum Village, the majority are people who do work in the social sector. They go to Plum Village because they are burned out."

As I gradually discovered, too many people in the nonprofit sector indeed lose their spark and succumb to burnout. Always selling hope and trying to convince others to take action can be emotionally draining. Most for-profit companies have a peak season and an off-season. The retail industry, for example, is busiest during the holiday season and usually during the end of the month, when paychecks are distributed. On other days, employees are able to relax a bit. But there's no such thing as downtime when it comes to serving the most pressing causes in the world. There is a steady stream of emergencies, and deadlines are to be taken seriously— in some cases they are a matter of life and death. The constant urgency of the work can force other important facets of activists' lives to take second priority. Partners, marriage, family, and friends end up competing for time and attention. Furthermore, many of the issues that nonprofits deal with on a daily basis have no tangible solution. Intractable goals (such as ending poverty) and the constant uncertainty as to whether their efforts are making any difference at all can also lead to frustration and eventual burnout.

The 2008 survey "The Voice of Nonprofit Talent" found that 84 percent of nonprofit job seekers saw work as part of their identities, and not just a way to make a living. This can be a very strong driver when it comes to working for social change, but it can also be a hindrance in finding a healthy balance between work life and personal life. As Jill Robinson said, she hasn't had a free weekend since 2003, and that schedule resulted in the end of her marriage. "I think that happens to a lot of people in this movement. We become so dedicated and so passionate, you leave the things you love a little bit behind until it's too late."

When it comes to motivation on the job, people who choose to work in the social sector start out with a clear advantage. They have passion for their careers and are devoted to their organizations' mission, and their jobs feed their idealistic nature. Most people who work in finance cannot say that, and admit they're only in their jobs for the money. One of the many differences between a "job" and a "calling" is that a job depletes you and a calling energizes you. But while nonprofit professionals benefit from a very natural energy source, how do they sustain their motivation, commitment, and passion in the long haul when what they do for a living barely makes a living and the grind never stops?

Indeed, there are some nonprofit job descriptions, such as undersea "explorer-in-residence" at the National Geographic Society, that make deskbound corporate drones seethe with envy. But most nonprofit jobs read more like "development director" or "research manager." Worse, many nonprofit workers end up doing everything because their organizations are understaffed. Sylvia Earle, who actually held the explorer-in-residence title, has implied in interviews that her scientific expeditions may have led to the dissolution of her first marriage. "It's hard to have a traditional kind of relationship when you are as motivated as I have been," she says. And the ever-smiling and ebullient Nick Vujicic, who was born without limbs and who uses his story to spread the message of hope to other disabled people, says, "I've got my issues. I've got things in my nonprofit I have to deal with and in my for-profit that I've got to deal with . . . and I have back pain too. I don't always wake up in the morning with a smile on my face— no way!"

Just because activists are mission driven doesn't mean they're happy all the time. Just because they love a cause doesn't mean they love their jobs too. It's not a constant state of happiness from saving the world and saving the children.

Burnout and Compassion Fatigue: When Helpers Get Tired of Helping

The psychological consequences of working in situations characterized by constant distress and crisis are usually classified into three categories: burnout, secondary traumatization, and compassion fatigue. The three are not exactly the same, and it's helpful to be able to distinguish among them.

Burnout is related to the job environment where one works, which includes stressors such as paperwork and poor supervision or support. Burnout syndrome is one of the worst consequences of working with people in distress, and one of the most incapacitating outcomes of professional stress of care workers. People in the nonprofit sector are made to feel guilty if they have decided to take a break. It's as though by signing up to work for the Red Cross they have waived all their rights to go on a nice vacation. The California Wellness Foundation (TCWF), based in Los Angeles, is one of the very rare foundations that gives cash grants to nonprofit executives so that they can take time off from their stressful day-to-day responsibilities. Now in its eleventh year, the foundation has been providing thirty-five thousand dollars to each executive director to cover salary and other expenses during a sabbatical, which lasts a minimum of three months. They are free, often for the first time in decades, to do with their time exactly as they wish. "TCWF recognizes the importance of supporting leaders in the nonprofit sector to allow them to rest, reflect, and recharge," says Judy Belk, TCWF president and CEO.

STAGES OF BURNOUT[6]

by Dr. Andrew Goliszek

Stage I

High expectations and idealism

Excessive enthusiasm for work

Dedication to work

High degree of energy consumption

Positive and constructive attitude

Great achievements

Stage 2

Pessimism and first signs of dissatisfaction with work
Physical and mental exhaustion
Frustration and loss of ideals
Reduced working morale
Boredom
Early psychosomatic symptoms of stress

Stage 3

Withdrawal and isolation
Avoiding contact with collaborators
Anger and hostility
Serious negativity
Depression and other emotional difficulties
Inability to think or concentrate
Exceptional physical and mental strain
A large number of stress symptoms

Stage 4

Apathy and loss of professional interests
Low self-esteem
Chronic absence from work
Negative attitude toward work
Complete cynicism
Inability to interact with other people
Serious emotional difficulties
Serious stress symptoms on a physical and emotional level
Thoughts of leaving the job or profession

Secondary traumatization (sometimes referred to as vicarious or indirect trauma) refers to the psychological effects that working with traumatized people has on care workers. Care workers often experience the same phenomena as the traumatized clients they work with, such as nightmares, intrusive thoughts, depression, anger, irritability, the feeling of helplessness, chronic exhaustion, digestive problems, being prone to infections, increased consumption of alcohol, smoking, addiction to prescription medicines, etc. These strong reactions are a result of the interaction between the experience that a person in distress is going through and the unresolved difficulties and previous life experiences of a care worker. Listening to dramatic stories, care workers may have to face feelings of their own, such as the fear of dying, or the fear that something similar could happen to their families and friends. This process triggers a number of defense mechanisms such as suppression, denial, and projection, which can manifest in dysfunctional professional behavior and impaired relations with colleagues. These strong emotional reactions on the part of care workers can hamper their work, rather than contribute to their understanding of clients and a creative use of professional skills.

People in helping professions are susceptible to stress because of the direct communication with people who need the help of other people. This communication entails a close relationship and empathy with the emotional states and the suffering of others. In the course of their work, care workers hear numerous sad and tragic life stories, with descriptions of traumatic experiences and devastating loss. They are often emotionally overwhelmed by these insights. In addition, they usually face very limited sources and possibilities to help traumatized people.

Daily encounters with the material presented by traumatized clients are a serious risk for the mental health of care workers. Some of them are volunteers who are not paid for their work. They are usually people of goodwill who help individuals in distress, but not as a regular job. To be sure, there certainly are professionals among these volunteers who do their job without pay. Most volunteers, however, are laypersons in the field of mental health, and are not mentally or emotionally equipped to handle the difficulties of dealing with other people's problems. Hearing about the devastating experiences of others often shakes care workers' sense of control over their own lives and their worldview assumptions. Care workers can thus become traumatized themselves and experience situations of crisis.

Compassion fatigue (CF). When burnout and secondary traumatization are both present, an individual is said to be experiencing compassion fatigue, a condition characterized by a gradual lessening of compassion over time. Nearly everyone who performs emotionally intense charitable work can be susceptible to compassion fatigue—and those who are exposed to the traumatic suffering of others, such as doctors, nurses, emergency-service personnel, counselors, social workers, clergy members, and animal-shelter workers, are at high risk. They forget why they wanted to help people in the first place. In the case of those who work in animal-related charities, such as shelters that euthanize unwanted pets, compassion fatigue is particularly common, contributing to high annual turnover rates at some shelters. Unlike every other type of charitable work, killing is a part of the job at most animal shelters, notes Diane Less Baird, president of Angels for Animals, a shelter and pet-owner education center in Canfield, Ohio. "You can only hold so many animals in your arms and feel the life go out of them," she says, "without it starting to suck the life out of you." What's more, says Carol A. Brothers, a clinical psychologist in Annapolis, Maryland, who conducts compassion-fatigue workshops for animal shelters around the U.S., shelters tend to encourage workers to remain stoic when euthanizing or turning away unwanted pets, and those workers may be less likely than other charity employees to get support from people outside of work. "People in their lives start saying to them, 'Oh, my God, it's only a dog,'" she says.

The signs of compassion fatigue can mimic those of post-traumatic stress disorder, which can afflict people who have survived a traumatic event such as combat, rape, or assault. Sleeplessness, irritability, anxiety, emotional withdrawal, avoidance of certain tasks, isolation from coworkers, feelings of helplessness and inadequacy, and even flashbacks are among the symptoms. Some argue that the media has caused widespread compassion fatigue in society by saturating newspapers and news shows with often decontextualized images and stories of tragedy and suffering, causing the public to become too cynical and resistant to helping people who are suffering.

There is another element to CF: compassion satisfaction (CS). Psychologist Beth Hudnall Stamm, Ph.D., explains this phenomenon as "being satisfied with doing the work of caring."[7] In other words, the gratification of helping others makes the strain of the work worth it. It is not uncommon to see social workers continue in their jobs after physical or psychological injury, or to find them reluctant to leave the field despite personal stress. The care that we give to the world is both the greatest risk and the greatest protective factor from long-term trauma.[8]

WHAT CAN WE LEARN FROM THOSE WHO STAY HAPPY?

But what can we learn from those who are truly happy? Here are a few things I have observed:

1. **They renew their energy by going deeper into the cause.** This is the most surprising thing I have noticed among nonprofit leaders who stay happy doing what they do. Distracting themselves by watching TV or playing a round of golf is only a temporary option. They find more "hands-on" opportunities that allow them to directly experience the positive outcomes of their work, or that bring them back to the very reason they got involved in the first place.

   Animals Asia founder Jill Robinson, the bear rescuer whose calm demeanor belies the gruesome scenes she has faced and chased in defense of animals all around the world nearly all her adult life, says that the greatest source of strength for her is the bears themselves. "I always say that the bears rescue us every bit as much as we rescue them." Jill will sometimes flee emotionally wrought scenarios and say she has to run to a meeting. "I'll just tell a lie and say, 'I have a meeting with Jasper.'" Jasper is one of the bears at the sanctuary, where every bear takes on anthropomorphic characteristics and has a name. "I'll just go off, and I just absorb all this amazing energy from a bear that was crushed in a cage for fifteen years with a catheter. I'll just suck up the bears' happiness as they lie on their backs in the sun in their enclosures and just look at them, and understand why we're here. They rescue us. They tell us why we're here. They have such a propensity for deep enjoyment of life. They have heavy emotions as deeply and as deep and profound as the emotions that we have, and I'm just overwhelmed by the fact that they don't hate us as a species for everything that we've done in their past. We've taken away their lives, we've taken away their youth, we've taken away their beauty, we've taken away their choices, and yet our presence no longer means harm to them. How can a species be so forgiving?"

2. **They take care of themselves first.** Truly happy activists take a break from work, exercise, do breathing exercises, and participate in other recreational activities that help them reduce stress.

Jill says that at the end of each day, she winds down by watching TV, having a beer, and simply relaxing. "Frankly, I don't want to watch another Animal Planet or National Geographic. I don't want to see more animal stuff, animal cruelty, or animals being eaten by other animals. I want to watch Simon Cowell shouting at people on *X Factor*, or *Downton Abbey*!" Animals are never really absent from her life, however, and her relaxation time is spent with Muppet and To Zhai, two dogs she rescued from the hellish dogmeat markets in southern China. "They're utterly gorgeous, and they make me laugh every single day."

Christy Turlington Burns, who has been an anti-smoking as well as a maternal health activist, says, "There's also the other side of giving and being in service, which is that it can be very depleting. People are attracted to this field because of a desire to help others, and yet they're very depleted by the system. I don't tend to feel depleted often. I mostly feel really energized, but I am conscious of what the impact of giving could have physically without knowing it. You just need to pay extra attention to caring for yourself to be able to do more."

3. **They know how to say no.** One of my mentors once taught me to learn to say no to the things that don't matter, so that I can say yes to the things that do. I have also observed among nonprofit leaders that saying no helps them do better with the things that are already on their plate. Saying yes too often not only affects the quality of their current projects but also adds a level of stress not worth taking on. They don't do more; rather, they do better. This safeguards their sanity and the level of passion they are able to sustain for the work that they choose to do. Do-gooders often feel the pressure to do more and more—there are invitations to get involved in this project or that movement, etc. Knowing how much need there is in the world, and how much opportunity there is to make things better, it can be hard to say no. The ones who keep their sanity choose to stay in their niche and do what is within their power, so that they can actually follow through and know what happens as a result.

4. **They find strength in a group.** It is incredibly helpful to surround yourself with people who can relate to your situation. Maintaining a diverse network of social support, from colleagues to pets, promotes a positive psychological state and can protect against

secondary traumatic syndrome. Healthy leaders have built a community of support around them. They are connected to coaches, mentors, and colleagues who care for them and can help them stay healthy. And it's helpful to have a few role models who inspire them with how they stayed passionate and committed over the long haul.

Jill says she finds strength in her team, whom she considers not just colleagues and professionals, but very good friends. "I encourage people to talk honestly and then again if people have got problems. I always encourage open dialogue because I think that this is really very healthy for us to get things off our chest and move on stronger, and it works." She is also a great believer in crying. "When you need to, I think you have to. I encourage the team to wear their hearts on their sleeves. I'm more worried when people don't cry than when they do cry."

5. **They don't suffer from "founder's syndrome," and they are not "the cause."** Many nonprofit leaders suffer from what is called "founder's syndrome," the propensity of an organization's founders (be it one person or a group) to have a deep sense of ownership over and responsibility for the organization. It's their "baby" and they don't want everybody's hands all over it. Founder's syndrome leads to a great deal of frustration and unhappiness among people working in nonprofits. Those who are happy realize this, and so develop strong teams that can function well without them. This is critical to the health of the leader and the organization. They need to maintain a sense of identity outside of work, and they know it's

dangerous to completely fuse their personal and work personas. Without boundaries, people end up seeing the leaders as "the cause" and don't know how to engage with them in any other way. Thus founders maintain and invest in relationships outside of work.

6. **They maintain a sense of humor.** The creators of the site When You Work at a Nonprofit say:

> We created it because we thought it would be funny. Of course, humor is the best way to communicate frustration, and we have a lot of that too. So we started [the site] because we wanted to highlight some of the problems we continually see, and let other nonprofit people share their experience about working in the sector. We had no idea it would take off the way it has. Clearly there's a ton of frustration, at every level. We get about two hundred submissions a week, as well as twenty to thirty e-mails each week with stories about working at their organization, and thanking us for creating the blog. Several people have told us that this blog is the only thing getting them through their day.

7. **They focus on the effect they are having.** They spend time with the recipients and see the results of their hard work.

> Katie Stagliano, the young founder of Katie's Krops, says, "When I'm down, I think about all the people that I'm helping. I think about the people who don't get meals, the people who wait in lines for hours just to get food. I think about the struggles people have to go through just

to have what so many of us take for granted. Knowing that I have the ability to help them keeps me going."

Jill Robinson says: "Personally, for me, what helps me, what strengthens me is to simply see what we do." To see at long, long last things coming home to roost. Jill has laugh lines, not wrinkles. "I'm just really, really happy with the fact that we have these incredible places of peace for the animals. We've got six bears sleeping now back in quarantine, with every chance of living. That makes me deliriously happy. We're able not just to rescue these animals just for their own sakes, but able to get the paperwork out there, the evidence out there, and use that evidence to end further suffering." Animals Asia collects vital scientific evidence on the physical and psychological effects of bile extraction. Reports and papers published by their teams have helped to raise the profile of the moon bear within the scientific community and to increase public awareness of the terrible cruelty involved in the bear bile farming industry.

Jill is so impassioned, her voice crescendos, and there are no pauses between her sentences. "We can smell success; we can taste it. We are now making a difference— it's very, very clear. I've never seen a transition like this in China, over the last couple of years, thank God! I strived a lot for this, there's no question. And we can see things developing; we can see change." Jill's original goal was to start a debate in China about the cruelty of the bear bile industry. Now, her Weibo messages (the Chinese equivalent of a tweet) go viral within seconds. "I've always been warned in China by Chinese that things happen slowly. I can see it happening and it's just indescribable. There's a great saying from Gandhi: 'First they ignore you, then they laugh at you, then they fight you, then you win.'"

8. **They think win-win.** Happy nonprofit workers don't think of themselves as constantly in a state of need, but think of what they have got to offer. Kate Roberts, senior vice president at Population Services International, says: "Develop win-win ideas. Nobody will help you otherwise—what's in it for them?" Richard Rockefeller says, "In the end, it has to be all about all of us. Desiring the happiness of every living being is a philanthropic impulse. If you approach every day that way and have a philanthropic goal that's about increasing happiness, then it's a source of pure joy. There's an expression, 'What goes around comes around.' You move it that way and then eventually it comes back to you, because you are connected with a person or group or cause that you are giving to. There's a circle so it's reciprocity rather than charity."

9. **They know it's a job.** Like it or not, they know they will need to get up and go into the office (or out in the field) every day. Some days will be a lot of fun, and some won't be. It will never be a nonstop adventure of driving around in a 4x4. They realize that there will be office politics no matter where they go, and that even though nonprofits are run by well-intentioned people, those people have flaws, egos, and mood swings.

10. **They have decided whether to sign a vow of poverty—or not.** Some of them realize that their passion for their job exceeds their desire for anything else—including the ability to have a big paycheck

and to provide for a family. Some know that they're not quite willing to give it all up.

Kate Roberts, a self-confessed lover of nice shoes and expensive travel, once gave a commencement address to the graduates of the George Washington University School of Public Health and Health Services (now the Milken Institute School of Public Health), in which she said, "I looked down at my Gucci loafers and made a mental note that they could probably feed a family for a year. Did I really need these shoes? Probably not! It was so clear what I had to do." She says of her current job in Washington, D.C., "You can do all this and still have your shoes! They're probably not going to be Gucci, but a nonprofit career also doesn't mean that you're gonna go completely broke."

Shouldn't the satisfaction derived from working for an NGO be reward enough? "Excuse me, but that's a load of crap," says Joan Salwen, whose family downsized their upper-middle-class lifestyle so they could give more to charity. "It's all very well to do a worthwhile job in the nonprofit sector when you're forty and you've provided for your retirement and your kids' education, but it's not easy for people. I see young teachers who are struggling to support families on thirty-five thousand dollars a year. Yes, we've worked very hard. But we were both born incredibly lucky. Although neither of us came from a lot of money or was given any, we were born in the U.S., we were born white, and all four of our parents were teachers, so we were very well educated. Even in our downsized state we're extremely blessed."

A PRINCE TURNED PAUPER . . .
TO PRINCE AGAIN

In 2004, Manhattan club promoter Scott Harrison left behind the streets of New York City for the shores of West Africa. "I'd made my living for years in the Big Apple promoting top nightclubs and fashion events, for the most part living selfishly and arrogantly. Desperately unhappy, I needed to change," he says. Soon, he signed up for volunteer service aboard a floating hospital with a group called Mercy Ships, a humanitarian organization that offers free medical care in the world's poorest nations. On Scott's website, he wrote:

> Top doctors and surgeons from all over the world left their practices and fancy lives to operate for free on thousands who had no access to medical care. I soon found the organization to be full of remarkable people. The chief medical officer was a surgeon who left Los Angeles to volunteer for two weeks— twenty-three years ago. He never looked or went back. I took the position of ship photojournalist, and immediately traveled to Africa. At first, being the Connecticut Yankee in King Arthur's court felt strange. I traded my spacious midtown loft for a 150-square-foot cabin with bunk beds, roommates and cockroaches. Fancy restaurants were replaced by a mess hall feeding 400+ Army-style. A prince in New York, now I was living in close community with 350 others. I felt like a pauper.
>
> But once off the ship, I realized how good I really had it. In new surroundings, I was utterly astonished at the poverty that came into focus through my camera lens. Often through tears, I documented life and human suffering I'd thought unimaginable. In West Africa, I was a prince again. A king, in fact. A man with a bed and clean running water and food in my stomach.
>
> I fell in love with Liberia—a country with no public electricity, running water or sewage. Spending time in a leper

colony and many remote villages, I put a face to the world's 1.2 billion living in poverty. Those living on less than $365 a year—money I used to blow on a bottle of Grey Goose vodka at a fancy club. Before tip.

YOU DON'T HAVE TO GO BROKE

At top-ranked universities around the world, students routinely express interest in working in the social sector and following in the footsteps of the likes of Scott Harrison—but are dead afraid of going broke. As with many career decisions, there is a threshold at which the need for financial stability outweighs the desire to pursue a meaningful career. Although there is now great respect accorded to careers in the nonprofit sector, it is still a financial risk, especially for college graduates who have huge student loans, or midcareer professionals accustomed to a certain standard of living.

But in some parts of the world, this is now changing. Says Kat Rosqueta, of the Center for High Impact Philanthropy, "Fortunately, there are now increased opportunities in the social sector. There's no longer a trade-off between earning a livelihood and making a difference. You don't need to be a martyr to a cause. There are all sorts of opportunities along the continuum. You can be earning a fine living in a commercial enterprise but knowing that even as you do that, you can still play a role as a volunteer, a grant maker, or someone who ensures that sourcing within your company is socially and environmentally responsibly done. It doesn't matter which sector you're in—whether you're in the commercial, nonprofit, or public sector, there are opportunities to do good there."

Furthermore, many nonprofits are also beginning to think about how to be sustainable. Boards are recognizing that in order to make a difference, they have to think about how to attract the people who will bring them forward.

Don't Confuse Social Sector with Social Impact

So many people have turned to me and said they want to quit their jobs in the for-profit sector in order to make a social impact. I say don't confuse social sector with social impact—we don't necessarily have to be in the former to achieve the latter.

Working in a nonprofit is no guarantee of finding meaning and purpose in your daily life. Many nonprofit workers lack purpose in their work and find that they are not really making a difference, while many people in the for-profit sector know that they are making a social impact and find great fulfillment in staying where they are.

The American clothing designer and entrepreneur Kenneth Cole, whose eponymous fashion label has long been known for ads featuring provocative messaging on everything from gun control to marriage equality to finding a cure for AIDS, says: "I just feel far more enriched as a result of [my social activism]. It's done a lot for me; it's done a lot for my family. It's not quantifiable but it's certainly given me a greater sense of purpose and a greater quality of existence. At the end of the day, [social activism] can be gratifying not just emotionally but also financially and professionally. And it's okay. It's not something to be embarrassed about—that you can provide for your family, that you can make a living, and at the same time that you're serving your community and making a difference."

The Antidote to Angst

By the middle of her senior year at Princeton University's Woodrow Wilson School of Public and International Affairs, Wendy Kopp realized she was going through life at such an alarming speed—and headed absolutely nowhere. At school, she was perpetually in overdrive, pursuing excellence and working obsessively around the clock on academics and extracurriculars. But she wasn't happy, so she began soul-searching. "I was in a desperate funk my senior year in college," says Wendy, who had, until then, led a very comfortable life. She was born in a wealthy part of Dallas, Texas, and attended an upper-middle-class school where a hundred-thousand-dollar scoreboard hung over a $3 million football stadium.

"I had never, ever been in that state before—but I realized I was so engaged in all these activities, but I really hadn't thought about what I wanted to do after I graduated. I found myself literally asking myself, What do I want to do with my life?"

There were only two things she was certain of: that she was going to work obsessively no matter what she chose to do, and that no matter how clichéd it sounded, she wanted to make sure all that hard work would go toward something that "makes the world a better place."

Meanwhile, she noticed that every Princeton senior seemed to be applying for a job in an investment bank or a management consulting firm. "Our generation was called the 'me generation'—at least that's what the media said. People thought that we just all wanted to go work on Wall Street and make a lot of money for ourselves." Back then, a number of writers spoke out critically against the culture of narcissism that they thought had permeated the youth, presumably as a reaction against the self-sacrificing culture of the older generation who had grown up in the Great Depression. But although these criticisms reverberated throughout American popular media, Wendy felt the moniker was misplaced. "I knew that many people were applying to those firms just because they didn't see the alternative."

Ultimately, her search for meaningful work led her to grow enamored with the idea of teaching. "I hadn't majored in teacher education, but teaching in a low-income community was the one thing I could think of." Wendy speaks so energetically, articulating every word as though she has given a dozen commencement addresses to inspire young people. It is hard to believe that back in the 1990s, when Teach for America, the nonprofit she founded, was just beginning, she grew concerned that her personality wasn't suited for a rigorous schedule of speeches and presentations. "Some of this is tried-and-true and trite in a way, but what can be more important than helping kids actually fulfill their true potential?" She began looking for a teaching job, but because she didn't have an education degree, she didn't get any offers. Wanting the security of a job after graduation, she reluctantly followed the norm and applied for a job in the corporate sector.

Wendy's experiences remind me of my own, when as a college senior graduating at the top of my class in Manila in 2001 I found myself being wined and dined at fancy restaurants and five-star hotels by McKinsey, Unilever, and other big-name companies. They took me, along with my other high-achieving classmates, to places we could never have afforded with our student allowances, and instilled in us the idea that as the crème de la crème, as they liked to call us, we should work for them, and only them. Brimming with idealism, sheer audacity, an excess of naïveté, and a dash of insanity, I spent my first year out of school teaching two college freshman courses—one on algebra, and one on the creative process. (I did actually apply for a job at McKinsey, but they turned me down.)

"Why don't we recruit people as aggressively as the investment banks do?" Wendy says. "Why don't we surround the choice to teach for two years in our highest-need communities with the same kind of aura of selectivity and status that we surround working on Wall Street for two years?" With that vision of making teaching "the thing to do" for America's top graduates, she proposed the creation of Teach for America, so named to underscore the national importance of the movement, in her undergraduate thesis, which she submitted in April 1989. The idea was to create a national teacher corps that places graduating college seniors as teachers in urban and rural areas across the country, modeled after the highly successful Peace Corps.

Evidently the universe did not want Wendy to be a banker—by the time she graduated in June, she hadn't gotten a single offer from any of the financial institutions to which she had applied. After receiving a rejection from Morgan Stanley, her last corporate option, she set her real aspirations into motion and simply moved forward with Teach for America step by step, believing that when an idea is meant to happen, the universe makes way for it. She moved to New York City in June 1989 with three trash bags of clothes and a sleeping bag, found a small room in a shared apartment for five hundred dollars a month, and worked alone in a skyscraper along Forty-fourth Street and Madison Avenue in an office donated by one of her earliest sponsors. There, she toiled every day from nine a.m. until past midnight mailing out hundreds of letters and making hundreds of phone calls to get a seed grant to launch Teach for America and reach her goal of five hundred corps members in training within twelve months. By August 1989, she had hired four staff. By April 1990, Wendy and her team had inspired twenty-five hundred people to apply to Teach for America, appealing to students with loads of idealism—and not the least bit of indecision about their plans after graduation. By June 1990, a charter corps of five hundred committed recent college graduates joined Teach for America and began fueling the movement to eliminate educational inequity.

"I was in pursuit of fulfillment. I'm a generally happy and optimistic person, but I wanted to ensure this kind of alignment between what I really valued and where my time goes," says Wendy, for whom "sleeping in" means rising at six a.m. "I think in a way, we're all probably looking for a way to align our values and what we believe is important with where our time goes. I think I have found the centeredness that comes from achieving that alignment."

Starting at least every third sentence with "I think," the forty-something Wendy seems highly cerebral, and not the type to spend much time reflecting on her existence. I ask her how giving her life to a cause has changed her in the same way it has changed the lives of so many others, and the question obliges her to contemplate. After a long pause, she finally says, "I really don't spend any of my energy in an angst about what to do with my life. I feel very lucky, and very satisfied with what I get to do every day. It's just an incredible privilege and it's almost just surreal, that I somehow, so early on, found my way to something that did in fact help me be part of a broader cause that is pursuing such a meaningful end." Having met so many young and old people feeling anxiety over the possibly meaninglessness of their existence, I tell her that what I find most fascinating about her is how she never spent time questioning what she wanted to be doing.

She attests that the same is true for everyone else in the picture. "I made this observation long ago. I spent a bit of time with some of the true veterans among the Teach for America people who had been at this for more than ten, fifteen, even twenty years, and I realized, I've never spent so much time with people who are so fundamentally fulfilled. These folks are centered in a community. They know their work is making an incredible difference." She surmises that if she went to their peers who chose a more traditional route, she would sense more angst among that group. "When I meet college students on campuses, and they're struggling with this decision of whether or not to do Teach for America, I just keep thinking to myself, If only I could help them truly understand and fastforward them to what they would be thinking in five, ten years."

As I reflect on my own experience of teaching, I remember that the hours I spent with my students in the classroom were the best part of my day. Back then I was in a relationship with a man who was verbally and eventually physically abusive, and because I had foolishly convinced myself that I "loved" him, I did not leave. I would stride into the classroom at eight thirty every morning brimming with excitement and purpose.

I tell Wendy that I could definitely relate when I read Teach for America corps members testifying, "I love my life," "I love what I do," "This is the best year ever." But from what I've seen, there is a downside too. Once, I volunteered to give a talk for Teach for Malaysia (one of TFA's offshoots in Southeast Asia) on one of their training days, and was struck by what I overheard. As the corps members sat on a secondary school's basketball court in a makeshift auditorium, an announcer gave out an emergency help line number that the teachers could call whenever they felt they could no longer handle the emotional demands of the job.

"I don't want to sugarcoat too much," says the ever businesslike Wendy, speaking with a consistently strong and clear voice. "This is the most challenging thing I've ever done. I've talked to a number of folks who say that the greatest intensity they've ever felt in terms of pressure and stress was when they were actually working in a nonprofit. At any given point, there is so much more to be done. It's impossible to be satisfied, so you can be achieving something, but you're constantly in pursuit of something even greater. If you are centered in the magnitude of the problem we're addressing, then you're always trying to raise the bar."

She says the way to get around it is to build a culture that helps people feel supported in the intense work. "The fact that I'm not alone in this and I'm surrounded by so many others who can support each other. There's no way to make the work less intense, but there's a way to create culture that supports all the individuals." Staying centered in the work is also key. "It's very easy to get overwhelmed by the administrative demands and whatnot. Just always finding the space to spend time in classrooms, in communities, and with the alumni program we're working in, and just constantly seeing the actual work is part of what creates the fuel to just keep pushing and to find the fulfillment and remember why this is all so important. What is fulfilling? It's to actually be a part of something that you realize is working!"

Not long ago Wendy met Ivy Martinez, one of TFA's corps members, and realized the plan was indeed working. Ivy was teaching fifth-graders in San Jose, in the Bay Area of California. They kids had been performing far behind, reading around first-grade level and already disengaged with school. At the same time, Wendy's son, Benjamin, was a fifth-grader in a school in the prosperous Upper West Side of Manhattan. "Ivy had started with her class when they were fourth-graders. She just got on a mission with her kids. She was just absolutely determined that she's gonna put them on a path to get themselves to and through college. She went to extraordinary lengths." By the time Wendy visited the kids, they were reading a novel. "They were reading it at such a level of higher-order thinking; and I realized, this class were ahead of my own kid and his classmates. I watched her kids giving each other feedback on their leadership, which they do each week in leadership circles. When I think about my own kid's class, they would be snickering through that."

But what about those who are unlike Wendy and Ivy, and have not mapped out their path, I ask. "I was just thinking about my own journey in this," she replies. "It was just so obvious and so simple. But I actually was very conscious about the fact that I was literally asking myself when I was a senior amidst this funk, What do I want to do with my life? There were no parameters at all. It was a big, wide, open space in my mind. So I think it's about each person asking themselves what matters to them, given where they are and just deeply reflecting on that, and then, starting somewhere. I think if I hadn't found my way to that early on, I would spend the rest of my life searching for the thing that would enable me to be in pursuit of something so meaningful. So I do wish for everyone to find their way to that, to be a part of a broader cause. I can't imagine anything more fulfilling than that or anything that would engender true happiness more than that."

Wendy Kopp is the founder and chair of the board of Teach for America. Under her leadership, Teach for America's nearly thirty-eight thousand participants have reached more than three million children nationwide during their two-year teaching commitments. Wendy is also CEO and cofounder of Teach for All, a global network of independent social enterprises that are working to expand educational opportunity in their nations by recruiting and developing their most promising future leaders to commit two years to teach in high-need areas and become lifelong leaders for educational excellence and equity. She has received numerous honorary degrees and awards for public service.

Teach for America is the national corps of outstanding college graduates, graduate students, and professionals who spend two years teaching in low-income urban and rural public schools and become leaders in expanding educational opportunity for all. TFA's mission is to build the movement to eliminate educational inequity by enlisting our nation's most promising future leaders in the effort. The organization's network includes corps members and alumni working in education and many other sectors to create the systemic changes that will help end educational inequity.

The Secret to Superhappiness

"Everything I did is so simple. People always get surprised and say, 'How come I didn't think about it?' I don't know. I did it, it worked, and people say it is big," says the Bangladeshi economist and professor Muhammad Yunus, with a befuddled look on his face.

"It" is none other than the concept of microcredit, or as Professor

Yunus puts it, "lending money to poor women," for which he won the Nobel Peace Prize in 2006.

The first few moments of our meeting are spent side by side in a makeup room at the CNN studios at the Time Warner Center in Manhattan, where we communicate by speaking to each other's reflections in a mirror framed with dozens of blinding incandescent bulbs, while he laughs as his face is being powdered in preparation for yet another TV interview. The day before, he was in a conference where he spoke in a panel alongside billionaire eBay founder Jeff Skoll, and where he received a Forbes 400 Lifetime Achievement Award for Social Entrepreneurship for his work, to thunderous applause from an audience that included Bono, Bill Gates, and Warren Buffett—mainstays in events he is invited to. So when I got the chance to trail him for a few hours in the midst of a frenetic day in New York before he flew off to Bangladesh, I gladly jumped at it.

Developing the concept of microcredit was "not a big rocket science," Professor Yunus says, but idealists around the world have accorded him the deference usually reserved for religious leaders and rock stars. It was something I saw in action in Singapore last year when, after giving a speech in a university, he was hounded by a throng of idealistic young students all wanting to shake his hand and have their pictures taken with him. A cursory glance at the website of the Yunus Centre reveals a staff list hailing from Cornell, Wharton, Dartmouth, and every elite school imaginable, and these Ivy Leaguers are happy to forgo hefty paychecks elsewhere for the chance to join his antipoverty brigade. And when he's beset by inevitable criticism for his methods, the likes of Steve Forbes come to his side, saying, "No good deed goes unpunished."

I wonder what it is about the gray-haired professor, ever smiling and always clad in his trademark kurta and Nehru vest, that invites all this devotion, as I watch the makeup artist press the last bits of powder onto his forehead. An aide leads us out of the makeup room and into the greenroom, where we sit with our backs against a tall window with a majestic view of Central Park, a calming scenery amid the chaotic holding area. We intermittently glance at a TV screen with a live feed of the program on which he is coming up next, as he tells me about his childhood.

Muhammad Yunus was born the third of fourteen children in 1940 in Chittagong, a busy seaport in what is now known as Bangladesh. His father, Dula Mia, was a tenderhearted and devout Muslim who owned and ran a successful jewelry shop on the ground floor of the family's small two-story home, while his wife, the strong, willful yet compassionate Sufia Khatun, helped him out at the shop, adding the final flourishes to the jewelry before they were sold. Because neither of them were very well educated, it was important to them that their children go to school. But apart from that, the children were free to choose which courses to take and which careers to pursue. "This is a fantastic thing. Usually parents are always planning for you," especially in the conservative society where he grew up, he says. To his parents' delight, young Muhammad was an excellent student and emerged as a natural leader and multitalented personality in school, engaging in music, theater, and graphic design, and discovering his first passion: being a Boy Scout. As part of a jamboree, he traveled abroad for the first time. "It was a very great experience for a young kid, to cross the Atlantic on a luxury ship and travel around, free as a bedouin. My parents didn't travel anywhere, so this gave me a little escape." He laughs as he recalls the happy memories.

But Muhammad's childhood was also marked by family tragedy. Five of his siblings died at a young age, and his mother succumbed to mental illness and struggled for thirty-three years. Even though Dula Mia paid for the most advanced health care available in Bangladesh back then, she never recovered. Young Muhammad was very close to his mother, who was always putting money away for their poor relatives, friends, and neighbors who came to her for help. It was she who helped him discover his interest in economics and social reform early on.

At the age of twenty-one, he was offered a post as a teacher of economics in his own college in Chittagong. "I always thought of myself as a teacher. I enjoyed teaching and I thought that would be my lifelong career," he says. As a child he loved tutoring his younger brothers and made sure they got top grades in school. Teaching at the college at such a young age put him in front of students practically the same age as he was, and some of them were even his classmates who had fallen behind. "That gave me a kind of a new connection with the young generation." Having grown up in an entrepreneurial family, he also tried his hand at setting up his own business, a packaging company that over time employed one hundred workers and made healthy profits. But even though the business was making money, he still wanted to teach. "Not as a job, see? I'm not taking it as a job that gives me some income. At no point in my life did I ever think I was doing a job. Teaching is something that I wanted to do. Salary was something extra for me. I never for a second thought it was a sacrifice; I was enjoying it all along," he says. In 1965, he was offered a Fulbright scholarship, one of the most prestigious scholarship programs in the world, and he seized the opportunity to get a Ph.D. in the United States. There, he learned from another teacher, Professor Nicholas Georgescu-Roegen, that things are never as complicated as they seem and that "it is only our arrogance that prompts us to find unnecessarily complicated answers to simple problems."

What followed is the history of the Grameen Bank, which began soon after Professor Yunus returned to a Bangladesh that was struck by famine. There, he accepted a post as the head of the Economics Department, and realized that the elegant economic theories he was teaching were useless in curing societal problems. "Skeleton-like people began showing up in the railway stations and bus stations of the capital, Dhaka," he writes in his memoir, *Banker to the Poor*. "In 1974, I started to dread my own lectures. What good were all my complex theories when people were dying of starvation on the sidewalks and porches across from my lecture hall?" Realizing that none of the economic theories that he taught reflected the reality of the city streets, he abandoned textbook-style teaching, and instead encouraged his students to go into the village and try to understand poverty at close range. In the village, he interviewed a woman who made bamboo stools, and learned that she had to borrow from loan sharks the equivalent of fifteen cents to buy raw materials to make each stool. After repaying the loan shark, she was left with a profit margin of about a penny. It quickly became evident to the professor that poor people became trapped in what he calls "financial apartheid": Because traditional commercial banks do not want to waste their time on lending the impoverished the few dollars and cents to raise themselves above subsistence level, poor people are enslaved by usurious loan sharks. Bothered by the absurdity of the situation,

Professor Yunus decided to lend twenty-seven dollars from his own pocket to forty-two people living in a tiny village—just enough credit to buy the raw materials for their trades.

"That was the beginning of it all. I never intended to be a moneylender. I never imagined that my micro-lending program would be the basis for a nationwide bank for the poor. All I really wanted was to solve an immediate problem." Now he is active in more than fifty other companies, ranging from agriculture to telecommunications, based on the same principles upon which the Grameen Bank was founded. "Every time I see a problem, I create a business to solve the problem." This leads to "superhappiness," he says.

"Superhappiness?" I ask.

"Superhappiness, yeah."

"Professor Yunus," I address him, mindful that nobody in Bangladesh would dare call a professor by his or her first name. I tell him that I have followed his story closely, especially because my grandparents set up a bank serving poor farmers in the Philippines. "When one is constantly trying to solve problems, doesn't that cause a lot of headaches? Where is the superhappiness in all this?" I ask.

"Yeah, I'll tell you." But before he is able to, a production assistant signals him that he's coming up next. He excuses himself, appears on the TV screen, and together with the crew, a documentarist who has been making a film about him, and yet another Harvard grad who has chosen to work for Grameen, we watch the ever-cheerful professor being interviewed on CNN. Ten minutes later he reemerges, and we walk outside and get into a car, where we continue our discussion as he makes his way to dinner with his eldest daughter Monica, an opera singer living in Manhattan, before catching an evening flight.

"All along I was happy, because I've been doing things I enjoy. People ask me, 'Do you go on vacation?' And I ask, 'What is a vacation?'" he says, oblivious to the scenes of midtown Manhattan showing through the car windows. "If I were a painter, I'd paint every day. Would you call it work or enjoyment? People, when they want to relax, go and paint. For me it's the same thing. I enjoy the work." And right there, as I am belted in the seat, the professor proceeds to deliver an impassioned lecture, loud enough that the driver can hear it clearly.

"Life is not about money. Life is about the purpose we want to set for ourself. Stacks of money cannot be a purpose, because money is a means, not an end result," he says, adding that Grameen's experience over the past three decades has shown that social consciousness can be as burning—or even more burning—a desire as greed. "Human beings are built in a different way. There are two things inside of us: selflessness and selfishness. Economic theory has been based on the selfishness part, not the selflessness part just yet," he laments. "Economic theory says that the only business there is in the world is business to make money, and there's no other kind of business in the world."

He says that there is a "new kind of business—business to solve problems rather than to make money. I call it social business. People argue that this is not going to work; the economy is going to collapse for the lack of money as an incentive. I agree [that] money is an incentive that keeps the wheels turning, but I disagree on one point. Money is not the only incentive. There are other incentives. Making money is a happiness; making other people happy is a superhappiness. But you don't know that yet because you haven't tried that, so you think there is only one happiness—making money."

"If it's all that fun, how come there are lots of social workers who get burnt out?" I ask.

"Because social workers are not in business. I'm not against charity, but this is better than charity. Charity has one life; this has an endless life. It's a machine that runs by itself. Even if I'm not there, it works. I created a lot of businesses, one after another, because I want to solve problems. I have always hated this problem of homeless people, so when I was in school, I thought, When I grow up, I'll create a business to solve the problem of homelessness. This was a self-designed incentive that I created myself."

"So many people are searching for meaning and happiness in life. Do you think this is the answer?" I ask.

"Yes. This is the answer. And the invitation is try it just once. A little one; see how it feels. Just a little one." He smiles.

"What if I can't come up with a Nobel Peace Prize–winning idea?" I tease him.

"No, no, just only a little one," he laughs. "For example, take five families out of welfare. Create a social business so they don't have to be in welfare anymore; they can be independent entrepreneurs so that they have their own business and so on. And if you're successful in taking five families out of that, then you can take twenty families, and so on." He names many other problems in which the same principle can apply: disabled people, drug addicts, human trafficking, torture, and the list goes on. "This is fun; this is enjoyment. You are solving people's problems. All I'm saying— take a bite of it; find out. Then if you know the superhappiness, you can decide which happiness you would like to go through, or you mix both: You have happiness from making money, and the super-happiness from touching people's lives and changing the whole world. You have the capacity of changing the whole world. You didn't know that because you are so busy taking care of yourself. That part is hidden to you, because our system never exposed that, so it built a wall. You didn't have any window or anything that you could see through. All I'm doing now is throwing out that wall. It's up to you; I'm not forcing you to do that."

As we approach the restaurant where he is to meet his daughter for dinner, I ask him if he ever feels drained by this nonstop action. "No—why should I? I feel strengthened; I feel that I have something that I can do for you. Otherwise, what is good for my life if I'm not useful to somebody else? If he's saying that I'm useful to him, and my life is worth living because I'm useful to some other people—otherwise, what is the use of my life? Just eat, and grow, and die. That's not life—not human life, at least." And with a big laugh and a jiggle he says, "I'm always in a dancing mood. I'm always dancing."

Professor Muhammad Yunus is the recipient of numerous international awards for his ideas and endeavors, including the Congressional Gold Medal, the highest civilian award of the United States. He is a member of the board of the United Nations Foundation. In Bangladesh today, Grameen Bank has 2,564 branches, with 19,800 staff serving 8.29 million borrowers in 81,367 villages. On any working day Grameen collects an average of $1.5 million in weekly installments. Of the borrowers, 97 percent are women, and more than 97 percent of the loans are paid back, a recovery rate higher than that of any other banking system. Grameen methods are applied in projects in 58 countries, including the U.S., Canada, France, the Netherlands, and Norway.

From Trauma to Triumph

For giving, not forgetting. A new way to deal with death,
terminal illness, and grave disability

If you light a lamp for someone else it will also brighten your path.

—BUDDHA

"I realized when I left Africa that it is not a crime to dream," says Djimon Hounsou, whose journey onto Hollywood's A-list seems so improbable, it could have come out of a movie. He was born in one of the poorest regions on earth—the small, unforested West African country of Benin, where "you wake up and the first thing you do is try and survive." He is the youngest of five children, and he only met his father, a cook, for the first time around the age of ten. "The dream was to escape that surrounding. Since your biggest need is having to sustain yourself that day to exist, a dream seemed like a luxury. In Africa, it's almost like a crime."

In search of a better life, Djimon, when he was barely thirteen, immigrated to France with his brother to study there. Soon after arriving, he dropped out of school, and because he lost his legal status as a student, he could not work and became homeless. "I lived on the streets for several years—fighting for survival, searching garbage cans for food, begging for money, and washing in a public fountain near the Pompidou Centre," says Djimon, a dark-eyed, dark-skinned, towering man with an Olympian's mighty body.

Four years later, while he was living on the streets, a photographer became so impressed by his exotic looks that he introduced him to the famed fashion designer Thierry Mugler, who then encouraged Djimon to become a high-fashion model.

Very soon after, he was walking on the catwalk and had an established career in Paris. Then he set his sights on another dream—to be an actor—and without knowing how to speak English he moved to the United States, where he landed parts in music videos for Madonna and Paula Abdul, and on popular television shows such as *Beverly Hills 90210*, *ER*, and *Alias*. His acting career kicked into high gear when Steven Spielberg cast him in the 1997 film *Amistad*. In the years that followed, he received two Academy Award nominations for his acting work, and has since become one of the very few African-born personalities who has won critical acclaim in the capricious world of Hollywood.

I meet Djimon for lunch at the Casa del Mar hotel, on Santa Monica Beach, on a day so bright and sunny, it was almost necessary to wear sunglasses indoors—which he does. Best known for his roles in movies that chronicle poverty, violence, and the fight against slavery, he has often been asked by directors to wield a weapon, scream in Swahili, and flash those "crazy" eyes. "I've seen both sides of success and failure, both sides of poverty and luxury," he says. Once, when he was homeless in Paris, he tried to make a phone call to ask for help, and asked a stranger for one franc to drop in a pay phone. "He looked at me as if I were what we call a *clochard*—they're basically just drinking wine and living on the street corners. He thought that maybe I was asking for money for drugs. He said no, but he turned around, laughed, and said, 'I'll buy you a drink but I'm not giving you a franc!' I thought that was odd," he says. "The challenges that I faced being on the streets were so great. The need for help was so great. It was heartbreaking." I ask him if his family was able to help at all. "Even if you're blood related, it's not a given nor a guarantee that a family member could even support you. I came from a very deprived family that didn't have much at all. I thought if my immediate family can't help me, I don't know who will."

When the film accolades started pouring in, UNICEF and Oxfam began to knock on his door, recognizing his potential, as one of the very few African-born actors with real leverage in Hollywood, to be a powerful voice against poverty and injustice in the developing world. They tapped him to be their goodwill ambassador, and he accepted. In 2005 he traveled to Mali, in West Africa, for a fair trade campaign, and thereafter he joined a vast succession of other campaigns for Africa.

Djimon candidly admits that his first foray into activism was one motivated by "having your image sort of be as a supporter of some kind. It's not that I had a great knowledge on whatever the topic is. I'm just trying to be honest and clear about it. I didn't fall into this because I had a strong desire to help. It sort of came as a result of one part business, and one part because I wanted to do right."

Eight years into his role as an Oxfam ambassador, he can't

imagine living his life any other way. "I really can't fathom the thought of not giving my time to a cause that I think is important to our evolution. I can't close my eyes on it. Over time I really understood the value of giving." Through his work he has made friends with many other activists (some of them famous, such as Brad Pitt and Angelina Jolie), and the experience of being around people who give generously has rubbed off. "Whether I am passionate about their cause or not, you can't help but be inspired."

We speak again seven months after our first meeting in Santa Monica. Djimon has been campaigning against the proliferation of weapons in South Sudan, and this time he has just returned home from a trip in the war-ravaged country, where hundreds of thousands of people have lost their lives as a result of armed violence made possible by the free flow of guns and ammunition. "It felt like a Hollywood movie to see young boys carrying AK-47s," says Djimon, who has a five-year-old son. "The vision of that was extremely shocking. It was a vivid reminder of what I could have become myself, if I hadn't left Africa." Over the next few minutes he gives me an impassioned primer on the need for an international arms trade treaty. I ask him if he ever feels burdened by the intractable problems that lie ahead.

"I definitely feel drained. I struggle with it." Decades-old political systems that predetermine one's economic fate, corrupt structures that seem impossible to undo, and nonprofit funds used only to "sustain the house of charity, the establishment" instead of going to the needy are all issues that make him feel restless. His passion for films that tell stories about Africa has brought him to movie set locations that "mimic very much the environment, and that's heartbreaking."

Djimon has also campaigned for the fight against climate

change, an experience he says "has brought me such a great awareness about what a disservice we're doing to our planet in so many
ways. But at the same time, the awareness has also made me a little
cynical about life in general. It's almost like a curse. You can't really
close your eyes on it. You can't really pretend now that you don't
know the damage that, for example, plastic, what it's causing
around the world. I mean, I'm trying to avoid plastic. Plastic is in
everything, everywhere!"

So why bother? I ask. "Because at the end of the day I feel like
the little bit that I do eventually offsets the system that is in place . . .
and redeems some aspects of the way that we go about life. The
more you dwell on what is, then you're basically part of the problem. The moment you create a world for yourself that you want to
change, then at that moment, change starts to come. But you certainly cannot dwell on the problems and expect a change."

To cope with the strain, Djimon recommends "a lot of meditation, reminding yourself of your basic needs, and trying to keep
serene." It is a process that he likens to how, as an actor, he clears his
mind each time he delves into a new character and tells a new story.
"I call it 'cleaning out the corrosion.' If there's a water pipe that's
been feeding your house, then over time it becomes full of corrosion. You have to work at balancing yourself in a way that you can
cope with the world. Keep yourself corrosion-free." Charity work is,
as he puts it, "a double-edged sword. I am deeply saddened by some
of the conditions I see. At the same time, supporting them brings
you such an emotional joy. It may be hard work, but the emotional
gratification and reward redeems and softens any hardship. There is
a blessing in helping someone other than yourself overcome something and move forward. It is intangible at times, but incredible.

"My greatest happiness often comes from helping others achieve," he continues, "or aiding others to succeed, accomplish their dreams, or overcome their struggles. There's definitely a tremendous joy and an emotional reward for contributing to someone else's advancement in life, in ways that I was hoping to be impacted when I was homeless also in France."

"What are your dreams now?" I ask.

"Most of my dreams are not so much about myself anymore. Most of my dreams are about creating a legacy for Africans. And now that my son is here, it's all about creating something so he can be proud of his father."

Djimon Hounsou is a two-time Academy Award–nominated actor for his work in the films *In America* and *Blood Diamond*. His company, Somnium Entertainment, is developing and is actively in production on a slate of feature films and documentaries focused on Africa.

How to Bounce Back from a Painful Past

I have found that among its other benefits, giving liberates the soul of the giver.

—MAYA ANGELOU

Not all people emerge from the throes of great loss to achieve growth. Many survive, but with significant impairment and psychic scars.

Generally, 25 percent to 30 percent of people exposed to serious trauma develop post-traumatic stress disorder (PTSD), a condition lasting months or years that is marked by agitation, fear, depression, and other symptoms severe enough to disrupt their lives. More than one-third of individuals with PTSD may fail to recover (even with treatment) over a decade.[1] Some people give up hope and end their lives prematurely or engage in substance abuse, avoidance, withdrawal, anger, and high-risk activities.

But the latest research on many thousands of traumatized people, from prisoners of war to rape victims to those injured in car accidents, has led desensitized clinicians to appreciate human nature's resilience. Some health experts point to recent, largely overlooked evidence on the psychological impact of violence: Many victims of trauma recover, and even say life is better and more meaningful than before disaster struck. As Nietzsche said, "That which does not kill us makes us stronger." Suffering has long been romanticized in literature, art, and folklore as transformative and empowering, and there are elements of truth to this concept.

"The bottom line is that people recover and go on to do amazing things with their lives," says Dr. Sandra Bloom, a psychiatrist who developed the Sanctuary Model, an inpatient psychiatric program for the treatment of patients who suffer from complex trauma-related emotional disorders. On a broader scale, social psychologists who have studied towns devastated by hurricanes or floods refer to "disaster rebound," the process of rebuilding a community so its members are more satisfied than they were before. Richard Tedeschi, of the University of North Carolina at Charlotte, says that people who survive or witness disasters can come away stronger emotionally. There are five ways in which people may grow after a trauma: They can develop a greater appreciation for life; deepen spiritual beliefs; feel stronger and more effective; grow closer to others; or pursue unexpected paths.

Simply experiencing suffering and trauma—and running as far away as possible from it—does not help. So what does? And what are these unexpected paths that people pursue that help them recover from their painful past? Although experts say it's hard to predict who will bounce back, they can identify some of the most distinguishing characteristics of resilient people. Those include a tendency to see crises as challenges rather than problems, optimism as opposed to pessimism, and a preference for socializing instead of withdrawing.[2]

But beyond simply trying to find the silver lining amid the trying circumstances, what factors allow trauma sufferers to achieve personal growth and happiness as a result of—and not despite—their experiences? Nobel Peace Prize winner Malala Yousafzai, the Pakistani schoolgirl shot by the Taliban who has astonished the world with her courage and determination to fight for education and equal rights for women, was once described by a reporter: "There is too, surprisingly for one who has experienced so much trauma, a constant undercurrent of amusement in her voice, as if she is on the verge of giggling."

Even Ted Turner, the media mogul and founder of CNN who gave a landmark $1 billion gift to the U.N., was a wounded person. When he was young, he witnessed the agonizing death of one of his sisters. His bipolar father, Ed, abused the young Ted with severe beatings using coat hangers and straps, and eventually committed suicide.

The approach that I have seen in common among so many people, which is also evident in the stories of Djimon Hounsou, Malala Yousafzai, and many who are described in this chapter, takes more than resisting the temptation to withdraw and brood. In the process, these survivors not only recover from a traumatic past but also actually grow from it and flourish.

The Hidden Power of Helping

Life and death are one thread, the same line viewed from different sides.

—LAO TZU

"My son Peter was still e-mailing with his sister Jane at 9:25 that morning. His e-mails seemed coherent and there was no problem then. And then they just stopped, so I don't know what happened. What eats me alive is that the three main things I want to know, I'll never know. I don't know how long he lived, I don't know how much he suffered, and I don't know how he died," says Liz Alderman, seventy-two, whose son Peter died on September 11, 2001. He was attending a conference at the World Trade Center, and was only twenty-five years old when he passed away.

"What happened to Peter was nothing like I expected. There is a void and a hole, and that's never filled. I knew that he was dead, but the 'neverness' of everything began to set in. All the things that would never ever happen. That I would never see him again, that he would never have a family, that he would never know the joy and pain of being married. That he would never have a future."

One of the first things Liz did after Peter was killed was train her dog to be a therapy dog for sick and elderly people. "I never even thought of that before, but I needed to do something positive, and I can't explain where it came from." A few months later, Liz, a former special education teacher before she married a doctor, got "very, very involved" with the Memorial Committee for Families of September 11, serving as cochair with a woman who lost a daughter the same age as Peter. "There was this burning desire to leave a mark for Peter, and I wanted to see his name written in stone. I knew that I had to make sure that the creation of the memorial would be something good and positive."

The experience, however, was not very positive, to say the least. "It was probably the single most frustrating experience of my life. It was all about money, and power, and greed, and politics. They couldn't care less what the families wanted. As a matter of fact, almost everything that was promised to the families never happened." A few months later, Liz quit, and decided to create her own memorial for Peter. "I wanted to leave a mark that he had been here, and I wanted the world to be a better place because he lived. That's what drove me, and that's what continues to drive me."

She and her husband started with fuzzy notions of how to memorialize their son. "We had been married for fifty years and never agreed on anything," she laughs. They considered building a playground, or endowing a chair at a university, but realized that wasn't Peter. Then, one night in June 2002, bleary-eyed from months of mourning, they saw a *Nightline* episode that featured Richard

Mollica, M.D., the director of the Harvard Program in Refugee Trauma and a world expert on the treatment of post-traumatic depression and PTSD in war-affected populations. He talked about the emotional wounds of survivors of terrorism and mass violence. "They were Cambodians, Iraqis, Rwandans, and Afghans, people whose psyches had been scarred by violence and trauma, just like ours." Shortly after the program, they tracked down Dr. Mollica. A week later they were meeting him and the staff of the program. "We remember remarking to each other afterwards that this was the first time we felt we were in an emotionally safe place following Pete's death." Soon after, they established the Peter C. Alderman Foundation as a 501(c)(3) nonprofit charity that would alleviate the suffering of victims of terrorism and mass violence in post-conflict countries.

"I always believed that if I ever lost a child I would never be able to stop screaming. The reality is, you can't keep screaming. Your throat closes up; you give yourself a headache—you just physically can't keep doing that. When we started the foundation, it was the work that got me through. There's no way you're going to lie in bed with all this work to do; you can't cry when you're sitting at the computer all day." Their family home has now become the headquarters of the foundation, with two rooms converted into offices for their executive director, administrative person, and their daughter Jane, who serves as the foundation's CFO. Interns also come in throughout the whole year.

In the course of Liz's work, she came upon a study of what helped build resilience and mitigate depression in Cambodian refugees. She says, "At the end of the study, they came up with three things: What helped people was spirituality, work, and altruism.[3] What really blew my mind was the altruism.

"We didn't start the foundation in any way, shape, or form to help ourselves. But it actually has helped us tremendously. It hasn't taken away one iota of the pain of losing Peter—that's always there. There are times I'm unhappy; there are times I'm always fighting with sadness. Sometimes I want to scream because it just never seems to go away; some days I want to go sit in a corner and suck my thumb. But what the foundation has done is it has given me a different life. It's a life that taught me things about myself that I never even knew before. It has been just an incredible learning experience. I never thought at the age of seventy-two, I would be working seven days a week, or eight, ten, twelve hours a day. I am learning that I am very capable. I am very strong. A whole new world opened up for me. I've learned I'm really a good public speaker—I can talk in front of a thousand people with no notes and be very comfortable; I can be comfortable on TV, you know? We started this knowing nothing. We knew nothing about the foundation world. We knew nothing about philanthropy except that I gave a little bit every year to Greenpeace and Amnesty International. We knew nothing about mental health."

Liz says she has lived "a very full life." She used to do many things with her hands, such as painting and architectural drafting, but says she hasn't been able to do them since Peter was killed. "I've replaced all those creative activities with all the creative stuff for the foundation. I design the invitations, the cards, the website, and that kind of thing. I'm not the person I was before; I will never be that person again. But I am someone new."

Liz Alderman and the author

I ask why she immerses herself so deeply in these issues. Would it not have been easier to just let go, perhaps go on vacation or retire quietly?

"No, that is absolutely the worst thing in the world for me. Busy is good; busy is very good. And I think busy is better than anything else. If I just retired, all I would do is think about Peter. And not that I don't, but I need to be doing something worthwhile in my life. Everything else just seems so insignificant. I look at friends of mine who will retire to Florida, and they go to exercise class and they play tennis and there's nothing the matter with that, but to me, I look at them as just being so empty."

"What's your advice to others who are grieving?" I ask.

"Number one, whatever you need to do to grieve, do it, as long as it doesn't hurt you or anybody else. Number two, busy is good; busy is really good. Number three, do something good, just do something positive, and it doesn't even have to be in the form of a foundation or a memorial. Just try to do some good in the world."

"Why?"

"Because, surprisingly, it made me feel better. That's why. There's no other reason; it's very selfish. You know what? My active altruism was very selfish. I believe that about human beings anyhow."

When I mentioned to Liz that psychologists argue that "empathy altruism" is ultimately selfish because of the emotional benefits it provides to the giver, she said that she has no problem with that, and that it is absolutely true.

"I do believe that when somebody does something charitable, they do it because it makes them feel better. I think we're completely motivated that way. We may not like to say it, but we are. I think about the experiences that I've had since Peter was killed, in terms of the foundation.

"I'm just a very ordinary, middle-class Jewish woman from Westchester, New York," Liz continues, "and now I've been in places in Africa where no one has ever been. I have adopted a former child soldier called James. It wasn't in any sense a true adoption, but my husband and I decided we would help him in any way we could to have a better life. He was representative of all the child soldiers we treat but would never actually know. We provided housing for him—he was living in an old bathroom that had begun to leak. We bought and sent him all sorts of art supplies for his painting. We paid to send him to school, and that ultimately was a failure. He was too old, the pressure was too great, and he began to drink. When we heard, we pulled him out of school, sent him back to the Kitgum clinic, and eventually sent him to work as an apprentice to a painting and craft shop, where he is doing exceedingly well. He wants to open his own place, but we feel it is much too soon. He has now married and has one daughter and seems to be a good husband and father. We really only communicate through his counselor and our once-a-year visit to Africa. He does not speak English—but when we see each other there are many hugs and great warmth. He feels that the work of our foundation has changed his life. But it's really the foundation that has changed my life. I'm happy about the work I'm doing; I'm really happy about the work."

The Peter C. Alderman Foundation (PCAF) operates seven mental health clinic sites around the world, including Cambodia, Uganda, and Kenya. PCAF established the first mental health Wellness Clinic in Liberia. The clinic sites and their community outreach programs treat survivors with traumatic depression and PTSD with culturally appropriate, evidence-based therapy. Working in partnership with Ministries of Health, local government, medical schools, local partners, and religious institutions, PCAF has trained doctors and clinics who have since reached more than one hundred thousand people suffering from mental health problems.

How to Cope with Collective
Grief and Public Trauma

A candle loses nothing by lighting another candle.

—ITALIAN PROVERB

The stories of Liz Alderman and Petra Nemcova are about grief that is personal and at the same time shared. The deaths of their loved ones occurred in the context of two very public tragedies: the September 11 attacks and the 2004 Indian Ocean earthquake and tsunami. For the two women, taking on a peer leadership or survivor advocacy role allowed them to build something positive into the present and the future.

Let us zoom out for a moment and understand what else was happening around them as they were grieving. When communities are struck by such national tragedies, calamities, or the deaths of public figures, many other people find themselves unexpectedly grieving, even though they are not direct victims. A witness at the scene of 9/11 described being unable to "get away from faces of innocent victims who were killed. Their pictures are everywhere—on phone booths, streetlights, walls of subway stations. Everything reminded me of a huge funeral."[4] Whether it's survivor's guilt or a general feeling of helplessness, the effects can be crippling. So many people are talking about what happened. The news updates keep coming in 24/7, and there's an outpouring of negative emotion—anger, frustration—after the incident. It's the only thing people talk about in elevators, cafés, everywhere you go.

Think of the last time a public figure died—and how immediately and spontaneously a shrine of flowers and hand-drawn posters and little notes were strewn to commemorate him or her. Even if it was someone like Princess Diana, Lee Kuan Yew, or Nelson Mandela, whom we may have known only from a distance, people have the urge to reach out in a moment of grief. These days online memorials emerge and quickly collect hundreds and thousands of comments. Our impulse to give during such moments of grief points to something powerful: Giving helps us cope.

I felt this myself in November 2013, when the exceptionally powerful Typhoon Haiyan devastated parts of the Philippines, where I grew up. It was the deadliest typhoon on record, killing at least six thousand people. Although I was all the way in Singapore, I could not help but feel depressed by what had happened, and this depleted feeling from the collective grief of the country impeded my ability to do my job. For a whole day I could not even bring myself to answer e-mails—I was just constantly on CNN, watching the devastation from fifteen hundred miles away. I was the last person I'd have expected to feel that way, but I did. I then realized that the only way to shake off those feelings was to do something. I signed up for a volunteer drive, and even just walking to the community center to help pack relief goods helped me feel better. I knew I was doing it for the good of the victims as well as for my own good. Distracting myself by flipping the channels was not going to work.

Research on growth and distress in social, community, and interpersonal contexts supports this phenomenon. Altruism and philanthropic behaviors have been found to help people create a more positive social script of traumatic events. Altruism can help people react proactively to tragedy, thus promoting the growth of both the individual and of society as a whole. Distress and growth can co-exist. For instance, many veterans who could not save buddies or civilians in combat are compassionate caregivers for family members, or they volunteer in their communities, often to honor those lost in battle or as personally imposed reparation.

The following passage about Ms. C, a New York City resident who was working and living less than a mile from the World Trade Center at the time of the attacks, is taken from a study called "Resilience and Thriving in a Time of Terrorism":[5]

For Ms. C, who experienced tremendous distress and psychological upheaval during and immediately following the September 11, 2001, terrorist attacks on the World Trade Center, her process of coming to terms with these experiences resulted in a deepened sense of personal authenticity and a greater appreciation for living a meaningful life. She recalls that on the morning of September 11, she was in her apartment on the phone when she heard a plane overhead that was "really loud, flying really low and in the wrong direction. I made note of it, but continued the conversation." Minutes later, she turned on her television to see the weather report and saw images that she assumed were from a movie. She turned the sound up and realized that there actually was "a big hole and fire coming out of one of the World Trade Center towers." She got dressed and was running down the stairs when she heard "lots of sirens, more sirens than [she] had ever heard at one time." For the next few minutes, dozens of her neighbors congregated on the sidewalk discussing what had occurred. She remembers being in a state of disbelief saying over and over "I don't think you're right, I think you're wrong, that can't be true." She recalls that within a few minutes "all the buildings had emptied onto the street, the streets were crowded with pedestrians, and it was a state of chaos." And then a few minutes later, "we started to see the zombies." Ms. C recalls seeing, "a huge mass of people, like a marathon running up 6th Avenue. People who had escaped the towers somehow, ran out of the building and just kept running." Ms. C recounts conversations with people who were hysterical, some of whom had only escaped by luck and were horrified by the knowledge that all of their coworkers must have been killed. "Over the course of an hour, the nature of it changed and there were more people who were cut and torn and bleeding and covered with soot. There was this huge black cloud of dust and the people were coming out just covered with soot."

Following her initial disbelief, Ms. C's immediate reaction was to problem solve. "I felt like I needed to do something. I felt unbelievably helpless just standing there watching the disaster." Ms. C describes what followed as feeling "more and more apocalyptic." "There was no way to help, we just stood around and then different risks that I hadn't thought about started to occur to me. It was just more frightening when it was dark. I was afraid to drink my tap water. The air didn't feel very safe; the water didn't feel very safe. It was so scary; no one knew what would happen next."

Over the days and weeks following September 11, Ms. C exhibited many of the symptoms of acute stress disorder such as nightmares, difficulty sleeping, mild derealization, and hyperarousal. These symptoms eventually subsided.

The most striking part of Ms. C's account is what she said next: "The turning point for me was getting back to work at the nonprofit, knowing that I was doing something to help."

Altruism is ironic. Sometimes helping others is the most selfish thing you can do, as NBC News national and international correspondent Ann Curry discovered in the wake of the Newtown tragedy. On December 14, 2012, Adam Lanza fatally shot twenty children and six adult staff members in a mass murder at Sandy Hook Elementary School in the village of Sandy Hook in Newtown, Connecticut. Before driving to the school, Lanza shot and killed his mother. As first responders arrived, he committed suicide by shooting himself in the head. It was the second-deadliest mass shooting by a single person in American history. As the country was reeling from the tragedy, experience inspired Ann to come up with a simple idea that led to a massive, unexpected wave of goodwill. "Imagine if we all committed 20 acts of kindness to honor the lost children of Newtown." She posted the message on Twitter and Facebook. The idea has evolved into a viral effort known as "26 Acts of Kindness," in honor of the students and faculty who died at Sandy Hook Elementary. "I know the truth," Ann says. "If you do good, you feel good. It's the most selfish thing you can do. Right now, this country wants to heal. I think the only thing comforting in the face of a tragedy like this is to do something good with it if you can. Be a part of that wave."

Websites promoting the idea suggested various basic, quick ideas to jump-start the kindness revolution, such as paying a thoughtful compliment to a stranger, popping a coin into an expired parking meter, helping someone with a baby stroller get up the stairs, paying a stranger's dinner tab, or donating blood.

Wayne Harriman, of Wallingford, Connecticut, said he felt helpless after December 14. "To shoot a six-year-old child for no reason is just, you know . . . Why? I can't understand the rationale behind it and I suppose we never will." Harriman then heard about the 26 Acts of Kindness movement and decided to show random kindness at the next possible opportunity. Seated next to a table full of strangers in a local restaurant, he was about to pay his bill when it hit him that it that now would be a great time to do something for other people. "I just turned around and said I would like to pay for these people's meal as well," he said.

Soon after, his wife, Pat Harriman, joined in as well. "I needed two pies, so I bought three, so I decided to give someone a pie because Wayne had told me the story about Ann Curry and the acts of kindness. So I got to the checkout and I paid for it and then I turned around and gave it to the woman behind me," she said.

In New Haven, photographer Karissa Van Tassel felt inspired by the pictures of the young and innocent Sandy Hook School victims, and decided to offer her clients candid pictures of their families free of charge. She gave each of them an eight-by-ten family portrait to make sure they have good family memories around them every day. "The meaning behind someone you don't even know, just saying I care about people, I think as a community created such an overwhelming feeling of love. Throughout the process I was so phenomenally moved by all of the things people were doing just to say, I care."

A year later, NBC reported the movement hadn't lost its momentum.[6] Newtown resident Betty Hallquist found a small envelope with a bag of cocoa outside the Town Hall. The note on the envelope read: "Kindness Warms Your Soul." Hallquist said it made her happy to know that people continued to carry on the 26 Acts of Kindness through small acts of giving. "We didn't forget; we still care," she said.

Harriman added that even the smallest gesture makes a difference. "It doesn't have to be something monetary; it could just be a deed you wouldn't normally do, something out of the ordinary, for someone who isn't expecting it. If you just take a few minutes out of your day to be kind to someone else, what a different world this would probably be."

A Mother's Love

In 1991, as the best-selling author Isabel Allende was in Barcelona, Spain, at a party to launch her most recent novel, her agent made her way through the crowd to tell her softly that her daughter, Paula, had been rushed to intensive care. Paula had been suffering from a rare hereditary enzyme deficiency known has porphyria, and complications had arisen from the otherwise curable disease. She slipped into a coma from which she never awoke, finally dying a year later at age twenty-eight in her mother's arms.

Born in 1942 in Lima, Peru, and raised in Santiago, Chile, Isabel is the niece and goddaughter of former Chilean president Salvador Allende. Considering her lineage, one can easily assume that Isabel's success was a by-product of birthright, but her memoirs reveal a life battered with "no lack of drama," as she puts it. When she was three her father disappeared, forcing her mother to relocate with Isabel and her two siblings to Chile, which she has described as "moralistic, class conscious, and having rigid social norms," and where her mother's single parenthood scandalized society. It was an unhappy childhood, one that Isabel credits as the reason she became a writer later in life. In 1973, following an extended period of social and political unrest, the elected President Allende was overthrown in a military coup, and subsequently committed suicide (or was assassinated, as many believe). Finding her own life in danger, Isabel fled Chile and found refuge in Venezuela, where she got married, continued work as a journalist, then became a TV presenter, a playwright, and a children's author.

"We were living in exile in Venezuela, and I had to do all kinds of small jobs to make a living for my children," says Isabel, who has worked nonstop since she was seventeen. She is sitting across from me wearing a blue chiffon dress, her nails painted red, her waist cinched with a wide belt, and her neck adorned with a playful silver necklace with seashell-colored charms. Beside us is a bookshelf brimming with multiple copies of the nineteen books she has written since 1982, when she came to international attention with the publication of her debut novel, *The House of the Spirits*. She began writing the novel in Venezuela as a series of letters to her one-hundred-year-old grandfather, who lay dying in Chile, in an attempt to preserve the memories of the country and the family she had lost. After initially being rejected by several Spanish-language publishers, the book became an international best seller that was translated into more than twenty-seven languages and was made into a major motion picture starring Jeremy Irons and Meryl Streep. By 1987, at the age of forty-five, Isabel was a well-established novelist living in Venezuela, known for her work in the "magic realist" tradition. Despite her literary achievements, however, her marriage deteriorated and eventually ended in divorce. The following year, she met her second husband, San Francisco lawyer Willie Gordon, while on a book tour in California, and moved to the U.S. to be with him.

"When she died, I was in shock," says Isabel, who has the superstitious habit of starting each of her books on January 8. But by the time that date came, she felt too depressed to even consider writing again. "I was just devastated, but my mother was here, and she said, 'If you don't write, you're going to die. So just write anything.' She left me, saying she wanted to buy a cardigan at Macy's, and disappeared for eight hours. When she came back, I had cried for eight hours, but also I had written while I was crying." And that was how she began a new book, titled *Paula*. Grief-stricken Isabel wrote: "By measures of our precarious humanity you, Paula, are more important to me than my own life, or the sum of almost all other lives. Every day several million persons die and even more are born, but, for me, you alone were born, only you can die."

Although Paula never awoke, *Paula* came alive. "When the book was published, nobody thought it would be successful because it's about death. But it's really not about death; it's about family, and love." Of all her books, *Paula* became "the longest-selling that is always in print, that would get letters every day," she says, glancing at the shelf of her best-selling works by our side. Money started coming in as the book sold. "I put it aside in a separate account. I didn't want to touch it, because I didn't want anybody to think that I had profited in any way from my daughter's death."

As the income from the sales of *Paula* came in, the grieving Isabel tried hard to think of a way to honor the memory of her daughter, but she could not come up with any specific ideas. "I knew that I could build a cathedral, and it wouldn't mean anything to her. I would have had to do something that she would've done, and would've been meaningful to her." Nearly four years after Paula's death, Isabel could not shake her grief, and was worried that it had been years since she'd written any fiction, her only livelihood. Her husband, Willie, decided it was time to take a vacation, which was to be in India, the country Paula had once visited and told Isabel was the "richest source of inspiration for a writer." Initially, Isabel did not want to go there. In her latest memoir, she writes about how she felt prior to the trip: "I didn't think I would be able to bear the legendary poverty of India, the devastated villages, starving children, and nine-year-old girls sold into early marriages, forced labor, or prostitution."

But off they went to India, which allowed Willie to indulge his passion for photography. Exhausted from an all-day road trip and picture taking, Isabel and Willie took a rest stop in a random village together with a local Indian driver as it was nearing sundown, and saw in the distance a group of women and children in the dry fields under a solitary acacia tree. Wearing curious expressions and threadbare saris and speaking no English, the women approached the foreigners with a warm smile, touched their hands and their faces as a gesture of hospitality that knew nothing of the Western concept of personal space. Moved by the otherworldliness of the experience, Isabel gave them all the silver bracelets that were piled on her wrists.

As Isabel bade the women good-bye, one of them followed her and handed her what she thought was a thank-you present for the bracelets. "I thought it was a bundle of rags, but when I turned back the folds I saw that it held a newborn baby, tiny and dark, still with the umbilical cord." Isabel realized that the woman had tried to give her baby away. Later, Isabel asked the driver, "Why would the woman want to give me her baby?"

"It's a girl—who wants a girl?" the driver said.

Soon after that moment, Isabel's idea to set up a foundation to protect women and girls was born. "I had this revelation that I could at least contribute somehow to help women and girls, because empowering women and girls can really change the world." In a 2007 TED Talk, the audience burst into laughter as she said, "By age five I was a raging feminist—although the term had not reached Chile yet, so nobody knew what the heck was wrong with me." On December 9, 1996, four years after Paula's death, Isabel set up a foundation to pay homage to her daughter, who as a young woman did volunteer work in the roughest slums in Caracas, Venezuela, places where even the police didn't venture after sunset. Paula, who wore no makeup, had waist-long chestnut hair, and was perpetually in white cotton shirts and long white cotton skirts, "would go off in her little car, carrying a bag of books, and I would be sick with apprehension. I begged her a thousand times not to go into those parts of the city, but she didn't listen because she felt she was protected by her good intentions and her belief that everyone knew who she was," Isabel says.

"Just by extending or enlarging the work she was doing, it was a much better way of honoring her."

I ask her whether setting up the foundation eased her grief, to which she answers, "My grief is a sort of subdued sadness that is always lying in the bottom of my heart, but it's a very rich soil where a lot of wonderful stuff grows."

A Model of Giving

In 2003, after a perfect pregnancy and a delivery that went just as she had envisioned, Christy Turlington Burns, founder of Every Mother Counts, experienced a complication that was frightening and totally unexpected. Thanks to the quality of care that she received in New York City, she recovered right away. But as she read more about what had happened to her, she learned that her condition, postpartum hemorrhage, was the leading killer of pregnant women around the world, including in the U.S. "Once I learned that hundreds of thousands of women around the world were dying each year I needed to know why. I realized that had I delivered my first child in a place without electricity, paved roads, or emergency obstetric care, I would have died." She then immersed herself in humanitarian issues and campaigned to end preventable deaths caused by pregnancy and childbirth, especially among women in poverty-stricken circumstances. "When I learned that almost ninety percent of these deaths are preventable I committed myself to doing all that I could to stop these senseless deaths," she says.

This was not the first time Christy turned a difficult situation into an opportunity to do good. In 1997, her father, a former Pan Am pilot, died of lung cancer. Still grieving, she called the American Cancer Society and the Centers for Disease Control and offered to help them launch a now-infamous antismoking campaign. In Christy's life, I saw a pattern of diving into charity after bouts with personal and family crises. "I was not conscious of it then, although I am conscious now. It happened so many times," she says, over a late lunch on a rainy spring afternoon in a Mediterranean restaurant in New York's City's Nolita district.

The first thing I noticed when she swung through the restaurant's glass doors was how reassuringly familiar her face was, even though I had met her only once before. It was like finally having a conversation with an old schoolmate you've never once spoken to, but whose face you've seen along the corridors year after year. Surely it was because every single time I had ever read a fashion magazine, Christy's face was somewhere in it. Discovered by a modeling agent at age fourteen, Christy says she never expected to have any staying power in an industry that puts a premium on youth. With the mind-set that modeling was a temporary gig, she always wanted to do something else. "So few of the days and years as a model were that satisfying. I always knew I wanted to do something more," she says. "It wasn't a question of do I want to do something meaningful. That was always a dream or a hope that I had. Even as I was a child, there was no how or why." Her father's death, and later on her experience with postpartum hemorrhage, "presented themselves to me as an opportunity. They just affected me so deeply that I felt I had no choice but to talk about and share what I had experienced with others.

"When I lost my father, I had already quit smoking," she continues, "but his death inspired me to go out and tell my story—not just my own struggles with addiction and the process of quitting, but what I learned about lung cancer and smoking-related diseases during my father's illness. I thought, maybe there was a way to use my personality as a model to make a difference." Only six months after her father passed away, a public service announcement came together. "It was very much a personal story, a testimonial, and it's very emotional," says Christy, who talks in a fast-paced elfin voice that makes even the direst of topics sound cheerful. "It has been great because it has turned so many personal negatives into positives for me. I was addicted to tobacco for many years and then lost my father to lung cancer due to his addiction to the substance. Then I was able to share my experience and struggle and encourage others to take better care of themselves. To this day, people come up to me and say they quit smoking because of that campaign. It makes me happy when I hear people say that they quit smoking because of me. That is so gratifying. I'm able to reaffirm my commitment to the cause and connect with people who have struggled with it. It is a tribute to my father and to his life and I feel really proud of it," she says.

"I've always kind of gone right in. I would say it allowed me to confront the fear that comes with the loss of a parent, or the fear that comes from having something happen to your body that you don't understand. It's a combination of being able to feel useful and have purpose and that experience of knowing that you are making contact or connection with others, and just that connection alone can make both of us feel better in the moment."

Coping with the Death of a Loved One

For *giving*, not forgetting

When we lose a loved one, the inherent compassion that friends and extended family bestow on the grieving family eventually fades. The first weeks following someone's loss can be filled with love, but the sympathy and empathy of a support network can only last for a few days or weeks as people have their own matters to attend to. The calls and greetings fade, the cards stop arriving in the mail, and the sense of loss becomes more palpable. Getting through the funeral was a challenging time, but how can one get through the next weeks, months, and years?

In the world of philanthropy, people have taken inspiration from tragedy, as evidenced by the numerous foundations that have been set up in the name of a deceased loved one. Memories of the dead have spurred surviving parents to do good works that benefit humankind while at the same time preserve the legacy of the loved one and maintain the bond between parent and child. Parental grief is particularly difficult, and many of the clients I have advised have described how the children they have lost continue to live on in their hearts.

The Daniel Foundation was set up by Harold Bush after his son tragically drowned at the age of six. He writes:

Parental grief is grueling and can lead to all sorts of mental hell. One has to work through multiple myths about this ordeal. People will say, for instance, that time heals all wounds. But about two years after Daniel's death I was feeling not better but markedly worse. I was so discouraged and often so physically and emotionally anesthetized that I began to do research on the clinical findings about parental grief. I undertook this research mostly as an attempt to figure out if I was losing my mind and if I would ever start feeling better about life. The findings of clinical psychologists helped me to understand several things. First, my reactions were normal and predictable. I was not losing my mind, but experiencing what the vast majority of bereaved parents experience. Feeling numb and short of breath, thinking incoherent thoughts—this is common. Looking around and expecting Daniel to run in at any moment is not a sign of mental illness.

Another piece of bad advice I heard was to "let go of the dead child and go on with your own life." This sort of advice has its roots in the modern theories of grief that considered extended and grueling patterns of grief to be pathological. In *Mourning and Melancholia* (1917), Sigmund Freud makes a famous distinction between mourning, which is the normal reaction to the loss of a loved one, and melancholia, which is a form of mental illness. According to Freud, grieving people need to break free from the deceased, let go of the past and reassert their individualism by charting a new course for life. A healthy grief experience, according to Freud, is one in which the deaths of loved ones will not leave "traces of any gross change" in the bereaved.

But Daniel's death left very intense and never-ending changes in my wife and me. More than eight years later we still think about Daniel every day, miss him a lot and refuse to let go of him. Clinical workers are now discovering that this is not only predictable but probably much healthier for the bereaved. For decades, counselors for the bereaved urged them to let go of the dead and get on with their lives, an approach that has been called the "breaking bonds" method. Oddly, this approach is still common, in spite of an abundance of clinical evidence showing it to be misguided. In reality, research has consistently shown that lifelong grief is normal in cases of the loss of close family members, especially children. Psychologists are recognizing the importance of maintaining bonds with the dead. In my own case, I still feel a deep connection with my son, and I have no intention of ever trying to break that bond.[7]

This is what we can learn from philanthropists. When they set up foundations named after their loved ones who have passed away, they do so to memorialize them, and not to forget them—"to let their legacy endure," as they often say. Some other notable foundations set up in memory of the dead include:

- The John Simon Guggenheim Memorial Foundation, founded in 1925 by the American businessman and politician Simon Guggenheim and his wife, Olga, in memory of their son, who died April 26, 1922.
- After the death of singer Amy Winehouse, her father, Mitch, announced plans to launch a foundation in his daughter's name, to help others battling drug addiction. Amy died at age twenty-seven, and they launched the foundation on September 14, on what would have been her twenty-eighth birthday. The family felt that it was important to "keep her memory alive."
- In March 2011, Finlay Connor and his mother Niki were hit by a bus within yards of Woodborough Primary School, in the U.K., killing six-year old Finlay on the spot. Soon after his death, his parents set up the Finlay Foundation, which raises money for toys, play equipment, and high-visibility jackets for hospitals, hospices, and charity-funded groups. "Having the Finlay Foundation gives me

a purpose and I love it when I go to give donations to places with money raised in his memory, as I feel he is right beside me and smiling. Even when he was very little he was always very generous and caring and I know he would be pleased that we are helping to make other children happy," says Niki.[8]

- Natalie Giorgi died in July 2013 after she took a bite of a Rice Krispies treat that she didn't realize contained peanut butter while at Camp Sacramento, in California. The thirteen-year-old had a severe peanut allergy; about twenty minutes after eating the treat, she started vomiting, then had trouble breathing and went into cardiac arrest. Natalie was taken to a hospital, where she was later pronounced dead. To honor their daughter and help bring awareness to food allergies, Louis and Joanne Giorgi created the Natalie Giorgi Sunshine Foundation. The goal of the foundation is to enlighten people about the dangers of food allergies. Natalie's parents say they have gone through excruciating pain since her tragic death and are now working to educate other parents and children.

What these bereaved parents demonstrate is that giving is a powerful way to cope with grief. It may not necessarily eliminate the grief, as Isabel Allende describes, but it certainly gives them the strength to keep living. The loss becomes a springboard people use to give back to others in some positive way.

These anecdotes substantiate experiments led by Stephanie Brown, which have shown that increased help given to other people after the loss of a spouse (i.e., providing instrumental support to others) predicts accelerated recovery from depressive symptoms among individuals during the eighteen-month bereavement period.[9]

The following is what one young woman said about her desire to give back based on the loss of her dad at an early age:

> I have been able to positively use the tragedy of my father in many instances. I am able to bring this situation up to people who have lost a parent or other significant people in their lives as a commonality and thus they have felt more comfortable confiding in me. While again, totally different situations, this bond has allowed me to be there to listen to those that have gone through losses because they have added comfort in confiding in me. This has been a wonderful gift and I am blessed that I have that to give. Maybe that has led me to volunteering for organizations like crisis intervention lines and mediation groups. And I am sure it has influenced my desire to work in social work in the future and applying for my master's in social work.[10]

You don't have to be a celebrity or a famous author to keep the memory of a loved one going. There are many other activities that we can engage in to honor loved ones and allow us to keep their memory alive. For most of us, setting up a foundation is not an option. Here are some other ways to do it:

1. Give funds for a project in the name of your loved one. For example, you may be able to donate to your local library, and depending on their policies, they may use a special bookplate with your loved one's name on it.

2. Think of activities and organizations that represent the kinds of things that your loved one cared about. Get involved with them. When starting a memorial fund at a community foundation or through a charitable organization, hospital, or college or university, focus on something your loved one cared deeply about, such as child welfare, animal rescue, or a certain medical condition.

3. If possible, consider organ donation. In 2008, Dr. Eric Yoshida, a liver specialist at Vancouver General Hospital, analyzed the psychological impact on families who consented to donating their relatives' organs. One of the study's aims was to understand whether the donation process hindered or ameliorated the bereavement process for organ donor families. The results conclusively showed that family members of transplant donors showed lower levels of depression, post-traumatic stress, and grief. As one bereaved mother said of losing her son, "Every day of my life I think of him and miss him but I believe something good came out of it."[11]

Facing Our Own Mortality

Sometimes it's not the death of a loved one, but rather our own mortality that we must confront. In late 2012, Sam Simon, the genius and cocreator of the long-running television show *The Simpsons*, was diagnosed with terminal colon cancer and was given three to six months to live. With this knowledge of his impending death, he wasted no time in living more through giving. He announced that he would be giving millions to animal charities. A dog lover, he had set up the Sam Simon Foundation in 2002 with a mission to save dogs and enrich the lives of people. Sam created what has been called the "grandest dog shelter in America," where he gave abandoned dogs a new lease on life. He announced that he would use all of his money to help animals and animal rights causes, to ensure that his efforts would continue and even expand long after he was no longer around. When asked about his motivation, Sam responded that it was simple: "One thing is I get pleasure from it. I love it. I don't feel like it is an obligation." Sam died in March 2015, leaving his nearly $100 million fortune to various charities he supported during his lifetime.

In 1992, the billionaire Jon Huntsman Sr. was diagnosed with prostate cancer. One day as he was on the way to the hospital for treatment, he made three stops, leaving a check at each of his destinations. First, he wrote a $1 million check to a homeless shelter. He then stopped by a soup kitchen and handed over another $1 million check. Finally, he dropped off a $500,000 check at the clinic where he was diagnosed. In fact, his charitable donations have already knocked him off the Forbes 400 list of the wealthiest people in America.

A woman named Kendall Ciesemier likewise discovered happiness and purpose while battling illness. As a girl, Kendall underwent not one but two liver transplants. At age nineteen she founded Kids Caring 4 Kids, a nonprofit organization dedicated to inspiring young people to care for children in Africa by helping to provide essential needs: food, education, water, shelter. For nearly a decade now, Kendall has been empowering and inspiring children through her speeches at schools, youth groups, and service organizations, challenging them to get involved in order to make a difference. She is teaching young adults the rewards of giving and how one can discover their sense of purpose. "Service is my power" has become Kendall's mantra. She did not want to be known as the "sick girl." Her foundation gave her a purpose to live beyond herself.

I asked exercise equipment mogul Augie Nieto, who was later diagnosed with ALS, how he recovered from the despair he felt after his illness was detected. Ninety days into his diagnosis, he was depressed by the prospect of succumbing to a long, slow, and debilitating disease for which there is no known cure, and he tried to take his own life by swallowing pills. "There are five stages of grief: denial, anger, why me, what did I do to deserve this, and acceptance. With acceptance, you are prepared to act. After I tried to take my life, [my wife] Lynne and I decided to take action by partnering with the Muscular Dystrophy Association to create Augie's Quest [to fund research and drug development for ALS]. It's this work that has kept me motivated and inspired to keep on living. I redefine normal every day. You can either mourn what you can't do . . . or celebrate what you can do."

Another such individual who emerged from difficult circumstances and whom I have long admired and been inspired by is acclaimed actor Michael J. Fox, who has been charming audiences since he achieved stardom in the early 1980s on the sitcom *Family Ties*. His career continued to flourish on the big screen and he returned to television in 1996 to launch the show *Spin City* and then assumed a recurring role in *The Good wife*. In late 1999, he announced that he had been battling Parkinson's disease for eight years. He then made an even bigger announcement, saying that he would be spending his time raising money and awareness for Parkinson's disease. In 2000, he launched the Michael J. Fox Foundation for Parkinson's Research, a nonprofit organization dedicated to finding a cure for the disease. The foundation is now recognized as the world's largest nonprofit funder of drug development for Parkinson's disease. Although his initial response to the diagnosis was self-pity and turning to alcohol, Michael eventually turned to philanthropy.

Asked if he could go back in time and change the fact that he got Parkinson's, he says, "No, I wouldn't; I absolutely wouldn't. I wouldn't at all because this path that I'm on is so amazing. . . . I would say I gave up my job to do my life's work." It's the givers like Michael J. Fox whom we hear saying, "I wouldn't have had it any other way. I am happy."

OTHERS:

- Cameron Cohen is a brilliant young computer programmer who was diagnosed with bone tumor at a very young age. While he was on bed rest after surgery for the tumor, he learned the C programming language and later developed an app for Apple called iSketch, with which you can draw sketches on Apple-generated gadgets. He then donated the application he had created to Apple's App Store to raise funds for the Child Life Program.
- Jessica Rees was only eleven when she was diagnosed with a brain tumor. One day, as she and her parents were driving

home from the hospital where she was receiving treatment, she turned to her parents and asked, "When do all the other kids come home?" When Jessica found out that many of them were very ill and would have to stay at the hospital, she wanted to help "make them happier, because I know they're going through a lot, too," she said. So she started making JoyJars—canisters full of toys, stickers, crayons, anything that might brighten a child's day. "She was really particular about what would go in the jars," said her mother, Stacey. "It had to be something cool; it couldn't be cheap or flimsy." Jessica created three thousand JoyJars before she passed away in January 2012, and her parents are carrying on her legacy. They set up the Jessie Rees Foundation, which by the end of 2012 had delivered more than fifty thousand JoyJars to young cancer patients.

- Alexandra "Alex" Scott was born in Connecticut in 1996, and was diagnosed with neuroblastoma, a type of childhood cancer, shortly before her first birthday. The doctors told Alex's parents that even if she beat cancer it was doubtful that she would ever learn to walk. But by her second birthday, she was crawling, and able to stand up with leg braces. In 2000, on the day after her fourth birthday, she received a stem cell transplant and told her mother she wanted to start a lemonade stand to raise money for doctors to "help other kids, like they helped me." Her first lemonade stand raised two thousand dollars and led to the creation of the Alex's Lemonade Stand Foundation. While bravely battling cancer, Alex continued holding lemonade stands in her front yard throughout her life, ultimately raising more than $1 million toward cancer research. She passed away in August 2004 at the age of eight. Today, Alex's Lemonade Stand sponsors a national fund-raising weekend every June called Lemonade Days. Each year, as many as ten thousand volunteers at more than two thousand Alex's Lemonade Stands around the nation make a difference for children with cancer.

Take Care of Yourself First

While grief is fresh, every attempt to divert only irritates. You must wait till it be digested, and then amusement will dissipate the remains of it.

—SAMUEL JOHNSON

Finding happiness through giving does not mean helping someone immediately after going through a difficult experience, whether it's a traumatic past, the death of a loved one, collective grief, or your own mortality. Psychologists say that the key to healing from traumatic experiences is to first achieve the "stage one" goals of personal safety, genuine self-care, and the capacity for healthy emotion regulation. We must give ourselves time to grieve. I have sat in many meetings in which my client's wish is to honor the memory of his or her dearly departed, and there are a few things I've noticed about these conversations. One is that it almost never happens very soon after a death. There is no set timetable—for some it takes months, even years. Most of the conversations I have with them occur several years after the death of their loved ones. Some people, such as the philanthropy advisor and heiress to the Pillsbury empire Tracy Gary, are able to do it immediately after personal tragedy strikes. On a late summer morning in 2005, while the world was overwhelmed with the devastating news of Hurricane Katrina, Tracy was overcome with the feeling of loss—her mother had also died that day, after a long battle with illness. With all that was happening around her, Tracy threw herself deeply into the Hurricane Katrina relief efforts. "Our family agreed that there could be no better recovery from our own personal grief," she says.

People will go through the list of feelings of grief—denial, bargaining, depression, and anger—and it is important to let those feelings run their course, and practice self-care first.

Even Zen Buddhist monks agree. My quest to understand how acts of giving can help us cope with our own challenges took me all the way to Bangkok, to meet with monastics from the community led by the Zen master and peace and human rights activist Thich Nhat Hanh. I asked the monastics whether, if one is unhappy, helping others can lead to happiness, to which they replied: "Take care of yourself first." Thich Nhat Hanh has said, "The first thing we have to do is come back to ourselves. We have to recognize that we have to take care of ourselves first. It's just like on an airplane when you have to put the oxygen mask on yourself first before you put it on your child. We have to take care of ourselves before we can take care of other people. If you are not capable of taking care of yourself, of nourishing yourself, of protecting yourself—it is very difficult to take care of another person."

Once that is established, ask yourself what haunts you. And go back. Help others going through difficult times, whether it is exactly what you have endured or something else. After you have taken steps to take care of yourself, help others. The grief might not go away. You might not recover from your illness. But you come full circle and will feel a renewed reason for living. When you are faced with the worst things in life, giving will give you reason to smile again. Entrepreneur Dan Gilbert, whose eldest child was born with neurofibromatosis (NF), a serious genetic condition, says, "Sometimes fate can deliver you a bad card, but what our family has learned from our experience is that there can be many 'blessings in disguise' waiting for you around the corner if you play the hand the right way. Had our son not been born with NF then we would have never known about the condition nor been in the position to help other kids who were also born with the disease. We feel honored to be able to give and help others in this world. It is truly a gift to give."

The Foundation of a Family

Why families that give together stay together

On the evening of September 18, 1997, a group of black-tie-clad diplomats and dignitaries sat in the ballroom of the Marriott Marquis hotel in Times Square, New York City, on the occasion of the annual United Nations Association dinner. That night, Ted Turner, the billionaire founder of CNN, was receiving a Global Leadership Award.

"I was on my way to New York to make the speech," Turner told *New York Times* journalist Nicholas Kristof. "I just thought, what am I going to say?"

So, in front of a stunned dinner audience, he defied expectations and shocked the audience by announcing that he was making a gift of a staggering $1 billion to benefit the United Nations. That $1 billion was, at the time, the largest single gift ever made, and I remember watching the news as a teenager and thinking what an insanely big deal it was back then. U.N. Secretary General Kofi

Annan called Turner "noble and extraordinary," and it helped transform the landscape of philanthropy. Turner's gift became the starting point for the modern era of high-profile, big-ticket giving, and revived the tradition of great philanthropists such as Rockefeller and Carnegie.

The donation was channeled not through a foundation bearing his name, but through the new United Nations Foundation, which has gone on to make significant advancements in addressing malaria, polio, family planning, and climate change. Soon after making the pledge, Turner began encouraging big-ticket philanthropy by publicly needling other billionaires, such as Bill Gates and Warren Buffett (who would later start the highly ambitious Giving Pledge). "If you're rich, you can expect a letter or a call from me," he said. Turner has fulfilled his pledge in its entirety as of 2014.

What not many people know is that seven years before his landmark U.N. gift, Turner had started his own family foundation. As a lifelong environmental advocate, he created the foundation to protect the planet from further degradation and "ensure the survival of the human species." But apart from that, it was created to ensure the survival of something closer to home. Divorced three times, with five children from two marriages, and having had a tumultuous childhood, he said in a speech I witnessed in Beijing that one of the main reasons he set up the family foundation was to bring his family closer together.

"Serving on the board of the Turner Foundation has brought my family closer together over the years," says Turner. All five of his children—Rhett, Laura, Jennie, Teddy, and Beau—sit on the board of trustees of the family foundation.

Family philanthropy can take many forms. It can be quite informal, with families meeting on an ad hoc basis to discuss which organizations to support. The family foundation model provides a more formal structure for grant making and is often adopted by families whose philanthropy is significant in scale and longevity. A family business may choose to establish a corporate philanthropy program, which in some cases may reflect the interests of not only the family but also other stakeholders, such as staff. Some families establish endowments for their family foundation and others establish family funds, such as a donor-advised fund within a specialist intermediary like a community foundation. In some cases families adopt more than one model.

Why Should a Family Give Together?

1. To establish a legacy.

Wealthy traditional families often wax poetic and use the lofty term *legacy*, which simply means what one is remembered for, or what is handed down from one generation to the next. Family philanthropy helps shape that family legacy and define answers to questions such as *What does our family stand for? What did my parents and grandparents stand for? What are the values and purpose that we hope will transcend generations and instill a sense of pride and tradition?* When a family gives together, a shared understanding and sense of pride develops. It may be, simply, that "we gave back to society." It may be that "we built this wing of the hospital for sick kids."

For the Rockefeller family, giving has been a central family value that has spanned an astonishing three centuries. The family's earlier generations believed that with great wealth comes great responsibility, and this ethos continues to influence the mind-set of the current generation. The family is now entering its seventh generation and has maintained its tradition of giving within each one. No wonder their name has been synonymous not just with great wealth but also with great philanthropy.

According to a wealthy Singaporean I met back in 2010, "Having a formal institution helps to bring the family together because they are fulfilling a common purpose as they realize that the family's wealth is being used for a worthwhile cause, to improve society. Philanthropy can give younger members of the family a new perspective on the harsh realities of life for underprivileged people, and helps family members learn and appreciate the family's legacy as well as their own fortunate circumstances."[1]

2. To strengthen family bonds.

Unlike bonding over a picnic in the park, a game of Scrabble, or a family holiday, the bonding that happens when a family works on a noble and higher purpose—especially when children, parents, grandparents, and extended family are all in on the act—is so much more powerful. A mundane family dinner, if turned into a

THE FOUNDATION OF A FAMILY

"family meeting" to discuss the next round of grants, is elevated to something extraordinary. Giving together does amazing things for the relationships between husband and wife, father and son, mother and daughter, and across entire families. It may not fix a damaged family, but it can surely strengthen bonds and compensate for the distancing that comes when the family life cycle sends kids off on their own across the globe.

Bloomberg adds, "If you want to do something for your children and show how much you love them, the single best thing—by far—is to support organizations that will create a better world for them and their children. Long term, they will benefit more from your philanthropy than from your will. I believe the philanthropic contributions I'm now making are as much gifts to my children as they are to the recipient organizations."

Augie Nieto, founder of the world's largest commercial manufacturer of fitness equipment, whose life took an unexpected turn when he was paralyzed by amyotrophic lateral sclerosis (ALS, or Lou Gehrig's disease), said that he and his wife have gotten much closer since they started getting involved in charity work together. In 2007, he started Augie's Quest, an aggressive effort focused on finding treatments and a cure for ALS.

"Because I have limitations with communication, Lynne was forced to be the spokesperson for Augie's Quest," Augie says. "When we first started, Lynne had a hard time living the disease in public. It wasn't something that came naturally to her as she is more of a private person than I am. While I wouldn't say it's her vocation of choice, I will say that I couldn't have asked for a better partner. She has given me unconditional love and gone outside of her comfort zone to become more engaged with what we are doing. She speaks to large groups often, communicates with other families fighting ALS, and involves everyone in our immediate and extended family in what we have going on. Most people with ALS only live three to five years. We are over eight years in. Most spouses would have said good-bye a long time ago but Lynne is more present than ever." He and Lynne have a blended family—both of them had two kids from previous marriages. "Family comes first. It wasn't always perfect but we worked hard at it and now I've never been more proud of our children. Just in the past few years, I would say our family and marriage have really changed for the better. I have never been more in love with Lynne."

And Lynne says, "Our marriage has never been better."

3. To pave the way for success.

Sixteen-time Grammy-winning music producer David Foster says that his wildly successful career in music has somewhat cast a shadow on his family life. "Remember the guy that won the Oscar, Roberto Benigni? He stood up when he won the Oscar and said, 'I want to thank my parents for giving me the greatest gift, of poverty.' My kids can't say that. My kids are spoiled." Indeed, it is a

commonly held notion that children of very wealthy people will grow up to be spoiled brats.

For wealthy families, doing philanthropic work together cushions children from the negative impact of
inherited wealth. The English businessman John Cauld-
well, who made his fortune in the mobile phone industry and who also signed the Giving Pledge, says, "I really
don't think it is healthy and desirable for children to
have such vast amounts of wealth left to them, and my
philosophy is very much to encourage my children to
forge their own success and happiness. . . . I also felt that
making them trustees for over half my wealth, with a letter of wishes as to how to use that money to help society,
would bring them far more pleasure than having the ability to spend vast amounts of money on themselves."

Parents attest that when children are actively involved
in running a family foundation, their participation gives
them a focus, a sense of purpose, and a wider understanding of the world around them. Involvement in the family
foundation provides a good training ground for young
people (especially when they are able to join the board),
helping build skills associated with financial planning,
governance, conflict management, decision making, and
leadership. Young family members start with narrow tasks
such as research, over time become involved in imple-
menting projects, and ultimately assume leadership roles.

A 2013 survey of high-net-worth and ultra-high-net-
worth Americans revealed that "shared values" are more

important than money to personal success.[2] Financial assets are not the only assets that wealthy families want to pass along. Many in the survey said that the values they inherited from parents—including a strong work ethic, financial discipline and skills, a commitment to family harmony, and an emphasis on education—were more important than money in enabling them to succeed. About a third (35 percent) said their families had instilled a commitment to charitable giving. Parents generally want to transmit these same values to their own children. In fact, two-thirds of wealthy parents said they would rather their children grow up to be charitable than wealthy.

Charles Collier, in his seminal book *Wealth in Families*, lists the best practices of successful families, which include the following:

- A focus on the human, intellectual, and social capital of the family
- Making each family member's pursuit of individual happiness a priority
- Work on enhancing intra-family communication
- The telling and retelling of the family's most important stories
- Creation of mentor-like relationships when establishing family trusts
- Collaboratively defining a family vision statement

All of the above happen when families give together—no wonder it has led to the success of so many families over the years.

4. To show, not just tell about values.

For parents trying to teach their children good values, engaging in family philanthropy is an excellent way to walk the walk. Talking about values does not take much effort or advanced planning—parents can start these conversations while the family is sitting down together for meals, doing household chores, playing games, telling stories, working on puzzles, walking the dog, and going on road trips. However, for children to truly understand what it means to be compassionate, fair, kind to others, and respectful, and to live whatever other values their parents hold dear, parents will need to show the deeds in action. Giving together is an excellent opportunity to demonstrate these values and put theory into practice.

Model Natalia Vodianova realizes that her children, Lucas, Neva, Viktor, and Maxim, ages 1½ to 14, are growing up amid wealth and privilege. Modeling, "which is not hard work," Natalia says, only takes up a sliver of her time. "I want my children to see that I am a working mother. Without my work at the Naked Heart Foundation, they will take the comforts of their home and the privileges of wealth for granted. And that's not good enough for me."

Seeing that their mother, Goldie Hawn, had been spending time working on her foundation, her children followed suit. Her daughter, actress Kate Hudson, age thirty-six, sits on the board of her foundation; her son, Oliver Hudson, thirty-nine, is doing it his own way. "I never knew it, but he was getting in his car and I asked, 'Where are you going, honey?'" says Goldie. She then found out that he was going to the local hospital to read to sick children there. "I just welled up. You can't teach these values; you have to be an example of it and of course speak about it and show the joy that you get and show the impact that you can have." As Augie Nieto says, "I believe your kids learn more from what you do than what you say, and my hope is that they are watching!"

The Generosity Gene

A peek into the Giving Pledges of some of the world's wealthiest and most generous people proves that parents have a very strong role in passing down values.

- Hedge fund tycoon William A. Ackman said in his pledge, "I don't think being charitable is innate. In my experience, it is learned from the examples of others. My earliest memories include my father's exhortations about how important it is to give back. These early teachings were ingrained in me, and a portion of the first dollars I earned, I gave away."
- Azim Premji, one of India's wealthiest people and most celebrated philanthropists, says in the very first paragraph of his pledge, "My mother was the most significant influence in my life as I was growing up. She was a strong woman, and a deeply committed person. Though she was a Medical Doctor, she did not actually practice medicine,

but dedicated a large part of her life, close to 50 years, in helping to build and run a charitable hospital for Polio and Cerebral Palsy Children in Bombay. It was not an easy task. It was very difficult to get the funding and even harder to organize everything and make it run efficiently. Yet she tackled every kind of challenge and never stepped back from her purpose."

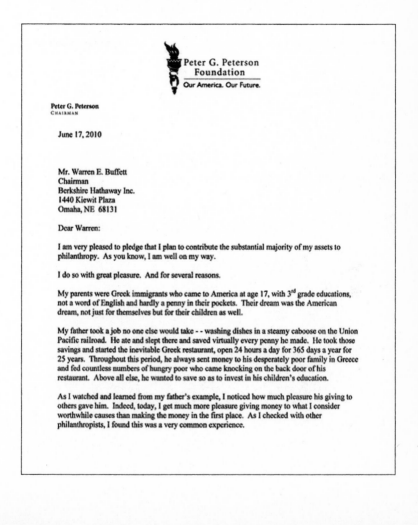

Peter G. Peterson
Foundation
Our America. Our Future.

Peter G. Peterson
CHAIRMAN

June 17, 2010

Mr. Warren E. Buffett
Chairman
Berkshire Hathaway Inc.
1440 Kiewit Plaza
Omaha, NE 68131

Dear Warren:

I am very pleased to pledge that I plan to contribute the substantial majority of my assets to philanthropy. As you know, I am well on my way.

I do so with great pleasure. And for several reasons.

My parents were Greek immigrants who came to America at age 17, with 3rd grade educations, not a word of English and hardly a penny in their pockets. Their dream was the American dream, not just for themselves but for their children as well.

My father took a job no one else would take - - washing dishes in a steamy caboose on the Union Pacific railroad. He ate and slept there and saved virtually every penny he made. He took those savings and started the inevitable Greek restaurant, open 24 hours a day for 365 days a year for 25 years. Throughout this period, he always sent money to his desperately poor family in Greece and fed countless numbers of hungry poor who came knocking on the back door of his restaurant. Above all else, he wanted to save so as to invest in his children's education.

As I watched and learned from my father's example, I noticed how much pleasure his giving to others gave him. Indeed, today, I get much more pleasure giving money to what I consider worthwhile causes than making the money in the first place. As I checked with other philanthropists, I found this was a very common experience.

- Pete Peterson, the Blackstone Group's founder, who eventually set up a foundation with a billion-dollar endowment, narrates in his pledge the values he learned from his parents, who, as poor Greek immigrants, nevertheless always managed to feed "countless numbers of hungry poor who came knocking on the back door of his restaurant."

- Lorry I. Lokey, founder of Business Wire, who was born during the Depression and has since given multimillion-dollar gifts to benefit higher education (including $134 million to the University of Oregon and $35 million to Mills College), said, "I remember vividly the worst of the Depression years in terms of how they affected my family. During even the Depression's worst years my parents gave money—about 8 percent of their annual income of $2,200. I remember saying to my mother that we can't afford that. But she said we have to share with others. I learned from that to share. Except for the first few years out of Stanford, I have given near the 10 percent mark for some 20 years. For the last 40 years the giving amounts to more than 90 percent of all monies earned."

- Billionaire John Paul DeJoria, who cofounded Paul Mitchell hair products in 1970, was raised in a European immigrant community in downtown Los Angeles. His mother once told him and his brother the three had just twenty-seven cents between them, but with food in the fridge, a backyard garden, and happiness, they were rich. For a time, DeJoria lived in his car while selling products door-to-door. He said, "One Christmas, when I was six years old, my mother took us to see the window displays and decorations in the big department stores in downtown Los Angeles. It was a big treat for us. We saw puppets that moved and trains that circled. . . . It was really special and added to the Christmas spirit, but it didn't cost anything. That same year, my mother gave my brother and me a dime. She told both of us to hold half of it and put it in the bucket near a man who was ringing a bell. We did, and then we asked my mother why we gave him the dime (at the time, a dime could buy you three candy bars or two soda pops). My mom's reply was, 'This is the Salvation Army that helps people who are really in need. Remember, boys, no matter how much you have, there is always someone who is more in need than you. Always try to give, even if it is a little.' Needless to say, that stuck with me in my adult life. Whether it's feeding thousands of orphans in third world countries, saving whales, helping the homeless find employment, protecting our waterways, rescuing young girls from prostitution, teaching and supplying families in Appalachia with equipment to grow their own vegetables, or any other worthwhile endeavor . . . giving back is a practice and joy I want my family to continue."

When Giving Leads to Love

In 1990, a young Harvard graduate by the name of Richard Barth was traveling around Europe, when his mother saw a *New York Times* article about Teach for America. Knowing about Richard's humanitarian aspirations, she sent him the article. Immediately, he came home and applied for a job at the organization. "He wandered into our office and said, 'I really want to be a part of this,'" says Wendy Kopp, who founded the organization in 1989.

Eight years after they met, they married, and they now have four children between the ages of six and fourteen. "Teach for America definitely led to our relationship. There's no doubt that there's just a fundamental alignment in our values and our view of the world in terms of what we should be prioritizing, that is foundational for our relationship." Smiling, she says it has done the same for many others. "If you knew how many marriages have been created not only in Teach for America, but across the Teach for All network, you would not believe it. If there were data on it, it would be really impressive. I mean there are just hundreds and hundreds! We're recruiting people at the front end of their career trajectory," she continues. "Most of them are coming straight out of college or just a few years out. Through TFA they meet people who share their values, and who are also undertaking something very intense."

A 2008 article in the *New York Times*, which is partly to thank for their union, dubbed Wendy and Richard "a power couple in the world of education, emblematic of a new class of young social entrepreneurs seeking to reshape the United States' educational landscape." After playing a crucial role in the early years of Teach for America, Richard now runs the Knowledge Is Power Program, or KIPP, a charter school network that turns low-achieving poor children into good students.

Teach for America is active in more than forty-six regions in the U.S., and Wendy is on the road nearly every week. "Richard and I have two very intense jobs and there's never any doubt at all about our supportiveness of each other's professional choices. When I think about the people I know who are most stressed, it's usually because their spouses aren't actually comfortable with their professional choices in terms of how much time or energy or mental space they put into their work. There's just none of that in terms of our relationship. There's just no doubt that he's incredibly supportive of my making professional choices that will drive other spouses crazy, just because he believes in the work," Wendy says.

She recognizes that the intensity of the work has led her to miss out on family life a little. "Even in small ways they know what we do—they literally will even process, like, 'Oh, you're going where? Why are you going there?' But then they'll understand, 'Oh, this is why you're making that trip and why this is important to the world.' They're getting into the thought process of realizing that it does make sense to make choices. It doesn't mean you don't love your family, but we're here because we want to make the world a better place." As we speak Wendy is getting ready for a trip with her oldest son, Benjamin, in eighth grade and on spring break. "I'm visiting some of the rural areas where Teach for America has been placing teachers, just to reflect with our teams about how to take the work to a higher level. I'm taking my son with me, and we're visiting parts of this country that most of the people don't even know exist—in Appalachia in the Mississippi Delta, and the Indian reservations in South Dakota. I just feel so lucky to be able to expose him to the realities of our country. I think we've given up some, in terms of family life, because you undertake these intense roles, but I think you gain so much more than you give up."

A Shared Passion

Four decades ago, Klaus Schwab, who was at that time the youngest professor at the University of Geneva, saw the need to bring together European and American business and political leaders to develop answers to the economic and social problems facing the world. With the help of Hilde, who was then his assistant, he inaugurated the European Management Symposium in 1971. The symposium has since been renamed the World Economic Forum (WEF), with the goal of "improving the state of the world," and its blue-and-white logo has become the coveted backdrop for snapshots of the heads of state, billionaires, celebrities, and other power brokers it convenes in its famed annual meetings. The WEF's signature once-a-year event has since evolved into a year-round discussion of regional forums, where a bevy of working groups tackle global issues such as climate change, cybersecurity, and fighting corruption and poverty. The forum also often provides a platform for political enemies to meet, gain mutual understanding, and even strike a peace deal.

Hilde said in a 2009 interview with *China Daily* news, "I am married to Klaus Schwab, but I'm also married to the World Economic Forum." Klaus later tells me that indeed, "We never had a clear separation of private and professional life. Hilde and I were both—despite challenges—always enthusiastic about what we are doing." The married couple is the driving force behind the WEF, which in some ways started out as a "family business" with a husband-and-wife team, and which Hilde calls "our life, my life, his life."

What exactly is the WEF? Think Queen Rania of Jordan, Al

Gore, Bill Clinton, Bill Gates, Tony Blair, Henry Kissinger, and Nelson Mandela huddled together in a snow-covered Swiss ski resort for one week. Throw in Bono, Paulo Coelho, and Charlize Theron for greater effect. The WEF is not the Cannes Film Festival, and there are no tuxedos or ball gowns in sight. The dress code says "smart casual," and since there are no really fancy hotels in Davos, Switzerland, even the ultra-high-net-worth participants stay in hotel rooms smaller than their closets back home. On any given day that week, the sleepy town of Davos transforms into one where it is normal to catch Filipino tycoon Fernando Zóbel de Ayala jogging at the crack of dawn, and hours later along the very same promenade see U.K. prime minister David Cameron on his evening stroll home. The January 2013 forum, for instance, brought together 2,630 participants, including 14 Nobel Prize winners, 37 sitting prime ministers and presidents, and 680 others with "chief executive" in their titles, many of whom paid many thousands of dollars to be invited. Anyone who has ever tried to organize a thirty-minute conference call between even two VIPs knows how challenging the task is.

For more than four decades, Klaus Schwab has gotten them all up there to spend a week in the mountains with temperatures dipping below zero. No wonder *Forbes* magazine has called him "indisputably the most powerful connector in the world."

Born in 1938 in Ravensburg, a city of towers and gates sitting in the shadow of the Alps in Germany, Klaus grew up amid the war. "My husband was born in Germany but of Swiss parents, so he saw both sides. He saw Germany, a war-torn country, and Switzerland, a peaceful one. This was very important to him," says Hilde. Although the door is shut and the blinds are pulled down, we are interrupted by one of many people knocking and asking for thirty-second chunks of Hilde's time for her to sign papers, confirm appointments, and receive files. Throughout she is courteous, even maternal, stopping whatever we are talking about to introduce her team and thanking them for the wonderful work they have done. "Klaus got very engaged in the German-French youth movement, because the worst friction was between Germany and France," she continues. "This really sharpened his sense for collaboration, for bringing people together, and that's what he has been doing his whole life." Klaus later adds, "I grew up during the war and the question of the new Europe based on reconciliation was paramount and certainly shaped my thinking. When I created the World Economic Forum, I saw that the real satisfaction in life is to be an entrepreneur in the global public interest and to have a positive impact—even in a small way."

Barely a month has passed since the annual meeting in Davos, and Hilde is nervously puttering about as she is about to leave for Peru for yet another forum. She takes me for a tour of the skylit, geothermally heated building whose construction she oversaw, beaming with pride over its eco-friendly attributes. The minimalist structure itself has only two colors—chestnut brown wood panels, stone ceilings and floors, and the rest is all glass. Understated as it is, the building gives you the sense that really important things are happening here. Dressed in a smart orange blazer and black skirt, with her chin-length ash blond hair neatly brushed back, Hilde seems prepared for the eventuality of a random prime minister walking in unannounced. On the walls are framed photographs of WEF events with various dignitaries shaking hands; colorful globes, maps, and paintings from all over the world brighten up the hallways, along with the cacophony of accents of its international staff (at last count, fifty-five countries), who stop by and say hello as we navigate the corridors. Like a proud mother, Hilde stops to introduce them, knowing precisely where they are from and what they are working on. She confesses that she doesn't actually hold office at the headquarters, preferring to work from home, across the street. She finds a tiny meeting room by a courtyard, shuts the door and closes the blinds, and we carry on with the discussion.

On working together, Hilde says, "It was a very hard beginning. It was not very easy. We started together without thinking it would continue. It does bring you closer, especially if you have the same aspirations, and more or less the same ideas about the world. It really brings you closer." As the WEF's "patriarch," Klaus is well regarded by his staff for being a visionary, and it is said that everybody in the office gets a personal phone call from him on the occasion of their birthday, no matter where he might be traveling. I ask if they ever switch off, and Hilde widens her eyes and laughs, "Yeah, of course—at home, we still talk about normal household matters, absolutely; we're like everybody else."

Hilde calls herself a "passionate housewife," who has had the privilege to be her husband's collaborator, while working at home and caring for their children. "I love everything about being a housewife, really—the house, the children, cooking, gardening, the dog, whatever. . . . I really do. But I have this chance to do more." She realizes that not all women have this setup, but attests, "I think you can find a cause where you can be involved, be it voluntary work or charity work or even something small, something else, where you just devote some of your time in order to get more fulfillment. Of course it's fulfilling to educate children, but even reading or watching interesting movies or having interesting discussions with other people is important for the children too, because there is something more coming out and that doesn't happen if you just sit at home. You have other perspectives and I think for the children's education, that's also very good."

Although their children have lived with the WEF all their lives and have spent time working there (son Olivier is in Beijing working for the WEF, while daughter Nicole was head of the Forum of Young Global Leaders at the WEF for two years, before deciding to do something else), Hilde says, "They were always free to create their own lives, their own destiny, their own professions. That was always clear, that they should not, do not need to follow our footsteps, but of course, we transmitted our values."

Established in Geneva in 1971, the World Economic Forum is a not-for-profit international institution committed to improving the state of the world through public-private cooperation and "engages political, business, academic, and other leaders of society in collaborative efforts to shape global, regional, and industry agendas."[3]

The Schwab Foundation for Social Entrepreneurship is a not-for-profit organization founded in 1998, with the purpose "to advance social entrepreneurship and to foster social entrepreneurs as an important catalyst for societal innovation and progress."[4] Annually, the foundation selects twenty to twenty-five social entrepreneurs from a pool of applicants through a global Social Entrepreneur of the Year competition. With more than 260 members, the Schwab Foundation community is the world's largest late-stage network of social entrepreneurs. They come from around the world and work in a wide range of sectors, but they have many challenges and characteristics in common. The foundation supports the replication of their methodologies among each other, and provides them with opportunities to connect with influential leaders in business, politics, academia, and the media.

While most of the preceding examples feature very wealthy families, a family doesn't have to be Rockefeller rich to reap the benefits of giving. Some of my most enduring memories from my childhood have to do with my mom's little charitable acts. I recall a scorching summer day when I was in the passenger's seat as she was driving down a long, treeless lane in our village. My mother spotted a woman and her child walking in the sweltering heat, and stopped her car to offer them a ride. It has been years, but I remember the startled woman thanking my mother profusely and calling her "one in a million," "a saint."

There were many other times when she performed these random acts of kindness. When I was about nine, my mother began monitoring, from a distance, an old beggar lady living in a shanty near the street where I grew up. Manila is a tale of two cities, and it is not uncommon to see shantytowns practically next to enclaves where middle-class people live. It must have been because the old woman looked particularly distraught that my mother singled her out, and she began to regularly drop by to give her clothes and food. This carried on for a few months, until the old woman mysteriously disappeared. My mother surmised that the old woman had probably passed away.

My mother did a lot of other things for other people. One year she celebrated her birthday at an orphanage. She said it meant a lot more to her to be there than to be in a fancy restaurant yet again celebrating the passage of time. And so no matter what, I will always know that my mother is a good person; I will always remember her for her good deeds.

When I ask Hilde Schwab what advice she can offer to families who want to make a difference but do not have so much money, she replies, "We were the same—we didn't have wealth, and we didn't have fame when we started the World Economic Forum. I grew up in Switzerland, in an affluent society, but my parents were not wealthy at all. We're just average. I was always educated in such a way that if you want to do something and to have a good life, you have to work hard for it."

Klaus and Hilde worked together for thirty years, and eventually were able to set up their own foundation, the Schwab Foundation for Social Entrepreneurship. Through the foundation, Hilde facilitates unknown but exemplary social entrepreneurs sharing the stage with presidents and prime ministers. "For ten minutes I can introduce four or five social entrepreneurs and just talk about what they are doing. After that, all the media comes, and they really can spread the message."

When Hilde noticed that the voice of the people working on the ground had yet to be integrated into the Davos agenda, she decided to do something about it. "I always thought that something was missing, the voice from the ground, the people who created organizations to help the poor people in a very immediate and direct way. I thought of Muhammad Yunus, who had created the Grameen Bank, but who was not well known in the West for a long, long, long time," says Hilde in her rapid-fire fashion. "I told my husband there must be hundreds, if not thousands of people who do similar work on the ground. That's how we came to create the Schwab Foundation with our own money. It's not a huge fortune, but it was good to start with it. If you're passionate about something, just do it."

THE STORY OF the Salwens, told in the book *The Power of Half: One Family's Decision to Stop Taking and Start Giving Back*, demonstrates that it's not necessary for a family to set up its own foundation to impact society—and its members—in a positive way.

One day in the fall of 2006, Kevin Salwen was driving his fourteen-year-old daughter, Hannah, home from a sleepover. They were at a busy intersection about a mile from their Atlanta home when Hannah noticed a shiny black Mercedes convertible parked right next to a shabbily dressed man holding a cardboard sign asking for food. "If that man had a less nice car, that man there could have a meal," Hannah said as they drove home.

At that time, home was 116 Peachtree Circle—a dramatic, three-story Greek Revival house with big trees on the front lawn and a sprawling garden round the back. The Salwens had bought it when Kevin was a reporter and editor at the *Wall Street Journal*, and his wife, Joan, was a partner at the global management consultancy Accenture, where she earned more than five hundred thousand dollars a year.

As the family ate supper that night, the young Hannah described the disparity she saw to her mother and her brother. "Dude, it sucks," she said. "We should fix this." Her parents had grown accustomed to Hannah's idealism, which started when she was eleven and a school project called Urban EdVenture took her to Cafe 458, an Atlanta diner that supports a local homeless project by providing free meals and donating its profits. She loved it so much she spent the whole summer there. Hannah may have also been inspired by her parents' own actions. A few years earlier, in 2002, Joan had quit her high-paying job at Accenture to become an English teacher at Atlanta Girls' School—a decision that entailed a 95 percent pay cut. Meanwhile, Kevin left the prestige of working at the *Wall Street Journal* to start a magazine about living life with more purpose.

But Hannah thought that her whole family could be even more generous. Days later, she raised the topic once again. "I really don't want to be the kind of family that just talks about doing things," she announced. "I want to be a family that actually does them." So her parents challenged her to give up some of the things she owns. "What do you want to do? Sell our house? Move into a smaller one and give what's left over to charity?" her mother asked.

And no matter how silly or impetuous it sounds, that is exactly what they ended up doing. Hannah's fifteen-year-old brother at first thought the house move idea was a joke. But soon, the family put their Peachtree Circle home on the market, bought one with roughly half the space they used to have, and over the course of the year studied hundreds of nonprofit organizations in Africa before deciding which one to help. As their plans were set into motion, Joan and Kevin noticed a change in their children. The discussions about spending the money turned into vigorous wider debates about cancer care, the environment, the effectiveness of foreign aid. "We were spending a lot more time together and the conversations we were having had shifted from to-do lists to meaningful conversations that reflected our individual and collective values," says Kevin.

They eventually decided to pledge eight hundred thousand dollars to the Hunger Project, a nonprofit that strives to eliminate poverty and hunger by helping people take control of their own futures. Their donation could fund two five-year programs that would move twenty thousand African villagers from poverty to self-reliance.

The move has had an amazing effect on the Salwens' relationships. As journalist Emily Hohler once described, "Outwardly the parent-teenager relationships look fairly typical—Hannah is ticked off for dropping crumbs on Kevin's laptop; Joe is congratulated for having a shower—but there is none of the sulky diffidence that teenagers so often display."[5] Kevin says, "We have all the usual arguments about messy rooms and unfinished homework, but the difference is that we now have a deeper level of trust and can all communicate openly." Hannah adds, "I'm the happiest, most upbeat person I know; that may be because I'm doing something to help."

Working on a noble, higher purpose together may not make everything perfect, but it can surely strengthen the bonds for many families by providing a deeply meaningful focus point.

But Wait . . . It Could All Go Wrong!

Happiness is having a large, loving, caring, close-knit family in another city.

—GEORGE BURNS

Back in 2011, I flew to Bangkok to facilitate a family meeting with the second generation of one of Thailand's wealthiest families.

At first it seemed like I was being welcomed into paradise. Upon landing in the airport, I was whisked off to a private oasis in the heart of Bangkok, and a guide took me to a secluded compound surrounded by palm trees and bougainvillea, eventually leading into an imposing meeting hall where paintings of gilt-clad Thai royalty gazed upon a massive, shiny solid wood table. One by one, the members of the family appeared. They were the sons, daughters, and in-laws of one of Thailand's most powerful, well-respected business leaders, and they were impeccable in their manners and dress.

But to my surprise, soon after the meeting started, I found out that the reason they wanted me there was to essentially have a "rehearsal." They had been wanting to submit a project proposal to their father, a very successful entrepreneur with a domineering, inflexible approach. Years back, he had started a foundation that the rest of the family did not necessarily believe in, and yet the whole family was expected to respect it as their "legacy." The children and in-laws may have been obedient and deferential to the patriarch, but his approach made it very difficult for them to feel passionate about the family's philanthropic work. There I witnessed how a multimillion-dollar foundation that had the potential to be one of Asia's best could not get off the ground.

Regardless of the good it brings, giving together doesn't automatically lead to a perfect family life. As this example demonstrates, it could all go terribly wrong. As opposed to doing it alone, giving as a family will bring about different sets of challenges, mainly due to the involvement of family members—who is involved and to what degree.

Conflict is natural. It occurs in all human relationships and can come from many sources—across generations, between siblings, and within marriages. In many cases, it arises when a strong patriarch or matriarch defines and controls the agenda and the purse strings for the family foundation, expecting deference from other family members. Older generations tend to be more conservative in the sense that they spend less, save more, and donate to familiar institutions. Younger generations might be willing to take more philanthropic risk and may want to see more direct impact from their giving.

Difficulties can also arise as a result of changing family dynamics, which can divide members. Children get married. Grandchildren are born. Extended family members become involved. And unavoidably, divorce alters the dynamics of families. Some families will want each member to have equal weight in decision making. Others will decide to have only their immediate family involved.

I saw a similar case in Singapore, when a successful entrepreneur wrote in his will that there would be a charitable trust to provide scholarships for poor students. After he died, his grandson, who was named the executor of the will, told me that "no one wanted this job. It was shoved down my throat." Although he cared about education, his main passion lay in helping the disabled.

Finally, not all family members will be willing or able to engage in the same way. In my own experience, I certainly learned values from my mother by watching her go to the orphanage and take care of beggars. However, I could not say that this was a bonding activity or a source of joy for us children, as we were not involved in her decision-making process. I recall sitting with my brother in the orphanage, feeling useless about being there as mere spectators to her charitable acts. We certainly felt sorry for the poor women and children, but we did not know what to do.

How to Do It Right

Why do philanthropy as a family at all? It's hard enough to run a household and take care of everybody, and even planning holidays with the family can sometimes be a chore. And as the previous examples demonstrate, it could all go wrong. Would it not be easier to just write checks?

In *Generations of Giving*, Kelin Gersick's study of thirty enduring family foundations, he discovered that the foundations that take their work most seriously are the ones that have the most positive impact on relationships. "The participants develop a sense of true pride. There are few bonding experiences more powerful than real accomplishment as a result of challenging hard work. In more than a third of the cases, the family credits the foundation with fostering closeness and perpetuating family cohesion across branches, geography, and generations."

With some effort, a family can reap the benefits of giving together, whether they are running a structured foundation or just giving informally.

LEARN FROM EACH OTHER. Family members must assume that they all have something to learn from each other, no matter the differences in age or philosophy. While conflict can be a source of angst, it can also be a source of creativity. Each person brings a unique perspective to the group, and has a specific set of experiences that shape his or her choices. Recognizing and providing for individuality to be expressed by family members in different ways can also make coming together on group decisions easier. Experiences, decisions, and lifestyles will vary among family members, so it's important to consider and respect what each person brings to the group. Families should recognize that although each member has individual interests, everyone has the overall goals and good of the family in mind. Establishing discretionary funds for family members is one way of allowing each person to fulfil his or her own philanthropic interests while also participating in shared family goals.

Teddy Turner, Ted's oldest son, recalls the first vote the trustees outvoted Ted on. "We thought it was the end of the world. But he thought it was the greatest thing. I think it was part of the transition he wanted—the trustees' passion is not only reflected in their involvement in the foundation, but also in their personal commitments."

SET GUIDELINES. Giving serious thought about who is involved in the family's giving process, what each person's role is, and how decisions are made will ensure that each member has a voice in the decisions and has a fulfilling experience. Determining how much or how little each family member will participate will help them understand what is expected of them, and thus allow them to be more effective with their contributions. Families need to decide who should be included in their family giving structure. Will it include extended family, spouses, and grandchildren? Clarify how decisions will be made, how inevitable differences in opinion might be handled, and what you are inviting and asking your family to do.

BE FLEXIBLE. Life gets busy for everybody. Understanding each other's commitments will help balance the interaction between more engaged members and less active members. Giving flexibility to family members will make giving more rewarding for each person, as their obligations and interests will change over time. Family members may need to be involved at differing levels depending on their talents, time, and personal preferences. All of us experience personal and professional demands on our time and resources that vary throughout the year and over our lifetimes. Having the understanding that family members may be allowed to enter or leave the charitable process ensures that giving together doesn't become a burden as people's lives and obligations change. There should be an invitation to participate, an agreement that each member is free to enter and leave the process, and an understanding that giving together should be a pleasurable experience.

MEET AND COMMUNICATE. Many families find it difficult to find opportunities to come together, whether because of their geographic dispersion or the demands of their careers. Families should make time for such meetings to make site visits, meet with charitable recipients, discuss their proposed annual distributions, review administrative issues or investment updates. These may be the only meetings that give families the opportunity to clearly articulate their reasons for working together, and to discuss financial issues and individual goals and desires in a fairly neutral context. Effective communication involves both talking and listening. I must stress the importance of actually planning out the meetings and not just letting them happen spontaneously.

In my own experience, it was clear that my parents and grand-parents were generous. However, their generosity became a source of unspoken conflict and even jealousy among us, and not some-thing that brought us closer together. None of us kids were told about the why, what, whom of the giving. My mom and dad would do their own thing separately, out of a sense of obligation to less fortunate people from the towns where they grew up. None of their charitable activities brought them closer together as a couple. As for us kids, we were not involved in any decision making, we didn't know the recipients, and at times we even felt resentful of the ben-eficiaries because we thought we had lost out to them.

Later on in my career I discovered that other families actually sit around the dinner table to discuss the charitable grants they are making. What a wonderful way for family members to get to know each other, exchange information and ideas, and become good prob-lem solvers!

INVOLVE OTHERS. Families need not do it on their own. Others can and will enter the picture as well. Doing charitable work together inevitably surrounds a family with like-minded people who can be a source of inspiration and positive reinforcement. If parents are worried about kids getting involved with the wrong crowd, this is one solution.

HAVE FUN. It doesn't matter what the cause is—addressing world hunger, reducing crime, helping the homeless, planting trees. If a family can find a cause that resonates with each member, and spend time together addressing that cause, the experience of giving becomes all the more satisfying. It is particularly important for parents to make sure that whatever the family is doing is what the kids actually want to be doing.

"I never pushed any member of my family to get involved in the foundation because I always believe that everybody should find their own route of life," says Mo Ibrahim, the richest black man in Britain. "But my daughter Hadeel insisted—against my wish, actually—to come and work on the foundation." Hadeel is now executive director of the Mo Ibrahim Foundation, and sits on several other boards. "This has given us huge energy."

Kevin Salwen says, "We want our kids to be idealistic, but we also say, 'Let's not go too nuts here.' We're not Mother Teresa. We're not taking a vow of poverty, or giving away half of everything we own. We gave away half of one thing, which happened to be our house. Everybody can give away half of one thing and put it to use. You'll do a little bit of good for the world—and amazing things for your relationships."

Jennie Turner Garlington, the youngest of Ted Turner's five children, describes her experience being involved in the family foundation as "one of the greatest opportunities that any son or daughter can ever hope to have." The other siblings also share their dad's passion for environmental causes. Said Beau Turner, "I think Dad thought it was very, very important to start giving money away while he was still around, so he could see what our interest was in all this. And so he could see his children enjoying the giving."

What Volunteering Can Do for Your Family

Families get a whole slew of benefits from community service. Volunteering as a family is an excellent way to spend time together. Family members get the chance to communicate more, enhance their problem-solving abilities, learn about social issues, and gain a new perspective on the world. Volunteering can draw family members closer together, forging new bonds through shared experiences that are outside the normal daily routines. Parents, children, and other relatives who volunteer together also learn more about each other while experiencing new activities. New friendships can be made and new interests may be awoken that can stay with the family for the long haul. At a basic level, volunteering as a family is a concrete way to apply and demonstrate shared values and beliefs while making a positive impact in the world around them. Volunteering as a family can benefit children in particular, in the following ways:

- Exposes children to positive role models.
- Teaches social responsibility. Volunteering helps children develop empathy and learn that one person can make a difference.
- Promotes a healthy lifestyle and choices. Children who volunteer are less likely to become involved in at-risk behaviors.
- Helps young people decide what they want to do with their lives.
- Enhances children's psychological, social, and intellectual development. Increases self-esteem, responsibility, and an

interest in learning and helps children develop new social skills. It also provides opportunities to apply newly learned material.

- Creates a lifelong ethic of service.

There are a number of volunteer opportunities that lend themselves quite readily to family involvement. Many schools, nonprofits, churches, and community groups offer opportunities for the whole family to volunteer together in a range of activities, from coaching sports or playing music to visiting the residents at a retirement home or assisting with a toy drive. It's a good idea to convene a family meeting and discuss what areas the family members are most interested in working with each other on. For example, environmental cleanups give the family a chance to enjoy the outdoors together while also doing something positive for the planet. Volunteering at a homeless shelter, a food bank, or a soup kitchen can not only help the needy in the community but can also remind the family members how fortunate they are to have one another. If a family member is planning to participate in a walk-a-thon or another charity fund-raising event, there may be openings to get the rest of the family involved (handing out water to racers or programs to attendees at a dinner ball, for instance). A family can also take the initiative and create volunteer activities, such as raking leaves from an elderly neighbor's lawn or helping a low-income family paint their house.

Families can engage in short-term or one-off activities, and for those who are willing there are also some volunteer positions that involve a longer commitment, which are most beneficial to charities who are looking for dedicated, reliable attendance. Also, when one family volunteers, it can be a tremendous example to other families, fostering a sense of community responsibility and perhaps even inspiring others to contribute their time and skills toward improving the community.

Voluntourism

Families need not leave their communities to volunteer. But for those who have the opportunity to do so, volunteering abroad can be a life-altering experience—an unforgettable, rewarding, and responsible way to vacation. Family members can learn about one another in a new and different way.

"I'd been married three times [now four], never really living with my kids full-time because I'd always been a divorced father. It's very difficult," says music producer David Foster. When his daughter Jordan was nine, he took her to Africa with UNICEF. "We went way deep into the camps, way past all the tourist places. And she still remembers it up to this day. She got to see the real disease and sickness. She then went to Fiji and built homes when she was fifteen."

Voluntourism for Couples

A word of caution: Make sure you both genuinely want to go. Just because it's your dream to volunteer abroad doesn't mean it's your partner's dream as well. Volunteering abroad together can make a couple stronger and closer to each other, but it also has the potential to cause tremendous stress in a relationship. What if one loves the outdoors and the other can't live without air-conditioning? Couples should work out the duration, location, cause, and what skills to contribute. Special attention must be paid to health and safety issues—secure accommodations, safe food and water, and a community that cares about your welfare. Finally, make sure that you are going to a place where your help is needed and wanted. If you do not know a charity directly, work with a company that operates under the direction and invitation of local nonprofit partners.

How to Make Celebrations More Meaningful

BIRTHDAYS

A birthday party with a charity twist can be an opportunity for parents to teach their child lessons in altruism, in hopes that those lessons will stick for life. Some ideas for these parties include asking guests to give donations instead of gifts, organizing activities such as baking cookies for the homeless shelter, planting trees, entertaining residents of a retirement home, or walking dogs at a local rescue.

But to get kids enthusiastic about helping others, parents should direct them to causes that reflect their interests, and if possible, let them meet the beneficiaries of their gifts. If it's not real to them, they won't understand it. If donations have been sought in lieu of gifts, parents should take the child to the drop-off location. The praise and encouragement that the children get from the charity staff is some well-deserved icing on the cake. Kids can also share details of their donations and their recipients in thank-you cards to their party guests.

Parents should note that while some kids don't mind giving up gifts altogether, some aren't quite ready yet. Judith Martin, who writes the Miss Manners syndicated column, fears kids may "grow up hating philanthropy because it's done [them] out of [their] birthday presents." As an alternative, parents can arrange a volunteer day when kids can have fun and learn from the experience.

WEDDINGS

In the same way, charity weddings are becoming more and more popular. Couples use their wedding day to highlight socially conscious causes in various ways: by asking for charitable donations in lieu of presents, by donating to charities on behalf of their guests in lieu of handing out cheesy wedding favors, or by giving their guests presents such as fair trade chocolate or tree seedlings to promote environmental sustainability. Weddings are about whom and what you love, and couples want to share who they are by highlighting the causes they care about.

A wedding can be an ideal place to gather attention for a charity. According to the Wedding Report, a research company focused on the wedding industry, there were 2.2 million weddings in 2009, with each event averaging 128 guests.

The I Do Foundation, a nonprofit group that helps engaged couples set up charitable registries, reports that about sixty thousand couples have established registries through its site. When the foundation began in 2002, couples could select from a dozen charities.

Today, the agency offers more than 1.5 million nonprofit groups to choose from. Couples can also shop from selected vendors, with a portion of their spending going to a charity.

The overall rise in interest in the social sector among young people may be one reason for the rise in charitable weddings, but it may also be that the trend is due to a larger cultural shift in marriage. More couples are cohabitating and marrying later. For example, in 2004, the average age for a bride was twenty-seven and the average groom's age was twenty-nine. In 2009, the bride was twenty-eight and the groom was thirty, according to a survey of twenty-one thousand couples conducted by TheKnot.com. By the time these couples are getting married, they don't need flatware, silverware, and candlesticks.

The Circle of Reciprocity

"It feels as though at some level, I won the lottery," said Richard Rockefeller, who grew up seeing his family name imprinted on countless halls, universities, museums, libraries, laboratories, and even national parks and forests across the country. Richard's great-grandfather was the legendary industrialist John D. Rockefeller, who is said to have been the richest man who ever lived. By today's standards, he would have been worth a dizzying $340 billion—not even Bill Gates or Warren Buffett could come close. "We lived in tremendous comfort. There was luxury all around us, as much as you'd ever possibly want," said Richard.

But very early on in his life, he discovered that there were just as many unhappy people in the Rockefeller family as there were anywhere else. He watched his relatives who owned five or six houses at a time spending all their time going from house to house and having too little time for friends. "Wealth didn't make them happy, and in many cases, burdened them. The things they own own them," said Richard, whom I met in 2013, the year before he died. We sat in an empty, borrowed office in one of the many New York edifices funded by his great-grandfather. The building's granite walls and wood paneling gave off a dense odor, somewhere between the smell of a wad of bills and a pile of gravel, the smell of a dynasty that has been impossibly rich for a century. "By the time I was twelve, I could say, 'There's no way!' People are crazy. Why would they want to be owned by their possessions? What I think a lot of people don't realize is, the very having of wealth can sap one's life of meaning," he said.

At age sixty-four, Richard's demeanor hinted at the same conviction he must have had as a boy quickly getting over the trappings of wealth. Throughout the four months that our interview was in the making, he personally responded to each of my e-mails, without a personal assistant and always signing off with *Sincerely, Yours*, and various versions of *Best wishes*. On the day of our interview he greeted me at the lobby of the Rockefeller Brothers Fund office wearing a blue oxford shirt that looked pleasant enough but slightly threadbare and in need of a bit more ironing. Leading me into the pantry, he offered to make me tea before making his own. In a city where space is one of the rarest commodities, there are miles in between the pieces of furniture spread across rooms overlooking the Hudson River. But as we walked past an eighteen-seat conference table, Richard eschewed the imposing space in favor of a small, windowless room that reminded me of a doctor's office, where he felt right at home.

Many years ago, Richard chose to pursue the path of what he called "normalcy." "I decided as a young man to get a career, and ignore the whole family thing and see what it was like to live as a middle-class person having to work for a living," he said, hunched over the desk and speaking slowly and thoughtfully, with a sense of tranquility honed by years of Buddhist practice. The young Richard went to medical school, and traded the Rockefeller kingdom of New York for the quiet New England town of Falmouth, Maine, where he practiced as a family doctor for seventeen years doing "the full gamut," delivering babies and taking care of children, adults, and old people. "People assumed I couldn't be related, because why would somebody who's part of the Rockefeller family be living in Falmouth, Maine, seeing patients for eight to nine hours a day? I got the best of both worlds, in a certain way. I got to have the luxury of living an observed life. I got to actually experience what it's like to live the way a lot of people do, which is to have a full-time job while raising a family, and being answerable to, in this case, my patients." Thanks to various trust funds that let the family members live off the principal's interest (or the interest of the interest), Richard did not actually need to earn his keep. "The only point in doing this is to do it as well as I possibly can. There's a wide gulf between slapdash, factory medicine where you just grind bodies through the system, see one patient every fifteen minutes, and get paid whether you solve a problem or not, versus really working on the fundamentals of primary care, which are prevention, early detection, appropriate diagnosis, and appropriate treatment."

While a German con artist and murderer once worked his way up through the highest echelons of New York society by living for years under the name Clark Rockefeller and claiming to be an heir to the famed family fortune, some of the real Rockefellers try to escape their family name, which Richard called a "fifty-fifty burden-privilege," particularly to young family members who were trying to find their way. His sister Peggy, a humanitarian who spent her student years working with the poor in the favelas of Rio de Janeiro, changed her last name altogether, "so as not to be judged or feel the pressure too much," Richard said. I told him about my own experience in Philadelphia of having a professor named Glenn Rockefeller, who on the first day of school immediately made clear that he was not part of that family, in case we only signed up for his class hoping to rub elbows with the rich and famous. "Yeah, yeah, I know exactly what you mean. All your life, you get the question, Are you one of the Rockefellers? And you have endless ways of deflecting the question, or answering it," Richard said. "It's been really most problematic for those who stayed and lived in New York, because Rockefeller and philanthropy are all just so in New York." Rockefeller Center alone is a complex of nineteen commercial buildings stretching over six blocks and covering more than eight million square feet of prime Manhattan real estate. Although the Rockefellers no longer own it, there are still grandiose assumptions about the family's wealth, which Richard said is nowhere near what they once had, as much of the money has been given away or spent by the more than two hundred members of the family. "The assumption is you have to be related, and then there are presumptions about your wealth and capacity. I wouldn't have known if I stayed in New York whether people are interested in getting to know you because you're actually an interesting person, or because of the fact of your heritage. If you took us all together, we still wouldn't have the wealth that a lot of new, newly wealthy families in America and elsewhere around the world have. And individually, we absolutely don't. People don't see it that way, and you can tell them till you're blue in the face and they think that can't be true, because they know that the name Rockefeller means enormous wealth."

Fortunately, the Rockefeller name also means enormous philanthropy. "Both my great-grandfather and grandfather at different times were overwhelmed by their possessions, and they both found their way out of it by effective institutional philanthropy, and found happiness. I'd never thought of it this way, but the water I swam in was of my male ancestors having come to this discovery. There is a pathway to happiness through giving." No doubt they have had their troubles, like any other family, but they believe that this collective focus on giving has helped them to avoid many of the problems experienced by other wealthy dynasties, and they remained a tight-knit clan.

While Richard's medical practice had already given him joy, the happiness he found through his charitable work was on a different level. "In medical practice you discover the feeling of tremendous joy when you see somebody sick, you are deeply involved in making them better. They're better, they're happy, they're grateful, they're just happier. It feels good." Richard's discovery very gradually unfolded starting in 1989, when the French medical humanitarian organization Médecins Sans Frontières, or MSF (now known internationally as Doctors Without Borders), sent a woman from Paris to open an office in New York. By coincidence, her father and the Rockefeller family had done business in the past, and in keeping with the family's philanthropic spirit, they offered her an office space at Rockefeller Center.

Soon after, MSF called on Richard to join their board of

advisors, because he was the only one in the family with a background in medicine. "I had never heard of them. It was sort of the sense of obligation that made me join, because I was extremely busy raising a young family and trying to carry out my medical practice in Maine, and they were in New York. It's not that I jumped in and did it eagerly because I thought, What a wonderful organization! I reluctantly agreed. I actually said, 'Well, okay, until you can find somebody else,'" said Richard, chuckling at himself. For ten years, he would meet with MSF about once a year, occupying a "mostly ceremonial" role in the organization, which opened doors using his last name—a name that Richard simultaneously embraced and admired from a distance. "There's none of us in our generation who can come close to what John D. Rockefeller and John D. Rockefeller Jr. did. They were equivalently generous, strategic, and successful in what they did. In our family, that tradition of philanthropy has remained strong all the way through and everybody feels it, whether they spend their life in there or not. Everybody feels that it's a duty and an honor, a privilege to use whatever gifts you have to give back," said Richard, who felt honored even just to bear a physical resemblance to his grandfather.

In 1989, MSF invited Richard to go on a mission to Peru to see what they were doing, and out of the Rockefeller sense of duty he went out in the field. "I saw how incredibly dedicated, hardworking, and effective they were. They were doing the kind of work that I trained to do and doing it in very difficult circumstances. It excited me as a scientist, as a doctor. But on the other hand, as a Rockefeller, I knew that the best thing I could do for them would be to use my name and my medical background as an advocate in government, and also as a fund-raiser."

Twenty-one years later, Richard was still chairing the board of advisors, and doing the work because it made him feel "switched on." When I asked him what that meant, he pulled out a piece of paper and a plastic blue ballpoint pen to attempt to diagram the idea. I was taking notes myself, and at that moment I felt a sudden compulsion to hide my gold-tipped fountain pen, which looked pretentious in comparison. He drew one small circle to represent himself, and next to it a bigger circle to represent the scale of the issues he was addressing. The illustrations by themselves made little sense, but as he traced lines from one circle to the other, I began to understand that he was referring to the enhanced capacity of the wealthy and well connected to impact the nonprofit sector to a degree that is unimaginable to the rest of us. "With a small amount of my personal effort, a little bit of my time, my skills, and what I can bring to bear, there's a likelihood that I can actually do something to help meet that need," he said, retracing the bigger circle to make the point. "Giving money away, actually, I find that . . . sort of boring. I do it because we owe it." Following the family tradition, he would give locally, nationally, and politically to more than three hundred organizations in the course of a year. "They tend to want to come back and meet with you and send you lots of letters and tell you how wonderful you are—none of that is a cause of happiness for me at all. My 'switched on' joy means having a personal connection with something very large and being in a community of people, but having a very particular role. I do find these days that the things that excite me are the things where I have a real history with them." Richard's history with MSF ran very deep, especially after the spring of 2000 when, after a trip to Uganda to visit a malaria program, he began to feel sick and was diagnosed with a rare type of leukemia that kills almost everybody. He credited his survival to a miraculous drug that was released months after his diagnosis, and he began to engage in a process of trying to support access to drugs for rare diseases, as well as a host of various other medical causes.

He said that each person has a unique set of circumstances that influence what kind of giving feels most right for him or her. "Thank goodness there's a huge range of people who want to do different things. We're not all trying to fight for the same philanthropy spot." For many volunteers, the appeal of MSF is in being in the field, and as its chair, Richard was inevitably exposed to field work. Is this what made him happy? Unapologetically, he explained that this was not what got him going, particularly at his age. "I think there are many answers for many people. There are MSF-ers who go back and back and back, even though they kind of ruin their family lives; they don't make any money. In a way, they are adrenaline junkies. They love being in areas of civil conflict, being in danger all the time, but they are absolutely saving lives every day. This is intense. It is like a drug; they become a little bit addicted to it. That is not what motivates me." A few years ago Richard, who was at that time already in his sixties, spent a month in Nigeria in a meningitis campaign. "We were out in 115-degree heat all day and I would come home completely drained and just want to eat and just go to bed, and the long-term MSF-ers would still be up all night going through all their paperwork, going over through everything, reorganizing the whole campaign. The lives that they live in the field, they're not the life that I want to live," he said. Once, he joined a campaign that eventually immunized eight million people across sub-Saharan Africa. It was the large scale of such a project, and the individual contact that it proffered, that he liked to get involved in. "I'm very happy to do that, at really a one-to-one level, but I'm just as happy doing it in Falmouth, Maine, as I would be in Nigeria or anyplace else."

While he was neither an adrenaline junkie nor someone who needed recognition, Richard found excitement in other philan-thropic pursuits, namely in cracking the cure for post-traumatic stress disorder. "I am doing what sounds almost like a crazy thing right now, but it's a perfect fit for me." The day before we met, he spent the whole day at the Pentagon talking the U.S. military into supporting the therapeutic technique and drug that he attested could cure 80 percent of the people who had been severely trauma-tized by war. "I could get in with my name, and they're taking me seriously because I'm also a doctor. Right now, we have a giant problem, but people can't see it. There's a potential solution that I and a few other people can see. How in the world do you bring public awareness and resources to bear on it?" he said, speaking a lot louder and breaking the monastic calm of the office, his hands stir-ring the air between us as he gesticulated in excitement. "A lot of the joy is working on that puzzle. I love seeing things that other people can't see, and rendering them visible to other people. I love going and delivering babies, but it's a completely different kind of joy than a five- or ten-year project bringing this to fruition and assembling a team or working with an already existing team to bring this to light. We're getting testimonials back from these sol-diers who were traumatized in the Vietnam War from ages ago;

they finally have a life. Reading those testimonials just moves me, and it makes me tearful. That's a huge pleasure, but it's a combined pleasure with this whole business of seeing something that I can do something about. It's not the giving that makes me happy; it's the lens of creating—that's the joy."

As Richard talked about how his charitable work had brought him joy, I reminded him that some people argue that giving is meant to be a sacrifice. "You can go on with that argument forever and it's just not a useful argument. I remember having that discussion when I was a thirteen-year-old with my roommates in school. We concluded that there was no such thing as altruism because you could always say that it was self-serving because it would make you feel good." He was careful to make a distinction between giving to make other people happy and giving just to feel good, without checking to see whether the gift has also had a good effect on others. "There is a question about efficacy. If you pursue things just to relieve your own anxiety in your suffering, that's an unskillful way of going about your life. This is not true, by the way, of Gates and Buffett—they are extremely concerned about the effect they are having. It's accountable and effective. If the focus is solely on what happened to the giver, never mind the object, then I think it's shallower. You really want to look carefully—why are you doing it and what is the real result of what you're doing? Because a poor person who has a rich person always in a power position of just giving to them, it belittles them further. You're poor to begin with and now you have to accept charity and be grateful to this rich person for the rest of your life." He recognized that some people give to fill the need for power and prestige. "I don't care about power and prestige, but if they're also highly effective with the way they're giving, then let them be."

Most people don't have his last name, I said, and can forget about giving to fill the need for power and prestige. "How can people partake in the kind of joy you have found in giving?" I asked.

"Anybody can have joy. There's nobody at any level that has nothing to give—everybody has something that they can share and give. I do not believe the amount of joy you get from it is proportional to the amount that you have to give. Can people who don't have the resources to be philanthropists find joy in giving? The answer is yes, but it has to do with two things."

One stems from what he learned in Buddhist practice. "All of Buddhism is about how to be happy. That's one of the things I liked first about Buddhism; it's the religion where it's about happiness and you're allowed to be happy. There's tricks in getting to be happy and one of the tricks is living in the present, and the other is living a life of compassion—compassion for yourself and compassion for other people. When I first started Buddhist practice I thought those were two separate things; I didn't see how they would fit together. At first, that's just an idea. But in time, you develop this sense of peace and happiness, and there is no question in your mind that the idea that other people's happiness is your happiness, that your happiness is my happiness. And my sense of philanthropy has moved into that realm as well." That is different from what he called giving in the "puritanical" sense. "The thing is, in the end, it has to be all about all of us. Desiring the happiness of every living being is a philanthropic impulse. If you approach every day that way and have a philanthropic goal that's about increasing happiness, then it's a source of pure joy. There's an expression, 'What goes around comes around.' You move it that way and then eventually it comes back to you, because you are connected with a person or group or cause that you are giving to. There's a circle of reciprocity rather than charity."

The next trick, Richard said, has to do with finding out who you are and what you can bring. "Not what people in general can bring, but specifically you—what are your gifts and how are they different from others? Over time, through clarifying practice you find out what it is that switches you on. Everybody has something that can switch them on. Some people get excited about something and some people don't.

"The greatest experience of giving is when all parts are in harmony." And that was exactly where Richard was the year before he died, helping veterans heal their wounds of war. "The work with trauma is taking everything I've got and I love every morning getting up and doing it. It doesn't feel like giving—that's the odd thing. It's using the skills that I have, and knowing that I'm increasing them and enhancing them, and the goal is something that I care deeply about and that my heart is in it. It's using my intellect, my spirit, and my heart, and my body, and there's a flow. It doesn't feel like you're giving anything away. It feels as though you are a vessel for something else moving through you to create something. What's moving through you might be money, if that's what you have, but ideally, what's moving through you is everything that you have. Money, skills, intelligence, love. What makes for really satisfying giving is where everything that you have is being used. When it doesn't feel like work, there's no difference between work and play; it's just what you want to do."

Richard Rockefeller, Ed.M., M.D., practiced and taught medicine in Maine from 1982 until 2000, and remained involved in a variety of health-related nonprofit activities until his death in June 2014. He founded and served as president of Health Commons Institute, a nonprofit organization dedicated to improving American medicine through the use of computer-based information tools and informed shared decision making between patients and physicians. He chaired the U.S. advisory board of Doctors Without Borders from 1989 until 2010, and served on the board of the Rockefeller University until 2006. Dr. Rockefeller was founder and former chairman of Hour Exchange Portland, a service credit barter program designed to rebuild trust, reciprocity, and civic engagement in Portland and throughout the state of Maine. He chaired the board of Maine Coast Heritage Trust from 2000 until 2006 and was past president of the Rockefeller Family Fund.

From Success to Significance

When throwing money at the problem works

There is no greater duty—nor pleasure—
than that of giving help to others.

—SAMUEL GOLDWYN

It seemed to me that the people who were genuinely thriving
in their lives were the ones who had made room for
well-being, wisdom, wonder, and giving.

—ARIANNA HUFFINGTON, *THRIVE*

We should often blush at our noblest deeds if the world
were to see all their underlying motives.

—FRANCOIS DE LA ROCHEFOUCAULD

"I thought that if I had financial independence, good health, good family, friends, enjoyed what I was doing, I'd be automatically happy," says Ray Chambers. It is Valentine's Day and we are sitting in his wood-paneled office on the Upper East Side of Manhattan overlooking Central Park as he tells me his story.

Born in 1942 in Newark, New Jersey, Ray is the son of a steel warehouse office manager and worked his way through Rutgers University by playing keyboard in a rock-and-roll band called the Raytones. He spent a few years as a tax accountant at the Newark office of Price Waterhouse, before founding his own financial investing firm with Bill Simon, Richard Nixon's former Treasury secretary. It was the 1980s—the decade of unchecked excess, nonstop glamour, and Gordon Gekko–style ruthlessness—and by 1985 he had made hundreds of millions of dollars by acquiring dozens of major companies such as Avis Rent A Car, Outlet Broadcasting, and Wilson Sporting Goods through Wesray Capital Corporation, his own firm on Wall Street, and become one of the wealthiest people in America.

"Isn't this great? We've made all this money; we're at the top of Wall Street," said Bill to his business partner, Ray. "But you don't look happy."

Bill asked what it would take for Ray to be happy. And without thinking, Ray replied, "If we could lose it all and do it again."

Bill shrugged it off and told Ray he needed a vacation. But from that moment on, Ray knew exactly what to do. "I knew there was something missing," says Ray, in a voice so grandfatherly and wise, it's like an inspirational book on tape. "That void was not going to be filled by making more money or building more assets."

What Happens When You've Made It?

As I started getting rich, I started thinking, "What the hell am I going to do with all this money?" . . . You have to learn to give.

—TED TURNER

Most of us will not find ourselves on the Forbes list of billionaires in this lifetime. But what can we learn about happiness from those who have reached the pinnacle of material success?

The Real Maslow's Hierarchy

It is quite true that man lives by bread alone—when there is no bread. But what happens to man's desires when there is plenty of bread and when his belly is chronically filled? At once other (and "higher") needs emerge and these, rather than physiological hungers, dominate the organism. And when these in turn are satisfied, again new (and still "higher") needs emerge and so on.[1]

—ABRAHAM MASLOW

In 1943, American psychologist Abraham Maslow attempted to explain the pattern of motivations that humans generally move through. Human motivation, according to his theory, is based on a hierarchy of five needs: physiological, safety, belongingness/love, esteem, and self-actualization. Maslow's hierarchy, as it came to be known, has for decades been a mainstay in textbooks, journals, articles, and pop culture, and has remained one of the most enduring and popular constructs to explain the patterns of human behavior. Anyone who has heard of it can imagine its most popular visual representation: a pyramid (although Maslow himself never presented his steps with any imagery), with the final step of self-actualization, or the fulfillment of one's personal potential, as the highest of human motivations.

But what not many people know is that in the late 1960s, after having done more research on human behavior, Maslow amended his model. The new model placed self-transcendence, in which individuals seek a benefit beyond the purely personal, as the final step, beyond self-actualization. As Maslow put it in his unpublished October 1966 paper, "The good of other people must be invoked."

Unfortunately, Maslow found very little opportunity to publicize his amended theory. In 1968, he was hospitalized in intensive care following a heart attack. He never quite recovered, and died two years later.

Now, researchers such as Mark E. Koltko-Rivera, of New York University, argue that the conventional description of Maslow's hierarchy of needs is inaccurate as a description of his later thought, and that the implications of this change must not be underestimated.

A Rectified Version of Maslow's Hierarchy of Needs

Motivational level	Description of person at this level
Self-transcendence	Seeks to further a cause beyond the self[a] and to experience a communion beyond the boundaries of the self through peak experience.[b]
Self-actualization	Seeks fulfillment of personal potential.
Esteem needs	Seeks esteem through recognition or achievement.
Belongingness and love needs	Seeks affiliation with a group.
Safety needs	Seeks security through order and law.
Physiological (survival) needs	Seeks to obtain the basic necessities of life.

Note. The earliest and most widespread version of Maslow's hierarchy (based on Maslow, 1943, 1954) includes only the bottom five motivational levels (thus excluding self-transcendence). A more accurate version of the hierarchy, taking into account Maslow's later work (especially Maslow, 1969a) and his private journal entries (Maslow, 1979, 1982), includes all six motivational levels.

[a] This may involve service to others, devotion to an ideal (e.g., truth, art) or a cause (e.g., social justice, environmentalism, the pursuit of science, a religious faith), and/or a desire to be united with what is perceived as transcendent or divine.

[b] This may involve mystical experiences and certain experiences with nature, aesthetic experiences, sexual experiences, and/or other transpersonal experiences, in which the person experiences a sense of identity that transcends or extends beyond the personal self.

The earlier, well-known model says that at the highest level, the individual ultimately works to fulfill his or her own potential. "There is a certain self-aggrandizing aspect to this motivational stage," Koltko-Rivera says. However, at the level of self-transcendence, the individual's own needs are put aside, to a great extent, in favor of service to others. "Certainly the image of the best-developed human being that emerges from Maslow's hierarchy is very different, depending on which of these two stages is placed at the top of the motivational hierarchy. It is time to change the textbook accounts of Maslow's hierarchy of needs. Incorporating self-transcendence gives us a theoretical tool with which to pursue a more comprehensive and accurate understanding of human personality and behavior."

Logically, we can imagine the world's wealthiest people—particularly those who are self-made—to have reached the very top of Maslow's classic hierarchy. Basic needs? Without a doubt, the super rich have those more than adequately met. For them it's no longer about having a roof above their heads and enough food to eat, clothes to wear, and air to breathe. Their roofs can be made of luxury slate tile; their food Michelin star quality; their clothes Loro Piana; and their air purified, ionized, and fragranced. Safety needs? If they had to, they could build an underground bomb shelter, hire bodyguards, or at the very least choose a Volvo. Belongingness and love? Subjective as these may be, we can reasonably assume that the wealthiest people feel enough of a sense of belongingness through their relationships with family and friends, or at least through work. Esteem? Many of the wealthiest are held in high regard for their accomplishments, and are effectively given social power and influence through their status.

As for self-actualization, the world's richest self-made men and women are realizing their personal potential by having made their ideas come to life in the form of the businesses that they created.

But after they have reached the peak of business success, the novelty of money wears off and they realize that they want something else out of life—just as Mo Ibrahim discovered shortly after he sold his telecommunications company, Celtel International, for $3.4 billion.

Is There More to Life Than Sitting on the Beach and Playing Golf?

Born in 1946 in Wadi Halfa, a village in northern Sudan, and brought up in Alexandria, Egypt, Mo Ibrahim grew up in an Africa that he described as having "no Obama," when colonialism was still rife, many American universities did not accept blacks, and they still had to sit in the back of a bus. At that time, young people were speaking out about their condition—*Why are we poor? Why are we colonized? Why are we exploited?* His father was a clerk; his mother, a housewife; and with five children to raise, she taught them that education and hard work were the only way out of poverty.

Six decades later, Mo Ibrahim is credited with transforming a continent, and is one of the wealthiest people not only in Africa, but in the world. After Celtel International sold, he became the kind of rich that made people look at him with "dollar signs all over their eyes," he says, widening his eyes as he sits diagonally across from me on a November morning at the Mo Ibrahim Foundation headquarters, in London. His office has floor-to-ceiling windows on two sides, and occupies a bright and airy corner on the third floor overlooking Portman Square, a quiet area steps away from the city's busiest shopping street. One of the windows opens onto a small veranda with two chairs and a table, on which sits Mo's pipe. It is the office of a man who has made it, replete with framed photos of him shaking hands with everyone from Prince Charles to Archbishop Desmond Tutu. A candid photo of Mo, sitting with who appears to be former Irish prime minister Mary Robinson, former U.N. secretary-general Kofi Annan, and various other dignitaries with their identities obscured by large white 3-D glasses, staring straight into a screen, occupies a prime spot on a console table and hints at Mo's playful nature. And although he stepped down from Celtel nearly six years back, his is the office of a busy man. Stacks of reports, books, and various bits of paper sit neatly, but not so much that they look untouched, on nearly every surface.

"In the beginning, business is about building something and making money, but after a while becomes more of an ego trip," he says. "Is it wonderful? Will you be very happy? I mean, you will not eat better, you will not dress better, you will not have a better car. What are you going to do?" Dressed in a cashmere vest and a dark gray suit, Mo looks as expensive as one can be, without the slightest bit of ostentation. "There comes a time when you think, Okay, I am secure. My children are fine. I have achieved what I want in business. Then the diminishing law starts to apply. It becomes even meaningless. Meaningless."

And so once he cashed in in 2005, the golf-loving Mo did not just go to a beautiful island to enjoy the sunsets and play golf. "For me that's not a satisfactory way of life. Yes, playing golf is nice, and beaches are beautiful. But I find none of that fulfilling."

Celtel's phenomenal success (its investors made eight times their initial investment, on average, and the company became known as one that gave "not a dollar in bribes") was proof that it is possible to build a great business in a completely transparent manner. This ethos foreshadowed the philanthropist that Mo was to become. Having earned his wealth by radically transforming Africa's telecom infrastructure, he thought of giving back. "I really, really wanted to help. And I wanted to help in a different way." Believing that Africa's problems stemmed from the mismanagement of its resources and the lack of governance and leadership, he set out to create a radical shift in the way the continent is governed. In 2006, he launched the Mo Ibrahim Foundation, with the aim of promoting good governance and leadership in Africa.

"Becoming a philanthropist changed my life immensely. Immensely," he says. "It takes you from this tight circle of myself, my kids, my family and out into the wider circle of humanity. You feel you are part of this wonderful human race. And suddenly, any personal problem you have appears to be absolutely ridiculous. Really! It's absolutely ridiculous, you know." He shakes his head. "You get frustrated at the traffic, you get frustrated at any small inconvenience to your very affluent and comfortable life. And then you see what's happening around you. How many kids are going to bed hungry, people having malaria or starving, people getting killed, women being raped . . . There are huge issues out there."

Before he became known for being philanthropic, Mo would walk into business meetings feeling that people just wanted to extract as much money from him as they could. "If you're running a restaurant and some rich guy came to you, you will double the price immediately." But after he began to speak up and stand for Africa, waiters in Khartoum would refuse to let him pay the price of a cup of coffee and taxi drivers would decline his cab fare, telling him he has done enough for the continent. "It's a dollar or two. Nothing, really. But it's just the feeling of appreciation."

Does charitable work make him happy? "Absolutely! It adds a new dimension to life. Whatever you are doing is not measured in dollars but by the effect you've had on other people. It's more meaningful. You really feel you have done something—children having immunization, less conflicts, less people dying, improving the life of a community, improving the standard of governments, managing to stop corruption. It's a wonderful sense of achievement. It's wonderful if we are able to use the money to really do something more meaningful than just leaving it in the bank. And if we manage to help change the environment around us, there's an immense sense of achievement. Immense. It's an emotional dividend, that's different from material dividend."

He tells me of the experience that has touched him the most. He was in Abuja, in the middle of Nigeria, when he fell very ill with malaria. Too weak to go out, he stayed in his room and ordered room service. "I remember the guy bringing the tray, and he set the food down, and I was sick like dog. Then he came back to pick up the plates. He moved to the door, stopped there and hesitated, and came back.

"'Sir, are you Mo Ibrahim?' he asked.

"'Yes.'

"'I pray to God that you become well soon. Please be well, because we need you.'

"And that really brought tears to my eyes. For this man to appreciate the kind of work that I'm doing—what more satisfaction can I ask for?"

Dr. Mo Ibrahim is an expert in mobile communications and the founder of one of Africa's most successful companies, Celtel International. Founded in 1998, Celtel has brought the benefits of mobile communications to millions of people across the African continent. The company operates in fifteen African countries, covering more than a third of the continent's population. In 2005, Celtel International was sold to MTC Kuwait for $3.4 billion. In 2007, Dr. Ibrahim stepped down as chairman of Celtel International to concentrate fully on his foundation.

The Mo Ibrahim Foundation was founded in 2006 to support good governance and great leadership to catalyze Africa's transformation. Every year, the foundation awards a cash prize to an African leader who has demonstrated excellence in leadership and is judged to have ruled fairly and resigned, with grace, to an elected successor. The first recipient of the prize was President Joaquim Chissano (2007), who led Mozambique out of civil war and through a decade of economic recovery. The foundation also awards scholarships to aspiring African leaders at a number of distinguished academic institutions, and produces the annual Ibrahim Index of African Governance, the most comprehensive collection of data on the quality of African governance. The annual index provides reliable information to help governments and policymakers do their jobs better—and to give citizens a tool to hold governments accountable.

BACK ON THE Upper East Side in Manhattan, Ray Chambers continues to tell me his story.

His hometown, Newark, was a city plagued by riots. After

World War II, the white, middle-class residents started to flee to nearby New York City, spurred by new interstate highways, low-interest mortgages, and better access to colleges. The neediest and most impoverished locals—mostly blacks—were left behind, facing severe discrimination in jobs and housing. Years of poverty and discrimination created in many black communities a powder keg of frustration that finally blew up on the hot summer night of July 12, 1967, when a black cabdriver named John Smith was pulled over and badly beaten by the police.

It happened within sight of the residents of a large public housing project. After Smith was dragged into the police station, an angry crowd quickly gathered outside. Five days of rioting followed. Stores were looted and some were burned down. After a policeman was killed, the governor sent in the National Guard with orders to use their weapons at will. Tanks and armored vehicles blocked off streets, keeping many people from entering the city. According to official figures, twenty-six people died during the riots. More than seven hundred were injured, and there were fifteen hundred arrests. Windows were shattered, shops were looted, buildings were burned down. These riots were a major factor leading to the decline of the city.

"I had never seen people as down-and-out as the people of Newark," says Ray, as we are cosseted in his tranquil office twenty-two floors up from the frenzy of Madison Avenue. In 1987, he began to donate anonymously to the Newark Boys & Girls Club, part of a U.S.-wide organization of local chapters that provide after-school programs to young people, and where Ray himself learned to swim as a child. Around the same time, he agreed to pay for the college tuition of one thousand African-American students. "I was so taken

by their lives and their mostly single-parent, welfare-mother households and by their families that I began to lose all interest in business and wanted to just spend time helping them." The next business
transaction at Wesray no longer had any allure for him, and in
1989, Ray retired from his firm and dedicated himself to the service
of the people of Newark.

"I've been a full-time philanthropist ever since. And that void
that I was experiencing has really filled in. The gap I felt was completely taken care of by helping other people, after twenty-three
years of full-time philanthropy," he says.

Beyond his involvement in Newark, Ray has extended his support to other causes, such as fighting malaria. "I got involved with
malaria six years ago because I saw a photo of three children in
Malawi that were in malaria comas. I thought they were asleep, and
they probably subsequently died. I'll never get that image out of my
mind's eye.

"I always avoid generalizing," he continues, "but for the most
part those who are very wealthy and are seeking more wealth
because they think the incremental additional wealth can bring
them happiness, they're only digging their hole of unhappiness
deeper. I've never felt this challenged; I've never felt this satisfied.
And I'm just gonna keep doing it until I can achieve very, very difficult goals." In a statement he made before the U.N. in April 2015,
he said, "I can honestly say that the single best investment I've made
over a long business career has been the time, resources, and energy
I committed to working with you on malaria." His goal is to end
malaria deaths for good.

Ray Chambers is a philanthropist and humanitarian who has directed most of his efforts toward helping children. He is the founding chairman of Points of Light and cofounder, with Colin Powell, of America's Promise Alliance. He cofounded the National Mentoring Partnership, the Millennium Promise Alliance, and Malaria No More. He is also the founding chairman of the New Jersey Performing Arts Center and is the former chairman of Wesray Capital Corporation, which he cofounded with William E. Simon.

RAY CHAMBERS' FIVE STEPS TO HAPPINESS

Ray Chambers shares his five steps to happiness, which he came up with after looking for common threads in the teachings of Deepak Chopra, the Dalai Lama, and others who have inspired him along the way.

STEP 1. Stay in the moment, because that's the only time there is. We can't redo or undo what we said or did, and we may never reach tomorrow. The only time is now.

STEP 2. Step back and become a spectator to your own thoughts. When you're feeling anger, take a deep breath. Step back and look at yourself. That player, that actor, is not you. The spectator is you. Invariably it breaks the chain of the anger, the chain of the thinking.

STEP 3. It is more important to be loving than to be right. This is so simple, but hard to execute. There's something in us that's probably ego-driven that requires us to demonstrate even to those who are closest to us that we are right and they're wrong. If you can remember that it's more important to be loving than to be right, it's incredible what it can do to your relationships

STEP 4. Go out of your way to help anybody in need.

STEP 5. Each morning, write down what you're grateful for, and read that list aloud. Before you're halfway through that list, whatever is bothering you is likely to have dissipated.

The Most Satisfying Thing You'll Ever Do

I thought I knew about the joys that fabulously wealthy people get from their money—big houses, fancy cars, first-class travel. Who among us doesn't wish we could turn left instead of right upon boarding an airplane? Apart from enjoying the best plane seats and other worldly luxuries, the wealthy find comfort in their safety, and in having the freedom to choose work that fulfills them and doesn't just pay the bills. No doubt, there is true enjoyment and satisfaction in simply being financially secure and independent. As the 1930s sex symbol Mae West once said, "I've been rich and I've been poor. Believe me, rich is better."

But as Ray Chambers, who was at least a hundred times richer than Mae West, says, "I thought that if I had financial independence, good health, good family, friends, enjoyed what I was doing, I'd be automatically happy." So if those aren't enough, what else do the wealthy need to be truly happy?

Something unexpected has turned up in so many of my conversations with the wealthiest people in the world: As they've talked about their philanthropic work, so many of them, independently of each other, have said something to the tune of "This is the most satisfying thing I have ever done." At first I thought they were just empty words. Perhaps these interviewees were just trying to make a good impression and be the inspirational characters the public expects them to be. But I heard it so often, I wondered, Is there real substance behind these lofty declarations of the impossibly rich? I set out to investigate, looked beyond my own experiences, and studied the remarks of people whom I have never even met.

The first stop was the Giving Pledge, the campaign that Warren Buffett and Bill Gates started in 2010 to encourage the world's billionaires to commit at least half of their fortunes to charity, which now has more than 122 signatories. Most of them have actually posted their written pledges on givingpledge.org, highlighting the very public and social nature of the promise. When I read these pledges closely, I immediately noticed that quite a number of them, whether they were written by hard-nosed hedge fund managers or creative entrepreneurs, were talking about the same thing: that the ultimate achievement lies in giving.

- Michael Bloomberg, founder of Bloomberg L.P., whose net worth stands at $33 billion[2] and who famously pocketed only a token $1 of the annual $225,000 salary to which he was entitled as mayor of New York:

  "Making a difference in people's lives—and seeing it with your own eyes—is perhaps the most satisfying thing you'll ever do. If you want to fully enjoy life—give."

- Hedge fund billionaire John Arnold, together with his wife, Laura:

  "There is no more worthwhile work and no greater mission [than philanthropy]."

- Groupon CEO and founder Eric Lefkofsky, together with his wife, Liz:

  "We recognize that perhaps our greatest accomplishment—with the exception of the kids we raise—will come not from businesses we started, but from the help we provide to people and causes around the world."

- Dan Gilbert, billionaire real estate investor, founder of Quicken Loans (the largest U.S. online home lender), and owner of the Cleveland Cavaliers, together with his wife, Jennifer:

  "There is nothing more satisfying and exciting than being able to positively affect people and noble causes in this world. . . . It has been exciting more than words can express living in this great country and being able to start, develop and grow businesses. It will be even more exciting to deploy the wealth these businesses created to improve our world . . ."

Even if the pleasure derived from giving is not accorded a description in the superlative, it is nevertheless described so positively.

- Hedge fund billionaire Bill Ackman:

  "Over the years, the emotional and psychological returns I have earned from charitable giving have been enormous. The more I do for others, the happier I am. The happiness and optimism I have obtained from helping others are a big part of what keeps me sane. My life and business have not been without some decent size bumps along the way, and my psychological health and well-being have made managing these inevitable challenges much easier."

- Jewish-Canadian billionaire Edgar M. Bronfman Jr., who was eighty-two when he signed the Giving Pledge and had worked for eighteen years as a philanthropist at the Samuel Bronfman Foundation:

  "I have found philanthropy deeply satisfying work . . . I encourage all people to engage in giving to others, be it through time or money. The point is to be involved. Helping is a joyful experience and enriches the giver as those who receive."

- Bernie Marcus,[3] cofounder of Home Depot:

  "To make quarterly profits is one thing but changing one life is so much better."

- Mobile phone entrepreneur John Caudwell:

"About a decade ago I made a decision to start focusing more on helping others in desperate need, rather than focusing on my own wealth creation. For this reason . . . I decided to sell my business in 2006. About the same time I decided that I was going to give at least half my wealth away when I died, as well as trying to change as many lives as possible during my lifetime. Philanthropy gives me far more pleasure and satisfaction than making money. In fact, making money is now largely driven by the knowledge that I will be able to leave even more wealth behind for charitable causes when I go."

- Hedge fund billionaire Tom Steyer:

    "Surely the pleasure we derive from . . . consoling, understanding, loving, giving, and pardoning far outweigh any selfish and passive pleasures of owning, having, or possessing."

- Businessman Jon Huntsman Sr.:

    "The desire to give back was the impetus for pursuing an education in business, for applying that education to what became a successful container company, and for using that experience to grow our differentiated chemicals corporation into the global enterprise it has become. The journey which began in poverty somehow led to my name's inclusion on the Richest Americans list for several years running. We progressed from being leveraged to the eyeballs to realizing a degree of wealth of which we had never dared to dream, always with the understanding that it was not ours to keep."

PAUL SCHERVISH, professor of sociology and director of the Center on Wealth and Philanthropy at Boston College, has interviewed hundreds of multimillionaires in the course of his decades-long research on the patterns of wealth and philanthropy. In a recent study that he calls "an extraordinary sample of confession, memoir, and apologia" from the super rich, roughly 165 households responded, 120 of which have at least $25 million in assets. The respondents' average net worth was $78 million, and two reported being billionaires. The goal, said the survey's architects, was to weed out all but those at or approaching complete financial security. As an article in *The Atlantic* described, "Most of the survey's respondents are wealthy enough to ensure that in any catastrophe short of Armageddon, they will still be dining on Chateaubriand while the rest of us are spit-roasting rats over trash-can fires."

Apparently, Schervish himself was skeptical too when he first started hearing multimillionaires say that giving made them happy. But he heard it again, and again, and again. After having concluded the study, Schervish said: "I have found that the most striking thing is the joy people have that results from their giving of time and money to the care of other people. People would say things such as, 'What I have just done I'm convinced is more fulfilling to me, and has done more for me than it has perhaps done for the beneficiaries.'"[4]

Over the course of my career, I have met with many other very wealthy, "self-actualized" individuals, and observed among many of them a disposition that they express in the simple yet heartfelt phrase "I want to give back." Behind that phrase is a certain unease that they feel until they know they have actually made a difference. And sometimes, the biggest regret is not having done it sooner, as a living legend told me one afternoon at Paramount Pictures, in California.

Why Didn't I Start This Sooner?

To get to my next interview, I drive through Paramount's grand double arches along Melrose Avenue, get a backstage pass, hop on a golf cart that takes me through the back lot, and traverse narrow corridors decked with picture after picture of Hollywood stars with bleached white teeth. Finally I reach a small makeshift office above Stage 30 and see sixteen-time Grammy-winning producer and composer David Foster sitting by himself, on a break in the middle of an all-day rehearsal for his next concert. He is wearing a gray sweater, torn jeans, and pebble-soled loafers, and he looks up and greets me with a big "Hiiiii!" I am especially excited about this interview because not only have I been a huge fan of his for years, I also know that he will answer my questions with complete candidness, and I am not disappointed that one of the first things he says is, "I'm kind of pissed at myself for starting my foundation late. So late. I pulled the trigger when I was thirty-seven, and it has profoundly changed me."

It was 1986, and David had just won his first few Grammys, was newly divorced, and was completely focused on his career. "I was just thinking about myself, just thinking about those Grammys, thinking about making money, thinking about buying houses, thinking about buying an expensive car. I had no real clue about helping anybody. My parents taught me well, but I got caught up in the humdrum of Los Angeles and the hoopla of Hollywood. I was hanging out with people like Elton John, playing hit records, and constantly being asked to go here and there. I got caught up with myself."

In the midst of all that, David's mother, Eleanor, called him to ask that he visit a sick little girl from his hometown of Victoria, British Columbia. The girl and her mother were at UCLA Medical Center's intensive care unit as she awaited a liver transplant. "My mother didn't ask me to do it because I was someone famous, but just because the girl's family was from the same town where I grew up," says David. Being a good son, he agreed to his mother's request and went to the hospital.

"Have you ever been in an intensive care ward for children?" he asks me. No, I have never been, and he tells me what his first experience was like. "There's a clichéd expression about something making you so weak that your knees start to buckle. But I'm telling you, the first time I went in there, I actually had to hang on to something as I got past about the second bed. I saw that girl. She was five years old. She was hooked up to a machine and was getting a liver transplant. I asked her, 'What do you want more than anything in the world?' thinking she would say, 'Let's go to Disneyland.' But all she wanted was to see her sister," says David. "That picture of her face is etched in my brain forever."

After speaking with the girl's mother, David learned that while the medical costs were looked after by Canada's health care system, nonmedical expenses were left to the family. The sick little girl's sister was back in Victoria with her father, while the mother was with her at the hospital. And so he decided that the best way he could help was to fly the girl's sister down from Victoria, so that the two could be together.

"That moment twenty-five years ago when I paid for a sixty-dollar airline ticket to have that girl and her sister meet in California was one of the happiest moments of my life," David says. Soon after, he decided to form the David Foster Foundation, which provides financial assistance to families with children in need of life-saving organ transplants. He was also influenced by two of his friends, champion hockey player Wayne Gretzky and tennis ace Andre Agassi, who both started their philanthropic careers when they were much younger than David was. (Agassi once said, "Tennis was a stepping stone for me. It gave me the chance to do this. Changing a child's life is what I always wanted to do. Winning a tennis tournament doesn't compare to the anticipation of what these kids will do with their lives."[5]) "I was a late-bloomer, for sure, but I've made up for it," David says.

The sense of fulfillment David gets from his charitable work is "ineffable," he says. "You cannot explain it. It's a feeling that is totally different from anything else you feel. It's not like winning a Grammy at all. It's a completely different feeling of, 'Wow! This is why I was put on this earth.' We're on this planet to love and be loved. The 'to love' part means you've got to help. Winning a Grammy is not doing anything good in the world; it's only serving me. It only makes me look better, it only makes me look more successful, it gives me more money—but supporting a child going through a life-saving organ transplant, that's doing good in the world. What did I ever accomplish in music that could ever equal a mother saying to me, 'Thank you for saving my daughter's life'? Can you imagine?

"I don't do it to be a Good Samaritan; I do it to feed my soul. Now I spend so much time on the foundation and it's so completely rewarding. It's so completely unlike anything else that I do. It's been twenty-five years, and I can show you hundreds if not thousands of letters that we get every year from parents who go, 'You literally saved my marriage,' 'You literally saved my daughter's life,' 'Without you, we would be on the street,' 'Without you, we could have never had our daughter live an extra three years,' 'Our daughter is twenty-seven now with a new heart. Without you, that would not happen.' You don't get that feeling with a Grammy. You don't get that feeling with a hit record. You don't get that feeling with anything," says David.

He moves closer, and attempts to make me vicariously feel what he has experienced many times. "Jenny, thank you for saving my daughter's life." He claps his hands once, leans back, and takes a deep breath.

"You probably haven't heard that yet. Have you?"

"Not yet," I say.

"Not *yet*. But you probably will. And it will blow your mind."

The Hedonic Treadmill

"Abundance, it turns out, is the enemy of appreciation," says Michael Norton, professor of business administration at Harvard Business School. "This is the sad reality of the human experience:

In general, the more we're exposed to something, the more its impact diminishes." Just as an intense smell usually gets less intense (and less pleasurable) with continued exposure, and the warmth of a fireplace is soon forgotten after it has offered instant relief from the winter's chill, material wealth ceases to confer pleasure after one gets used to having it.

Over the past three and a half decades, inflation-adjusted "real" per capita income in the United States has risen from just over seventeen thousand dollars to almost twenty-seven thousand dollars. Within the same period, the average new home in the U.S. grew in size by almost 50 percent; the number of cars in the country increased by more than 120 million; the proportion of families owning personal computers rose from zero to 70 percent; and so on. Yet, since the early 1970s, the percentage of Americans who describe themselves as either "very happy" or "pretty happy" has remained virtually unchanged. The average level of self-reported happiness, or "subjective well-being," appears to have been flat going all the way back to the 1950s, when real per capita income was less than half what it is today. So why aren't we happier?

In 1978, psychologist Philip Brickman conducted one of the first studies testing the theory that we're all stuck on a "hedonic treadmill," a term he coined to describe the notion that good or bad events don't permanently affect our levels of happiness. He assembled two groups of subjects: The first group comprised Illinois state lottery winners who had pocketed jackpots between fifty thousand and a million dollars. The second group was one that we'd imagine to be pretty miserable: victims of devastating accidents, some paralyzed from the neck down. Brickman and his team asked members of both groups a series of questions, such as: *How happy were you before these events? How happy are you now? How happy do you expect to be in a couple of years? How much pleasure do you take in daily experiences such as talking with a friend, hearing a joke, or reading a magazine?*

His study yielded results that surprised many psychologists, making his theory of the hedonic treadmill popular to this day: Lottery winners were not any happier than their neighbors or any more optimistic about the future. In fact, they weren't any more optimistic about their future than a group of people whom we'd imagine to be pretty miserable. The lottery study is one of the prime pieces of evidence that support why we aren't any happier even though there have been tremendous advances in technology and our overall quality of life. People rapidly adjust to improved situations; thus, as soon as they acquire some new possession—a second house, a better car, an upgraded model of their mobile phone—their expectations only keep increasing, leaving them no happier than they were to begin with.[6]

Another theory is that people are relativists: Their interest lies not in simply having more stuff, but in having more compared with those around them, and the pleasure of consumption depends heavily on one's frame of reference. So if everyone in Pleasantville is given $1 million to spend, nothing has really changed because no one is better off than anyone else. Most of us, for instance, occasionally spoil ourselves with outbursts of deliberate and excessive consumption: a fancy spa treatment, dinner at an expensive restaurant, a shopping spree. In the case of the very wealthy, such forms of consumption can become so commonplace as to lose all psychological benefit—constant luxury is, in a sense, no luxury at all.[7] How much happiness can $1 billion (or in the case of Mo Ibrahim,

$3.4 billion) buy? As Mo says, "You will not have a better car, you will not eat better, you will not dress better."

"The story about the unhappy, squandering [lottery] winner primarily functions as a cautionary tale," says Dr. Anna Hedenus, a sociologist at the University of Gothenburg. In general, while we anticipate being overjoyed by events that we dream of, we find ourselves unmoved when they actually occur, and the pleasures of consumption wear off in time. In the high-risk world of finance, succeeding wildly is so rare that it can be tantamount to winning the lottery—and the sentiments over newfound wealth are the same.

Note, however, that the original study by Brickman involved only twenty-two lottery winners, and it didn't reveal whether their happiness changed. It measured their feelings at only one point in time, typically within a year of hitting the jackpot, and it compared them at that point with neighbors whose names were chosen at random from a phone book. Dr. Brickman and his coauthors noted the limitations and urged more rigorous research tracking winners' feelings over time.

Decades later, that research has finally been done, and these recent studies debunk the idea of the curse of a sudden windfall. The feelings of hundreds of lottery winners were tracked in two separate studies, both drawing on a British national survey of adults who were extensively interviewed annually about their states of mind and about events in their lives. Even though there's a very small chance we might hit the Powerball jackpot, the findings are nevertheless useful to all of us who want to get off that hedonic treadmill.

One of the studies, by Bénédicte H. Apouey and Andrew E. Clark, of the Paris School of Economics, found that the stress levels of lottery winners declined over two years while their positive feelings increased, so that their general psychological well-being was significantly higher two years after winning than it had been beforehand. The other study, by Jonathan Gardner and Andrew J. Oswald, of the University of Warwick, in England, found that winners' psychological well-being dipped slightly the year they won the prize, but rebounded significantly the next two years. The winners ended up much better off psychologically, and also better off than both the general population and a sample of lottery players who hadn't won a significant prize. The curse of the lottery was further debunked in a survey of more than four hundred Swedish lottery winners by Dr. Anna Hedenus, who found that most winners refrained from splurging, preferred to save or invest the prize money, and reported being quite content.

We have so often heard that money doesn't buy happiness. There is a popular notion that once material needs are met, income over a certain threshold (often stated as seventy-five thousand dollars) does not make us any happier. And although studies have discredited the idea that winning the lottery is a curse, no researcher has ever found that people are happier in the first year after winning the lottery. "Big jackpot winners say everyone they ever met comes out of the woodwork and asks for money, especially their family," says Michael Norton. He reports that giving away money is one of the surest ways to increase your happiness, but he doesn't see much joy in a jackpot winner being hounded the rest of his life by people looking for a slice of the pie. Norton discovered, however, that money can buy happiness[8]—if you spend it right.

"A lot of spending choices people typically make are not providing much in the way of lasting happiness. This was one of the most surprising findings I came across. It's quite striking that what so many of us are pouring our incomes into turns out not to have that big an impact on happiness."

How to Spend Money for Maximum Happiness

Based on his research, here are the five key principles of how to spend money for maximum happiness:

- Buy experiences. Research shows that material purchases are less satisfying than vacations or concerts.
- Make it a treat. Limiting access to our favorite things will make us keep appreciating them.
- Buy time. It turns out that giving away our time (through volunteer work, for example) can ironically make us feel that we have more time—a condition Norton calls "time affluence."
- Pay now, consume later. If anything, we want to consume now and pay much later—which is why people get saddled by credit card debt. But paying now and consuming later—forcing ourselves to wait (i.e., for a pre-paid vacation) allows us to experience the thrill of anticipation.

And finally:

- Invest in others.

As Norton's experiments discussed in chapter 1 confirm, spending money on other people makes us happier than spending it on ourselves. From giving money to a homeless person to buying coffee for a friend, spending money on others has a larger impact on well-being than spending that money on TVs, cars, and houses.

"We often make the mistake of believing that the measure of success in life is how much stuff we have, how much money we have, how many cars we have, and all these sorts of things," he says. "It turns out that when people really reflect on their life, very often they don't talk about their possessions. They actually talk about the impact that they have had on other people, whether they are family, friends, employees, or even random people that they helped in their lives. What really makes us happy is giving rather than getting, and that's what we've seen in our research. When you're affecting someone else in a positive way that really can lead to happiness."

Anonymous vs. Public Giving

When we do give, is it better for us to do it anonymously or with our name up in lights?

In 2011, Cornell University received an anonymous donation of $350 million. Frank Rhodes, who was Cornell's president at that time, knew the source of the donation, but was sworn to secrecy. "I had to convince the board of trustees that it wasn't Mafia money, and that the source was reputable."[9]

The clandestine donation was part of New Jersey–born entrepreneur Chuck Feeney's scheme to give away his $7.5 billion fortune derived from his global empire of airport duty-free shops. Since 1984, his foundation, the Atlantic Philanthropies, has directed $6.2 billion into various projects around the world, including bringing peace to

Northern Ireland, modernizing Vietnam's health care system, and turning New York's Roosevelt Island into a technology hub. And while other tycoons hire people to publicize their good deeds, Feeney was obsessive about his anonymity—never has he had a building named after him, and he has given only a handful of interviews in his entire life. To keep his identity secret, he went to obsessive lengths, incorporating his charitable foundation in Bermuda and attaching airtight confidentiality agreements to his foundation's grants. No giant checks were paraded onstage to showcase his largesse, no black tie galas were celebrated in his honor, and no congratulatory speeches were made to commemorate his legacy. He wanted none of that.

And for more than a decade, Feeney pulled it off so well that even his longtime business partner did not know about his big-ticket gifts. But eventually, all the complications of anonymous giving came to bear on him. When he first transferred to his foundation his 39 percent stake in his company, Duty Free Shoppers, hardly anyone noticed because the company was relatively unremarkable. It was only in 1997, when the company was sold, that the scale of his generosity became clear. He could have been the newest billionaire in America, but his stake—which had ballooned to $1.6 billion—belonged to his foundation. Thanks to astute financial management, the foundation's assets swelled to $3.7 billion at a certain point, making the organization far too sizable to stay under the radar. Feeney gave a single interview in 1997, then clammed up and disappeared again.

Few living people have given away more, and no one at his level of wealth has ever given their fortune away so completely during their lifetime. While many business titans obsess over piling up as many riches as possible, Feeney flies coach, wears a fifteen-dollar watch, uses a plastic bag for a briefcase, doesn't own a car, and is working double time to die broke. As of now, he is worth only about $1.5 million. By 2016, the approximately $1.3 billion that remains in his foundation will have been spent on four causes: disadvantaged children, aging, health, and human rights; the foundation will be shut down by 2020.

As he told *Forbes* magazine in a rare interview in 2012, "People used to ask me how I got my jollies, and I guess I'm happy when what I'm doing is helping people and unhappy when what I'm doing isn't helping people."

In today's culture, in which so many people obsessively self-promote, those like Feeney who prefer to remain in the shadows rather than having their names carved in stone seem refreshingly humble, even saintly. Indeed, giving anonymously is one of the most ancient and esteemed philanthropic practices around the world, whether stemming from cultural norms or religious convictions. Among wealthy families in Japan and China, there is a deep-seated tradition of anonymous giving, deriving from the cultural value of modesty. Catholics, Christians, Muslims, and Jews have long considered blind donations the highest form of giving, and many other religious traditions caution against self-promotion. The gospel of Matthew advises against announcing one's giving with trumpets; rather, "When you give to the poor, do not let your left hand know what your right hand is doing, so that your giving will be in secret; and your Father who sees what is done in secret will reward you." The medieval Jewish sage Maimonides said that it is best that the giver and receiver not know each other's identities—in this way, the receiver's dignity is preserved: The rich person shouldn't feel superior for giving, and the poor person shouldn't feel inferior for receiving. Anonymous giving, according to him, is the second-highest level of charity (second only to helping a person reach self-sufficiency by entering into a business partnership with him or helping him find employment).

"Anonymity dissolves the power imbalances in these relationships," says Georgetown University philanthropy professor James Allen Smith.[10] In giving anonymously, donors get no chance at currying political or social favor, and can derive no satisfaction from seeing their name up in lights. Recipients are also freed from any burden: Organizations need not stage elaborate thank-you gala dinners, nor do individuals need to feel the shame of indebtedness.

Yang Lan, a powerful Chinese media entrepreneur and journalist who has been called "the Oprah Winfrey of China," is leading a movement to encourage the growth of philanthropy in her country. "When I donated the royalties of my first book to sponsor children's education, the school actually asked me, 'Do we need a ceremony so that we could give those scholarships to these kids with them present?' I said I don't want that, because I think making children receive material help in public may have some impact on their dignity and their pride. And I think people who receive help have all the right to their dignity and privacy. As long as I'm able to help them, I'm fine. I don't need any publicity concerning that."

For donors, there are other benefits to staying anonymous. A 1991 survey of anonymous giving conducted by the Center on Philanthropy at Indiana University concluded that the primary reason donors like to keep their identities a secret is to avoid getting badgered by fund-raising requests. The study showed that 50.6 percent of people who gave anonymously did so to minimize solicitations from other organizations. (The next most frequent motivation cited in the study, at 5.3 percent, was a deeply felt religious conviction.) Other donors are concerned about kidnapping attempts if people find out they are wealthy, or they want to avoid hostility from people ideologically opposed to the causes they support. Some wealthy people prefer to give anonymously because they are aware of their own fortunate circumstances and want to set the balance straight without taking a lot of credit for it.

Despite the pervasiveness of religious and cultural admonitions against public giving, and the many other good reasons to stay anonymous, many donors choose to be public about their gifts. Anonymous givers can't become leaders who inspire other people with their charitable behavior, and they deprive foundations of the chance to use the gift as leverage to attract other donors.

Surely we would have fewer buildings, libraries, and park benches if we did not offer naming rights to donors. As society is the ultimate beneficiary, I do not disparage the self-promoting giver.

What Kind of Giving Makes One Happier— Anonymous or Public Giving?

Back at Paramount Pictures, David Foster tells me about his internal debate between staying public about his giving and being anonymous.

"Obviously, I like doing good. I must on some selfish level like the accolades; I admit that as a flawed human being. People tell me, 'Oh, it's so great you do all these charities.' It's kind of an overused phrase to say, 'I get more out of it than they do,' but yes, I am getting so much out of it myself. I'm not just doing it out of the goodness of my heart. I do get things out of it," he says, apologizing for giving what he describes as "shallow" answers. As he rubs his temples, his sleeve falls below his wrist, revealing a *D* tattoo in a medieval Gothic font. "I admit that if I saw my name on a building, I'd probably be, 'That's pretty cool. Something my grandkids could go visit.'

"Somebody once told me, if you want to test yourself, go where there's a crowd of people. Quietly place down a fifty-dollar bill on the floor right beside a homeless person, but don't let anybody see that you did it. Throw it down and then make sure the homeless person sort of sees it but he doesn't see that you dropped it. Then walk along, and watch him pick up the fifty dollars. Then grab it and tell him, 'Hey, buddy, I found it first!' And he's going, 'No, you didn't. I was here first.' And argue with him. The people will rally against you because you're such a dick for trying to steal a homeless person's fifty dollars. Finally, you relent and go, 'Okay. I was there first, but go ahead. I'm not going to fight you anymore for it. You're wrong.' And then walk away. That is the real, true art of giving," says David.

This reminds me of what happened to Steve Jobs, who was often rebuked for not giving enough to charity even after Apple became enormously successful. Only later did people discover that he, together with his wife, gave away millions without going public about it. Jobs kept quiet about his charitable giving even when he found himself under attack for his apparent lack of philanthropy.

After his death, his widow, Laurene Powell Jobs, spoke for the first time about the couple's charity in an interview with the *New York Times*. "We're really careful about amplifying the great work of others in every way that we can, and we don't like attaching our names to things," she said. Jobs reportedly donated $50 million of his own money to hospitals in California. According to his successor, Tim Cook, the cash went toward building a children's medical center and a new main building. It was also revealed that Jobs gave generously to the fight against AIDS. But he was so private about his charitable giving that he didn't even discuss it with his biographer.

"To not only be anonymous, but to have a crowd of people thinking you're an asshole. I have not gotten to that place yet," says David.

And it seems he'd be happier if he stayed just where he's at. According to a 2013 study by researchers at the University of British Columbia and Harvard Business School, making a charitable donation directly to someone you know in a way that builds social connection creates much more happiness than donating anonymously to an organization.[11]

According to Norton, who was part of the team of researchers, "People differ on which kind of giving they think is more ethical. But it turns out that giving publicly, where the recipient knows and everybody else knows that you gave, is better for one's happiness than is giving anonymously. Now, giving anonymously still makes you happier than spending on yourself. So again, giving tends to be being selfish, but if you are going to give, it can actually be better to get social praise for giving rather than doing it anonymously. It's a basic human response: We like people to smile and say thank you to us. When you give anonymously, you're leaving out that source of happiness. But when you give publicly, not only do you get that glow of giving to others, but you get praise from others, which we also know is important for happiness."

Philanthropy: The Door Opener

It's not just about the pleasure of giving, but about the people you meet when you give. "You meet a lot of wonderful people whom you would have never met before," says Mo Ibrahim. "When you meet in the context of philanthropy, there's no personal interest. It's just How can we improve what we're doing? How can we leverage on each other's work? How can we make one plus one equal three?"

As he mentally flips through the list of people he has met, he is not name dropping, but genuinely flabbergasted at the number of celebrities, rock stars, and Nobel Peace Prize winners who have somehow found their way into his life after he became recognized as a philanthropist: Desmond Tutu, whom Mo describes as "a man who always speaks the truth, truth to power. That's very rare. The truth can be inconvenient, impolite, shocking—but he does not shy away from that. But at the same time he has the most engaging, the most disarming smile, and sense of humor, and humility." Nelson Mandela is described as "an amazing character, a wonderful man with an amazing capacity to forgive, even his enemies." Former Irish president Mary Robinson makes her own coffee in Mo's office, and once described the work at the Mo Ibrahim Foundation as "fun." "I mean, Bill Gates came to see us here!" Mo says, pointing to my seat, where the Microsoft founder sat last month. And finally, "this guy Bono," whose depths of knowledge on developmental issues amazed Mo, and corrected his suspicion of rock stars as "people on drugs, really trivial people who would trash hotel rooms and go about philandering."

Mo discovered that being a giver has opened doors not just in the philanthropic sector but to the business sector as well. "Any business would like to partner with you. You have, like, a certificate of good health that makes many businesses want to associate with you. I'm unfortunately unable to take advantage of that because I really want to spend most of my time here at the foundation."

Goldie Hawn says of the people she has met through her journey as a philanthropist, "The people that you meet along the way are your soul mates: They're fortifying, they thrill you, they make you happy. You're meeting people that are doing things like yours. It creates connectivity, which also is lasting joy. There's a tremendous gratitude that you have but also what you realize is that there's a world out there, more and more that have a shared love of our future and of humanity. They're optimists; they believe in change, they think that they can help make a difference. Those are great attributes as a human being."

Tom Freston, cofounder of MTV, adds: "When you give, one door opens to ten other doors. It's made my circle of friends and acquaintances much more diverse and interesting. And as you keep going down that path you find more good things to do and more good things will happen to you in return."

In some cases, giving away money has paradoxically caused people to earn more money. As Ted Turner says, "Being generous always made me feel great, and it seemed like every time I gave money away, I somehow made that much more." And according to Bill Ackman in his Giving Pledge: "While my motivations for giving are not driven by a profit motive, I am quite sure that I have earned financial returns from giving money away. Not directly by any means, but as a result of the people I have met, the ideas I have been exposed to, and the experiences I have had as a result of giving money away. A number of my closest friends, partners, and advisors I met through charitable giving. Their advice, judgment, and partnership have been invaluable in my business and in my life. Life becomes richer, the more one gives away."

Philanthropy: The New Status Symbol?

Don't hate all rich people. They're not all awful. Believe me, I know some evil poor people too.

—JOHN WATERS

In a fifteen-square-mile area of desert south of the Dead Sea in Israel's Arava Rift Valley, researchers from Tel Aviv University have been studying a species of bird, the Arabian babbler, for more than three decades. Arabian babblers are small grayish-brown birds who live together in stable groups with strict orders of rank. What the researchers found out in the desert has led a number of scientists to call the babblers the "ultimate Mr. Nice Guys." They live in groups of up to twenty adults, each group having its own territory that it defends against marauders from other groups. All the members of a group work together to raise the young of a few dominant birds, and their cooperative behavior extends well beyond feeding the young. Adult babblers also feed each other, preen each other, watch over each other, and even keep each other warm at night.

But what truly surprised the researchers was that not only are the birds so nice to each other, they also compete for who can be the nicest, and are ultimately willing to sacrifice their lives for their groups. The babblers compete with unrelated group members to be the group's sentinel, who is responsible for watching for predators from treetops in order to warn the group of potential danger.[12] The sentinel's duty entails putting itself at a much higher risk of death than other babblers. Astonishingly, rather than avoid this self-sacrificial job, the birds compete for it. In the animal kingdom, where only the fittest survive, this kind of behavior seems dysfunctional, even strange.

What lies at the root of the birds' altruistic behavior?

One guess is that they help each other because they are related. An individual can gain some sort of genetic legacy by promoting the survival of other birds with whom it has genes in common. As these relatives are likely to share genes for helping behavior, the trait will flourish. But the researchers have tracked the breeding history of individuals in more than twenty groups of babblers, and they know that not all the members of a group are related—so this first explanation is out.

A second possible explanation for the babblers' generous acts is the survival of the species. Groups of babblers that help each other may do better than groups that do not because they are less susceptible to attack, or because they do a better job of feeding the young. But researchers object to this explanation because a babbler would get the same benefit (of being less susceptible to predators) at less cost to itself by letting others do the work. Yet, far from exploiting fellow babblers' proclivity to help, the birds actually waste energy stopping others from helping them.

A third possible explanation for the babblers' behavior is reciprocity: Perhaps the babblers all help each other because they expect their favors to be returned in the future, either in kind or in another form. However, this does not appear valid either, because within the babbler social system, the favors all go one way, and babblers are hostile to birds who try to reciprocate their good deeds. For

example, a dominant babbler that has relieved a subordinate sentinel responds aggressively if a subordinate later tries to relieve him of
his duties.

Babblers have an elaborate social hierarchy primarily based on
age and sex, with males taking precedence over females, and older
birds dominating younger ones. But within this rigid framework
there is another system operating. Between birds of the same age
and sex, social status depends on how nice each bird can manage to
be. As the *New Scientist* explains:

> Since being the recipient of good deeds may actually lower sta-
> tus, the business of being nice is fraught with contradictions.
> For example, a subordinate bird may refuse to be fed by another,
> even when it is hungry, because by doing so it effectively lowers
> its standing. Subordinates spend as much time as possible feed-
> ing the young, because this raises their social status. But when a
> dominant bird is at the nest, the lesser individual moves away. If
> it does not, the dominant helper will ward it off by preening
> it—a non-aggressive display of social status. The birds compete
> in the same way for sentinel duty. It is the alpha male who is
> most often to be found sitting high up on a branch watching for
> predators. Occasionally he will be replaced by a less dominant
> bird, but when he wishes to return, he will approach the sentinel
> and relieve him of his duties by feeding him.

So what's behind the babblers' behavior? The Israeli evolutionary biologist Amotz Zahavi, who has been studying babblers since
the 1970s, rejects the preceding three possible explanations in favor
of a much simpler one. He argues that a babbler's niceness is a signal

of its quality or biological fitness—just as the majesty of a peacock's tail is a signal of its health. Being nice is a signal that cannot be faked; a sick or weak bird cannot pull it off. This type of signal demonstrates to a potential breeding partner what a great mate an individual would be. In other words, babbler "altruism" has evolved as a social signaling system that brings direct advantages for the individual. The further a babbler climbs up the ladder, the more likely it is to get a chance to breed. "Signaling is probably the motivation in most cases of animal altruism, although researchers have been blind to it, because of the dominance of theories of kin selection and reciprocity," says Zahavi. This conclusion may be disappointing, but the pattern is reflected in the human species.

In the Native American Kwakiutl tribal practice of potlatching, tribal chiefs compete to give away their possessions.[13] Accordingly, the person who is able to give away the most resources is regarded as the highest-standing member in the group.[14] Anthropologists have observed similar cases of "altruistic signaling" in numerous hunter-gatherer societies, including the Aché of Paraguay and the Meriam of Australia.[15]

Competitive altruism proliferates across historical and contemporary cultures, from the sponsorship of trans-Atlantic voyages and opulent operas by European royals, to conspicuously large donations made by modern-day tycoons such as Ted Turner and Bill Gates, and the small-town housewife's desire to be the nicest dinner-party hostess.[16] Research has shown that self-sacrifice for the benefit of a group of strangers increases the self-sacrificer's status in that group, including the likelihood that the person will be selected as a leader.[17] And in cities like New York, London, and Hong Kong, countless charity galas demonstrate that "being nice" can certainly be a display of social status. All around the world, there are signs that philanthropy is the new Prada, and that having your own foundation is the ultimate signal of high social status, achieving far beyond what luxury goods can in signaling prestige, luxury, and exclusivity.

The Most Important Thing
You Can Ask Yourself

If you would not be forgotten, as soon as you are dead . . . either write something worth reading or do something worth the writing.

—BENJAMIN FRANKLIN

In 2011, while I was working at a private bank, I led a team that surveyed more than two hundred individuals engaged in substantial philanthropic activities in mainland China, Hong Kong, India, Indonesia, Japan, Malaysia, the Philippines, Singapore, Taiwan, and Thailand. We asked the respondents to rank, in order of priority, the reasons why they engage in philanthropy.[18] What emerged as the number one reason?

I presumed the top answer would be "to make a difference," "to help the needy," "to fulfill religious obligations," or perhaps, as skeptics often assume, "to fulfill tax obligations." Wrong. The number one reason, cited by 42 percent of the total respondents (and a whopping 73 percent of our Hong Kong–based respondents), was "to ensure the continuity of family values or to create a lasting legacy."

"Legacy is a stupid thing! I don't want a legacy,"[19] said Bill Gates to an interviewer in 2011. But he is an aberration, because the topic of legacy, or what a person will be remembered for, has come up in practically all of the discussions I've had with wealthy individuals around the world, including and well beyond the ones I met while conducting the 2011 study. *How will I be remembered? What will people say when I'm gone about how I behaved and responded, and the impact I had on others?*

Many wealthy, successful, and famous individuals are surprisingly hesitant to embrace their success as their lasting legacy, and do not wish to be remembered for the reasons they are remembered now. David Foster says, "I want my legacy to be my foundation, not my music. I stick by that, although it's probably not going to happen in reality, and my music will probably overshadow any philanthropy work that I do." Tom Steyer, who created the world's fourth-largest hedge fund, and who has a personal fortune estimated at $1.5 billion, said in an interview, "I really don't want the highlight of my life to be my success as an investor. Genuinely. My idea of death would be that person who is still telling you about that goal he scored in 1974."[20] Even the singer Katy Perry said, "I can't just be the girl who sang 'I Kissed a Girl.' I have to leave a legacy."

"Begin with the end in mind," as Stephen Covey writes in his perennial best seller, *The 7 Habits of Highly Effective People.* Thinking of one's legacy involves imagining the end of one's life as the frame of reference by which everything else is measured. Many of us wonder: What mark will we leave in this world?

It is probably the most important question you can ask yourself, to ensure that in the end, you won't have regrets. Knowing the answer to this question helps you live every day in a way that will result in what you truly want, rather than in emptiness, pain, and regret—and for many, giving is the answer. As Michael Bloomberg said in his pledge, "Giving allows you to leave a legacy that many others will remember. Rockefeller, Carnegie, Frick, Vanderbilt, Stanford, Duke—we remember them more for the long-term effects of their philanthropy than for the companies they founded, or for their descendants."

What Will I be Remembered for?

"You have to ask yourself, 'What will I be remembered for?' If you're just successful, you might not be missed. But if you're significant, you will be missed. Being significant has more to do with being *worthy* of the attention and importance placed on your success," said Augie Nieto in an e-mail he sent me in September 2013. Although I have been a speed reader since high school, I read Augie's message very slowly, and in my mind I took a snapshot of every perfectly typo-free word, knowing that he was unable to speak, and that in order to respond to me he had to type on a special computer by maneuvering his big toe.

8/20/13

Hi Jenny,

Sorry I haven't gotten back to you sooner . . . we had another grand baby arrive on Friday so it's been a hectic week! I've answered your questions below. Please let me know if you need anything else. I can't thank you enough for taking an interest in my story! . . . Augie

. . .

AUGIE IS ONE OF the most successful innovators in the history of the U.S. fitness industry. In 1977, when he was only nineteen years old, he bought the marketing rights to the Lifecycle exercise bike and shortly after, cofounded Lifecycle Inc. Over the next twenty years, the company, now called Life Fitness, grew to be the largest commercial manufacturer of fitness equipment in the world. Practically everyone who has ever had a gym membership has seen the Life Fitness logo displayed prominently on elliptical cross-trainers, treadmills, and strength equipment. They were the equipment of choice for serious gym buffs, professional athletes, and even Olympians. Business kept growing, and the handsome, powerfully built, bungee-jumping, skydiving thrill seeker Augie was the perfect poster boy for his business of designing and distributing high-end fitness equipment and other products related to healthy living.

But in March 2005, his life took an unexpected turn. In an unfortunate twist of fate, he became something diametrically opposed to the image of robust health that he used to embody. It happened shortly after he had been in Vietnam. While waterskiing, he kept falling down, and when he got home, he couldn't even shave his own face. After spending a week undergoing a battery of tests at the Mayo Clinic, Augie was diagnosed with amyotrophic lateral sclerosis (ALS), a rare, degenerative illness that slowly kills the nerves giving strength to your muscles. It's punishing because as your body shuts down muscle by muscle, limb by limb, your mind remains sharp, witnessing everything that is happening to you. Typically, patients become completely locked in within five years. Unable to eat and breathe on their own, they eventually die. Soon after the diagnosis, Augie progressively lost the ability to climb the stairs, hold on to things, feed himself, chew, swallow, wash his hair, brush his teeth, pull on his pants, even wipe his rear end. He became wheelchair bound, and he lost the ability to speak. He could only blink (once for *yes* and twice for *no*), and wiggle his toes just enough to operate a computer.

Around thirty thousand Americans have ALS. The figure is too small for big pharma to bother investing millions to find a cure, and that's the way it has been for years—until Augie Nieto decided to apply his sharp business acumen to change the situation. He approached the Muscular Dystrophy Association with an offer: He would raise millions of dollars for them if he could control how the money was spent. They agreed, and so he formed Augie's Quest, an aggressive, cure-driven effort focused on finding treatments and a cure for ALS. He started making numerous public appearances to raise funds for other ALS sufferers, and wrote two books, typing with his toes. He has now raised more than $40 million—more than anyone has in the history of the disease. "Before I was diagnosed with ALS, I had success. It wasn't until after my diagnosis and my involvement with Augie's Quest that I became significant. Before it was all about me," Augie says. "Since then, it has been about the whole world. There is a sense of urgency with the work I'm involved with now. People's lives are at stake, including my own. I communicate with other families fighting ALS every week. I hear their horror stories . . . dealing with the challenges that ALS brings, battling with Medicare and not being able to afford caregivers and proper medical equipment, no longer being able to communicate with their loved ones as they once did, feeling isolated from the world and frustrated that more isn't being done to find a cure."

I asked him how he was feeling, to which he replied, "Today I'm feeling great! Lynne and I just welcomed our 2nd grandchild, Michael

Andrew, to our family on Friday! A typical day for me goes like this: At 6AM I wake up and begin the morning routine with my nurse. I won't go into the details but it's a 2–3 hour process to get out of bed using a lift, shower, bathroom, suction, and get into the wheelchair. On Mondays, Wednesdays, and Fridays we drive about an hour to the Claremont Club, where I work with a physical therapist at Project Walk. On Tuesdays and Thursdays, I do my own workout at home of leg presses and calf raises on a machine designed specifically for my needs by my friends at HammerStrength, Life Fitness, and Octane. The rest of my days are filled with board meetings, answering e-mails, fund-raising meetings, and other visitors. I use WebEx and Skype to do most things virtually from my home." Augie has managed to keep his sense of humor intact too. (Toward the end of our interview, when I asked him if he had any parting shots, he said, "ALS only effects voluntary muscle movement. Therefore, my Willy still works!")

"The main thing was that my persona wasn't based on my life as the founder of Life Fitness," he says. "Now I would be known for something else. I'm an inventor with over 45 patents. I've been able to take my background as an entrepreneur and inventor and create things to make my life (and other people's lives) easier with ALS. One example is the bite switch. It's a small tool I sleep with in my mouth that allows me to alert a caregiver that I need help. This gives me peace of mind during the night, which can be a scary time for someone with ALS! I have shared this tool with others who are now using it. I enjoy coming up with new ideas and bringing them to fruition. Augie's Quest is my main business now. I'm on many boards but everything is really centered around finding a cure for ALS through our research at the ALS Therapy Development Institute in Cambridge, Massachusetts." As Life Fitness's current president Chris Clawson puts it, "Augie was the cofounder of Life Fitness and piloted our company to prominence as the leading fitness equipment manufacturer in the world, but his greatest accomplishments came after he was diagnosed with ALS."

According to Steve Perrin, who directs ALS TDI, the research institute funded by Augie's Quest, "We're on the cusp of what happened in the midnineties with multiple sclerosis." Back then, multiple sclerosis was a death sentence, like ALS is today. Then one drug was developed that allows patients to live forty to fifty years. Now there are more than a dozen drugs helping multiple sclerosis patients. "The impact could be a game changer," he says. "And once the first major breakthrough happens, you'll see multiple drugs that are going to be effective."

"My purpose is to live each day celebrating what I can do instead of focusing on what I can't do, to make sure that my family and friends know how much I love and appreciate them, and to beat this SOB called ALS," Augie says. In 2013 I asked him what was on his bucket list, and the first thing he said was "To walk my daughter, Lindsay, down the aisle at her wedding next summer." He did exactly that in July 2014. Next on his list: "Change it from 'Lou Gehrig's Disease' to 'Augie Nieto's Cure.'"

Donor Fatigue: When Giving Makes You Feel Depleted

Ah yes, giving is supposed to feel good. And it does, for so many. The words *joy* and *pleasure* spring to mind, and some of the most generous people I know give back because they draw deep personal satisfaction from their charitable work, and it's incredibly fulfilling.

But if giving feels so great, how, then, do we explain "donor fatigue," or that general weariness and diminished response to requests for aid for charitable causes?

It runs so contrary to this picture of happy giving that I have presented so far, yet donor fatigue is a very real phenomenon. There isn't a day that goes by that the mail doesn't include a solicitation from some charitable organization looking for help. One volunteer said, "I have to admit, I'm getting really close to philanthropy burnout. I do still want to contribute, though, and I am hoping this is just a wave I can ride out. But I've been feeling it for a while. It just seems to be about money, money, money, and even when I give all I can, it's not enough. I'm trying to do better, but again, it's just really hard to shake this feeling." A Singaporean philanthropist called his work in his family foundation "a thankless job." And in the aftermath of any major natural disaster, whether it is the 2004 Indian Ocean tsunami or Hurricane Katrina, thousands of donors become frustrated by constantly being solicited for donations. Personally, I have found some of my experiences with charities to be annoying, frustrating, boring, or, worse, saddening. Everyone here sounds like a moaner, but all of them, including me, are just honestly expressing their feelings.

How can we possibly reconcile these two dramatically different impressions of giving? There are two things I have learned along the way.

1. **First of all, donor fatigue doesn't happen because donors are broke.** It is far more likely that they have become fatigued because they are skeptical of whether most of the money they are giving away will ever reach the needy. Practically none of us can say that the feeling of donor

fatigue is because we're already giving away too much money to too many charities. Nearly all of us can give just a little more.

2. **The biggest reason for donor fatigue is that a person's generosity is not well matched to his or her passion.**

   Too often, charities aggressively seek out affluent people in their communities and ask them to give simply because they have the ability to do so. Charities do not spend enough time trying to understand why a specific cause might be a good match for a particular donor. And most donors spend no time at all trying to understand what causes might be a good match for them.

   Cindy Weber, vice president of mission development at the Door County YMCA, in Wisconsin, says, "I believe that people give because it feels good. I can't remember anyone ever giving me a check with a frown on their face. But we can't expect everyone to connect equally to our cause, as hard as it may be for you to believe." She continues, "There are some individuals who may not care about dogs and cats, or kids or seniors or art programs or music or preservation or history. That does not make them a bad person; it just means it doesn't make them a committed donor to [a certain] cause."

Implications for Fund-Raisers

One of the hardest things to do as a fund-raiser is to listen. Most fund-raisers want to tell their story, share their outcomes, and talk about the impact they are making. These are all extremely important, but often, the first thing that needs to be done when visiting a prospective donor is to shut up and listen. Amazing things can happen when the fund-raiser stays quiet and lets the prospective donor do the talking.

To make the donor's experience rewarding and meaningful, fund-raisers should try and ask potential donors a series of questions such as:

- Why did you first become a supporter?
- What aspect of our work excites you most?
- What would you like to see us do if funds were not an issue?
- What do you see our organization looking like in ten years, fifty years?

When the charities are neither informing donors of how their money is being used nor inspiring them with the organization's mission, giving can indeed feel like a burden. Donor fatigue can happen when charities take their donors for granted. But when charities treat their donors with gratitude and respect, giving becomes an incredibly fulfilling experience.

The Worries of the Rich

One must be poor to know the luxury of giving.

—GEORGE ELIOT

Schervish's decades-long research on the patterns of wealth and philanthropy presents a compelling case that being exceptionally wealthy—especially when the wealth is inherited rather than earned—is not a great deal more fulfilling than being merely comfortable. Among other woes, the survey respondents report feeling that they have lost the right to complain about anything, for fear of sounding—or being—ungrateful. Those with children worry that their children will become trust fund brats if their inheritances were too large—or will be forever resentful if those inheritances were instead bequeathed to charity. A friend of mine whose net worth is more than $3 billion said, "I want my kids to be hungry—not in the literal sense. They're good kids, but I'm just worried they're too comfortable." Very wealthy people fear that their money might be a curse, producing drifting, purposeless, drug-addled trust fund babies.

The respondents to Schervish's survey also confide that they feel their outside relationships have been altered by, and have in some cases become contingent on, their wealth. "Very few people know the level of my wealth, and if they did, in most cases I believe it would change our relationship," writes one respondent. Another notes, "I start to wonder how many people we know would cut us off if they didn't think they could get something from us." Some friends disappear, and others—perhaps attracted by the newfound wealth—appear. If the rich do take jobs, they sometimes find that coworkers resent them on the grounds that they're "taking away" the jobs of people who need them.

Others suffer from an affliction that many of us long to have: Sudden Wealth Syndrome. Psychologist Stephen Goldbart coined this term to describe the stress, guilt, social isolation, and confusion that often accompany a giant windfall. It strikes lottery winners, rags-to-riches celebrities, and overnight dot-com millionaires. While coming into money ought to be a good thing, it can take a bad turn. Many who find sudden fortune become overwhelmed, start to overspend, grow suspicious of those around them, become bored, and, finding themselves never needing to work again, question the very purpose of their existence.

Reaping Emotional, Not Material Dividends

I resolved to stop accumulating and begin the infinitely more serious and difficult task of wise distribution.

—ANDREW CARNEGIE

No person was ever honored for what he received. Honor has been the reward for what he gave.

—CALVIN COOLIDGE

Eventually, a number of wealthy people discover the satisfaction that results from engaging in philanthropy. What these wealthy philanthropists experience, says Schervish, is that virtue inherent in caring for others, which, no matter what our income, opens the path to our greatest happiness. "I found out in every instance that there was something truly deeper going on: care for others in which wealth was used as a tool," he explains. "I started looking more deeply at the meaning of philanthropy. What I found [is] not just joy, but hope, and fulfillment. I found people were experiencing fulfillment through a connection to something more profound than their usual daily life." As the London-based socialite and philanthropist Renu Mehta bluntly puts it, she engages in philanthropy "to satisfy both the selfish gratification of feeling worthy and the purist aspiration of deploying one's relevance." Or as Mo Ibrahim puts in a nutshell, "It's an emotional dividend; that's different from material dividend." These reaffirm British social policy pioneer Richard Titmuss's belief that people can be motivated by a spirit of public service rather than the expectation of something in return. For example, there is a successful system of voluntary blood donation in Britain in which the donor gets nothing except some free tea and biscuits.

The American businessman and Portland, Oregon, native Lorry I. Lokey, eighty-eight, who founded Business Wire in 1961 and has donated in excess of $400 million to various charities and schools, says, "At several of the colleges, the grants have been so large that the recipients use the word *transformational* to describe their effect. This has been especially true for University of Oregon [$134 million] and Mills College [$35 million]. What a good feeling this gives me. I would have it this way any day before wanting a jet plane or yacht. I have bought myself more happiness in the past twenty years doing this than I ever could've if I had instead spent my money on a boat or jet plane or country club membership. I refused to do any of those things."[21] (Indeed, Lokey flies coach and drives a hybrid.)

Meanwhile, H. F. "Gerry" Lenfest, who founded Lenfest Communications and sold the company to Comcast in 2000, and who has frequently been on the list of the most generous people in America, says, "One is not measured by how many homes, yachts, or airplanes you have. The ultimate achievement is how you feel about yourself. And giving your wealth away to have an impact for good does help with that feeling." Over the past ten years, he and his wife, Marguerite, have created a scholarship fund to send needy young scholars from rural areas to the better colleges, sponsored research used by others to introduce legislation protecting our oceans, started the Lenfest Center for Sustainable Energy at Columbia University, been the principal supporter of Teach for America in Philadelphia, and given to more than a hundred other causes. When asked why he and his wife have given the bulk of their fortune away, he said, "The first and [most] compelling is the joy we experience in giving to worthwhile causes."

The Privilege of Giving

"It was 1997, the year I went back to China after my graduation from Columbia University. My husband and I just had our first child. We read in the newspaper a story about a young girl who was studying very hard and doing well in school, but with both her parents having been laid off from China's state-owned enterprises, she was living in hardship and did not have enough money to continue her education. We were very touched by her story and wanted to help her. So we sent her some money. Her mother, who was unemployed and ill at that time, received us in their very small home," says Yang Lan, as we sit in the lobby lounge of the Mandarin Oriental hotel in New York City. Yang Lan is dressed impeccably in an understated gray cashmere skirt and a white silk blouse. With her fame, fortune, and regal demeanor, she is the picture of the woman who has it all. "'I don't have anything worth a lot of money that I can give back to you to show my gratitude to you for helping my daughter,'" Yang Lan recalls the woman saying, "'but I read in a newspaper that you have just given birth to a little baby. The winter in Shanghai can be very cold, so I knitted a sweater and pants for your newborn.'

"I was very touched, because at that moment I realized that compassion or helping others is never a one-way thing. It works both ways. That was the start of my conscious involvement in philanthropy and in charity. When the mother, who was very ill, gave me back this little sweater for my newborn, I knew that we were totally equal. You receive so much from those people. It's not just one person giving something to another; it's about helping each other at the same time. I feel enriched. I feel I'm the lucky one. When people allow me to enter their lives and share some of their most intimate aspirations, it's a privilege."

Back to Basics

To give away money is an easy matter and in any man's power. But to decide to whom to give it and how large and when, and for what purpose and how, is neither in every man's power nor an easy matter.

—ARISTOTLE

Not all of us have been or will be as successful as the Ibrahims, Rockefellers, Bloombergs, and Steyers of this world, retiring at forty-six to devote our lives to a cause that gives us great fulfillment, or spending down our family foundation's endowment to support pet projects that make us smile. But what can we learn from the collective experiences of so many wealthy individuals who have awakened to the joy of giving?

We could take a tip from American businessman Ray Dalio, sixty-six, who has been on both sides. Ray was born in Queens, New York, the son of a jazz musician. He began investing at age twelve when he bought shares of Northeast Airlines for three hundred dollars and tripled his investment after the airline merged with another company. In 1975, he founded the Westport, Connecticut–based investment management firm Bridgewater Associates, which in 2012 became the largest hedge fund in the world with nearly $120 billion in assets under management. Dalio has been labeled the Steve Jobs of investing, and in 2012 made it onto the annual *Time* 100, a list of the one hundred most influential people in the world. In 2011 and 2012 he was listed by *Bloomberg Markets* as one of the 50 Most Influential people. Institutional Investor's Alpha ranked him No. 2 on its 2012 Rich List and as of October 2014 he had a net worth of $15.2 billion. But it wasn't always so rosy. As he puts it in his Giving Pledge:

We were lucky enough to have experienced the whole range of financial circumstances, from not having any money to having a lot. Fortunately that happened in the best order. At first we experienced the worry about not being able to take care of the basics. When we earned more money, we experienced relief and then the diminishing benefits of having more money. We learned that beyond having enough money to secure the basics—quality relationships, health, stimulating ideas, etc.—having more money, while nice, wasn't all that important. We experienced directly what the studies on happiness show—that once the basics are covered there is no correlation between how much money one has and how happy one is—but there is a high correlation between having meaningful work and meaningful relationships to one's health and happiness.

Ray gives money to a wide array of organizations including NYU's Tisch School of the Arts, the Dalio Talent Identification Fund, the World Community for Christian Meditation, and Teach for America.

Sonja Lyubomirsky, a professor at the University of California, Riverside, is the author of one such study that Dalio alludes to. "The über-rich may control a huge chunk of America's wealth but they do not have a monopoly on happiness. The difference in money is huge but the difference in happiness is not," Lyubomirsky says. "You just don't get as much happiness per dollar," she adds.

It doesn't take research to know that not having enough money causes emotional pain and unhappiness. Among life's misfortunes made worse by lack of money are disease, divorce, and being alone. But a recent study points to what seems like a magic number. After this number is met, there is no correlation between money and happiness. The study, published in the *Proceedings of the National Academy of Sciences*, analyzed Gallup poll data from more than 450,000 U.S. residents in 2008 and 2009. The two researchers—Daniel Kahneman, the 2002 winner of the Nobel Prize in economics, and Angus Deaton, past president of the American Economic Association—explored the question of whether money can buy happiness in two, examining both how people evaluated their day-to-day happiness and their overall satisfaction with life. The happiness tipping point is about $75,000—more money than that can help people view their lives as successful or better, but it doesn't make a person cheerier.

With every doubling of income, people tended to say they were more and more satisfied with their lives on a ten-point scale—a pattern that continued for household incomes well above $120,000. But when people were asked to assess the happy hours of the previous day—whether they had experienced a lot of enjoyment, laughter, smiling, anger, stress, or worry—money mattered only up to about $75,000. After that, money didn't buy more (or less) happiness. (About one-third of U.S. households had incomes above $75,000, according to the U.S. Census Bureau's American Community Survey. The average household income of study participants was $71,500.)

"Beyond $75,000 in the contemporary United States, higher income is neither the road to happiness nor the road to relief of unhappiness or stress," say Kahneman and Deaton.

You Don't Need to Cure Malaria

I asked Ray Chambers how we can find happiness in giving if we don't have the kind of money that can cure malaria. "I don't think you have to do something anywhere near this grand a scale as solving malaria. Just getting involved in one other person's life and knowing that you can help that person with their career, with their emotional difficulties, is completely satisfying.

"The longer and deeper I allowed the relationships to go with

people that I'm helping," he continues, "the better I feel. It doesn't
have to be a charitable act—it could be a kind word, a kind thought.
And the more I let myself disappear, and I focus on somebody else,
the better I feel. The Dalai Lama has said that the most direct route
to happiness is in service to others. I feel much more inner peace
than I've ever experienced."

Tom Freston, cofounder of MTV, adds, "It's easier than you
think to find something small. . . . It's not going to require you to
put up a lot of money, it's not going to require a ton of time, but it's
going to make your life more interesting, it's going to make you feel
more capable, it's going to allow you to meet a lot of other interesting people, and things begin to happen to you that you could not
have imagined at the start of it. So give it a go, you don't really have
much to lose."

Your Turn

The action plan for happy giving

When I do good, I feel good; when I do bad,
I feel bad; and that's my religion.

—ABRAHAM LINCOLN

Up to this point, I have been talking about how giving is so good for the giver. In his best-selling book, *Give and Take*, Adam Grant writes about why giving in a business context leads to career success, and why some people who give burn out while others are on fire. Some givers end up being exploited by takers, and never see the rewards of their efforts. The same holds true in the social space: The reality is that giving doesn't always feel good. Donors get disenchanted, many charities are cheerless, many nonprofit workers burn out, and asks get annoying. There have been countless times when I have cringed while listening to jargon-filled pitches from so-called "social entrepreneurs," or halfway through a black tie charity gala I've made an excuse to go to the bathroom and rolled my eyes in exasperation as I trudge my way out in a long gown. It has been said that by making ourselves poor we become rich, but sometimes I just really want my time and money back. I'd like to think that, of all people, I should really love everything to do with giving money, giving time, giving gifts, and just overall giving back—but the fact is that as much as the world of giving makes me tick, there is just as much about it that ticks me off.

In the biography *Steve Jobs*, author Walter Isaacson reveals that Jobs found philanthropy annoying. I am not at all surprised. The Apple magnate quickly abandoned the foundation he started in the mid-1980s. Why? "He discovered that it was annoying to have to deal with the person he had hired to run it, who kept talking about 'venture' philanthropy and how to 'leverage' giving," the book says. A nonprofit blogger once remarked that the drawbacks of the social sector "include the breathless rhetoric that its promoters employ in describing it, coupled with their insistence that everything about it is innovative, even revolutionary. MBAs often are comfortable with the language of 'leveraging' and 'outcome metrics' and 'social return on investment,' while many of the lawyers—even those who are excited about the development of the [social sector]—grit their teeth."

Here are just some issues regarding giving that cause us exasperation, annoyance, anger, frustration, disappointment, and fatigue in varying degrees:

1. **Giving without getting thanks.** It sounds very basic, but so many of those we give to—individuals and organizations alike—neglect to say thank you. Whether we have spent an hour mentoring a college student on his or her career or spent a small fortune to back a coworker's pet project, there are times we never receive an

acknowledgment or a simple thank-you note expressing gratitude for our support, much less a progress report about what has happened since we stepped in.

2. **Caregiving.** Looking after our loved ones during illness and degenerative processes is an incredibly important task. But when we do it merely out of obligation, coercion, or guilt, without seeing it as part of our purpose (see chapter 2), caregiving can make us feel emotionally and physically drained.

3. **Lending money to friends and family.** "Neither a borrower nor a lender be," Shakespeare wrote in *Hamlet*. Why not? "For oft loan loses both itself and friend." When friends or family members ask us to help by lending them money, we often feel inclined to do so. After all, they wouldn't be approaching us if they weren't in a pinch. If they are coming to us instead of to a bank, chances are they do not have strong enough credit to seek a loan through official channels, and there is great risk that the loan will never be repaid. Worse, when they cannot repay, they may make us feel obliged to simply consider the loan to them a gift. Many of us have learned the hard way that family, friendships, and finances make a poor mix, and this is hardly the way to give our way to happiness.

4. **Giving after being shamed into it.** We have all felt the dread that comes from being cajoled into giving. Sometimes it happens after a mad dash to the supermarket, when all we want is a pint of milk and the cashier asks if we want to support a charity by adding a dollar to our bill. Other times, aggressive street fund-raisers,

or what the media call "charity muggers," take the enjoyment out of our walk on the high street. In these cases, we are more likely to give out of the avoidance of public humiliation rather than out of sheer generosity and concern for the charities they represent. Why doesn't this type of giving give us a glow? It is charity without contemplation. There's no time to make a reasoned decision about whether a particular cause is deserving of a donation or aligned with your passion. The real issue, as I see it, is not about coercing or pressuring or frightening people into giving.

Christy Turlington Burns, who raises money for her charity, Every Mother Counts, says, "The last thing I want to do is put my friends on the spot and make them feel obligated, because I know people are being pulled at constantly by this cause or that cause."

And Bill Gates once said, "Philanthropy should be voluntary." No one, he says, is going to take up giving "because someone scolded them or they heard Bill Gates say something mean."

5. **Passive giving.** The passive giver exists at all socioeconomic levels, from the airline passenger who drops the remainder of his foreign currency in the charity can before flying back home, to the religious donor who gives $1 million in unrestricted funds to the church. Once the funds have been donated, the act of giving is complete. When the giver does not make an effort to learn more about the beneficiaries of her gifts, or follow through by volunteering her time for the cause, she is unlikely to feel the joy of her generosity.

6. **Giving to someone we hardly know.** David Earnshaw, a student at the University of St. Andrews in Scotland, couldn't have said it

better, in his article "Why Is Charity Becoming More Annoying?": "Almost every day, someone I barely even remember from
primary school decides their previous twenty-two years of complete and unashamed apathy to the problems of the world can be
forgiven if they can only raise eighty quid for walking five miles
of the Leeds Country Way in a Pudsey Bear costume." It's not
just our Facebook contacts who are guilty. I am constantly baf-
fled by how some foundations named after families, companies,
and individuals aggressively solicit funds from the general public. We all want to leave a legacy, and when a loved one passes
away, we want to honor theirs. But do you really want to give to
the John Smith Foundation to enhance the legacy of John Smith?
Unless John was your dearest friend and college roommate who
was the foremost advocate of gay rights before he died at the
hands of the Taliban, I would not blame you for seeing this as a
joyless activity. The exception, of course, is if the John Smith
Foundation were actually doing an excellent job, and you are
convinced that your funds are better off given to them than to
any other organization working in the same field.

7. **Writing a check after being forced to watch "poverty porn."** It's a cli-
ché in the nonprofit world: images of starving children in Africa
with their ribs poking out, sallow-skinned AIDS patients moan-
ing with pain in overcrowded hospital wards. "Poverty porn" is
the name given to these stereotypical images that practically
define today's perception of the humanitarian world. When there
are catastrophes on the scale of Hurricane Katrina and Typhoon
Haiyan, showing people in desperate need is quite possibly the
easiest way to make people donate. But depictions of people

fraught in despair are so ubiquitous that we are quite possibly growing immune to them, and the stereotyping creates an "us and them" sense that prevents us from feeling connected to those who need help. Similarly, listening to postapocalyptic scenarios described by environmental conservationists can be very frightening at first, but eventually they just become draining.

I'm absolutely not discouraging people from giving to good causes just because they don't cheer us up. If we gave only to get something back each and every time, what a dreadful, opportunistic world this would be. Neither am I saying we should not be part of the solution to intractable problems such as climate change, poverty, and incurable diseases—we certainly should. There are things we will and should do out of obligation, sympathy, and a sense of responsibility, and in the spirit of public service. But then again, there are ways to give that not only make a difference to the lives of others but also bring us great joy. "There is a sweet spot where generosity feels organic and gives everyone warm fuzzies," says activist Christopher Bergland.[1]

This begs the question, how can we give in a way that leads to happiness and fulfillment?

How to Give in a Way That Leads to Happiness and Fulfillment

It's not how much we give but how much love we put into giving.

—MOTHER TERESA

I am only one, but I am one. I cannot do everything, but I can do something. And I will not let what I cannot do interfere with what I can do.

—EDWARD EVERETT HALE

1. Find your passion

I strongly believe that your passion should be the foundation for your giving. More commonly, though, we become part of something because someone asked us to do it, regardless of how interested we are in the cause. Or we give year after year as though we are paying taxes, never paying much attention to whether we are giving to something that deeply matters to us.

When I asked Goldie Hawn what advice she can give to others who want to make a difference, she said, "First of all, find out what you care about, who you care about, what matters to you, what is your passion, how do you want to see change." Many people who have founded their own charities immediately try and enlist support for their own, but she knew all too well that what tugs at her heart may be very different from what other people are drawn to. "When you truly look at these things outside of yourself, then you may find your charity, your time, your volunteer period. Find out what it is—is it with children? Is it with hospitals? Find out."

Mark Vermilion, who ran Steve Jobs's foundation for the brief time it existed, said that Jobs wanted to support projects focused on nutrition and vegetarianism, while Vermilion, whom Mr. Jobs reportedly hired away from Apple to run the foundation, wanted him to promote social entrepreneurs. Can you imagine how different things would have been if Steve Jobs had been encouraged to pursue his philanthropic passion?

Harvard Business School's Michael Norton, who has been working with businesses to maximize their staff's volunteer experiences, says, "We often see companies send their employees out to help with nonprofits. For example, an accounting firm will send their accountants to help build houses. It turns out that accountants, first of all, don't know anything about building houses. Neither do they like building houses, and so it's not necessarily even the most rewarding opportunity for them to volunteer. Yet there are so many poor people who actually need help with their taxes—and that's something that accountants can help with and actually enjoy helping with, because it's in their area of expertise."

Giving should be personal. You care about this and not so much about that, and that's okay. It should not be simply a matter of choosing the right thing, but also a matter of choosing what is right for you. If your heart isn't fully into it, you're very likely to get bored, distracted, and apathetic. You're also very likely to give up when the going gets tough—and things will get tough. If you don't feel like going totally bald to support a cancer charity, you shouldn't feel bad about it. Perhaps you can offer your marketing skills for the same charity, or a different charity altogether.

Watching you grow and discover the world seemed a thousand times more interesting than the United Nations and their ambitious plans to improve the fate of the planet.

—ISABEL ALLENDE, ON HER DAUGHTER, PAULA

We need to reflect on our personal experiences in order to decide what issues we want to focus on, whom we want to help, and where we want to act. The process is very personal, often evoking difficult memories or experiences. For many people, it is an intensely emotional act.

To identify your passion, answer these questions:

- What experiences have shaped your life?
- When you were in school, what did you most enjoy studying?
- What is your greatest accomplishment or triumph? What is your greatest loss?
- If you could change one thing about your past, what would it be?
- What is the greatest lesson you've learned in life?
- Who has been a role model for you?
- What do you cherish most in life?
- How would you describe your values and morals?
- What keeps you awake at night?
- What makes you angry?
- When did you last choke up at the movies?
- What moves you?

2. Form your vision

A vision describes what you want the world to look like. It is both idealistic and long term, and it serves as both inspiration and motivation. Your vision will be of central importance to you as you explain and share with others what you hope to accomplish. It helps to actually write down this vision. It is the written manifestation of your intentions and enables you to check constantly if you are staying true to your course. The best vision statements make a bold, clear-sighted statement about how things should be. They are generally:

- Aspirational—describing how things should be, rather than how they are
- Focused—setting out the what, where, and whom that will anchor efforts
- Concise—summing up intentions in a crisp and understandable way
- Memorable—catching the attention of potential partners and inspiring their actions

My vision is a world where people see giving as a pathway to happiness and fulfillment in life. What is your vision? It will remain a working document for a long time and will drive the planning of your giving. So don't rush it, and keep in mind that a vision statement is never fundamentally right or wrong. It represents your choice.

3. Find your niche

In an effort to broadly categorize all nonprofit organizations, the National Center for Charitable Statistics created the National Taxonomy of Exempt Entities classification system, dividing the universe of nonprofit organizations into twenty-six major groups under ten broad categories representing sectors such as the arts, culture, and humanities; education; environment and animals; and health. Within these major groups, organizations are further broken down into divisions and subdivisions. Take any one of these categories, such as education, and you will find subcategories such as elementary and secondary schools, preschools, libraries, alumni associations, parent and teacher groups, remedial reading, and many others. So if we have identified education as our core philanthropic passion, there is still a long way to go in terms of figuring out exactly how and where to give. So how?

You have to start somewhere. Armed with an understanding of your motives and what you can contribute, decide on the focus of your giving. Once you do get started, you have a better chance of refining your course of action and ending up doing what you really want to do. There will be some refinement along the way.

To identify your niche, answer these questions:

- What theme or topic will you engage on? What is the cause Hyou want to address?
  - ☐ Health, environment, social justice, education, arts and culture, disaster relief, social welfare
- Where? Geographic focus?
  - ☐ At what level? Global, regional, country, community
- Whom? Who are the beneficiaries?
  - ☐ Age group—e.g., children, youth, adults, elderly
  - ☐ Gender
  - ☐ Populations—immigrant, rural, ethnic, or religious communities
  - ☐ Socioeconomic communities

THE NARROWER YOUR FOCUS, the easier it will be for you. Being specific about what you will focus on, where you will act, and whom you will help has two benefits. First, it increases your chance of success by concentrating your efforts on something that is achievable. Second, it makes it easier to determine what you need to do to get there, as well as how to measure progress.

Your desire to engage may be based on a particular experience, or an affinity for a country or a specific community, or it may stem from your wish to use your professional expertise in a social context.

Immediately after her father died of lung cancer, Christy Turlington Burns said, "I have learned that I can be most effective through my anti-tobacco work. I also continue to help a variety of other not-for-profit, grassroots organizations in areas involving children, education, the environment, and animal rights, but given my time constraints and desire to focus on making the most impact, anti-tobacco remains my platform."[2] Her focus has since shifted more toward maternal health issues, after her experience with post-partum hemorrhage inspired her to campaign for women's health. Our focus can evolve over time, but we are more effective when we concentrate our efforts on just one or a few core issues instead of spreading ourselves too thin.

4. Give your time

Giving is by no means limited to gifts of money. The gift of time is sometimes even more valuable to the receiver, and more satisfying for the giver. "There's always something that you can do. You don't have to have a lot of money or notoriety to give back," Goldie adds.

We don't all have the same amount of money, but we all do have time on our hands, and can give some of this time to help others, whether that means we devote our lifetimes to service, or just give a few hours each day or a few days a year.

Before he turned ten, Joshua Williams already knew the importance of giving time. "We encourage people not to only donate but to come out and help. We want your donation and we want your time. If you speak to any of our volunteers you will see they give their time and money because they want to see the impact, and this makes them happier."

5. Chunk your giving

In a study led by psychologist Sonja Lyubomirsky, people performed five random acts of kindness every week for six weeks. They were randomly divided into two groups: Half chunked their giving into a single day each week, and the other half sprinkled it across all five days each week. At the end of the six weeks, despite performing the same number of helping acts, only one group felt significantly happier. The "chunkers" achieved gains in happiness; the sprinklers didn't. Happiness increased when people performed all five giving acts in a single day, rather than doing one a day. So although performing random acts of kindness can give us a high, we can reach greater heights if we actually schedule our giving.

6. Give with more focus and intention

"I realized early on that I can't fund every single cause out there. I need to have laser-like focus on one main goal. For us, that goal was to fund the best ALS research in the world," says Augie Nieto. "We haven't been able to help every family that reaches out to us for financial assistance or resources but we do connect people with others who can help and try to give them hope." When we choose where and how to give, the choice is difficult because we are choosing between good and good.

According to Norton, "Giving to a cause that specifies what they're going to do with your money leads to more happiness than giving to an umbrella cause where you're not so sure where your money is going. You really want to feel like you're having a specific impact on somebody when you give. For example, the feeling of buying a malaria net for someone—even for an anonymous person who can't give us thanks—leads to more happiness than giving to an organization where you can't visualize where the money is going."

Once we have already decided to give, choosing where to give involves a decision between right and right. There are thousands of worthy charities, and we should not feel bad about taking our time in choosing where we'd like to give, how much, and how. Many generous people prefer to give in different ways, knowing that some donations have more impact than others. It helps to do things more purposefully.

7. Align your giving with your interests, motivators, and skills

Your motivators (security, public recognition, etc.) and your skills (communication, quantitative analysis, etc.) are very important as you consider what kind of giving suits you. For instance, Lynne Nieto, who graduated with a degree in accounting, cofounded Augie's Quest with her husband and has played a pivotal role in its success through her focus on the bottom line, where her accounting background has been key.

Be true to yourself and address issues that matter to you, no matter how radical they are. Auto insurance magnate Peter B. Lewis says, "If there is one area that is taboo for most philanthropists yet exemplifies disastrous public policy, it is our nation's outdated, ineffective marijuana laws. A majority of Americans are ready to change marijuana laws, yet we continue to arrest our young people for engaging in an activity that is utterly commonplace. I have funded much of the movement to enact laws that give patients access to marijuana as relief for pain and nausea—and have made no secret of being one of those patients myself, using marijuana to help with pain following the amputation of my lower leg."

8. *Find ways to integrate your interests with the needs of others*

"Selfless giving, in the absence of self-preservation instincts, easily becomes overwhelming," says Adam Grant. It is important to be "otherish," which he defines as being willing to give more than you receive, but still keeping your own interests in sight, and using them as a guide for choosing when, where, how, and to whom you give. "Instead of seeing self-interest and other-interest as competing, find ways to integrate them. When concern for others is coupled with a healthy dose of concern for the self, givers are less prone to burning out and getting burned." This is especially true when we interact with the needy, ill, and less fortunate. Many of these interactions can be emotionally distressing and physically taxing.

Christy Turlington Burns says, "Most people that I work with on my issue are not people that have wealth and fame; they're people who come from a lot of different walks of life. All they have is the desire or the recognition that there's a problem, and they see that there's not someone else doing anything about it, or not enough people doing anything about it, and so they have created an opportunity for themselves by just looking at gaps and seeing that their voice matters and makes a difference and then jumping in and trying in their unique way to gain support and make it bigger. To me that's the answer; it's sort of not thinking too big. Starting with yourself first, educating yourself, feeling that whatever it is that resonates most with you. What do you read about in the paper that makes you want to cry? What injustice do you feel is the most pulling?"

9. Find your tribe

When choosing which organization to support, be aware of its organizational culture. Many people overlook the fact that the satisfaction of giving often has so much to do with the culture of the organization you align with—and not just its focus area. It is overly simplistic to assume that if you love animals you should volunteer for an animal welfare charity. There are so many animal welfare charities with so many different strategies, led by so many different personalities. You will find that you are more aligned with some, and less with others. Think of whom you will be working with. Most issues are complex and intractable, and require many different people to work on them in order to get results.

"When I think of the folks who are successful in making a difference and are clearly deeply satisfied, they are not lone rangers," says Kat Rosqueta of the Center for High Impact Philanthropy. "They view themselves as part of a community—whether their peers, their network, other people who care about the social issue that they care about. The sense of belonging to a community keeps people committed."

10. Ask for transparency

Giving is not risk free. There is a likelihood of failure. Even the best projects led by the most dedicated people can fail, or even unwittingly make things worse. To mitigate risk, it is important to conduct due diligence on potential recipients and partners. For many of us, this simply means asking for transparency.

11. Do something that makes a real impact—
and see it for yourself

The greatest reward is often said to be the impact one has on an issue. This is why it's better to give while you live, rather than waiting for people to do things on your behalf once you have gone.

The magnitude of your impact depends on what you are willing and able to do. For example:

- Buying beds for a hospital so that it can serve more patients has a direct and often immediate impact on those served.
- Supporting a university to create a nursing program to increase the number of medical staff has a longer timeline for impact, but once achieved, it benefits thousands of lives.
- Advocating for better health care policies in a country could take years, if not decades, but it can eventually improve millions of lives.

"Many of the folks who have created new solutions to social problems, or who have spent a lot of time volunteering, or have given money generously often say that they are the biggest beneficiary of their gifts. The people who get the most satisfaction are those who are confident that they are making a difference," says Rosqueta. "If you are stuck in a situation where you are constantly being pitched by causes that all sound good, but you don't have a strong sense that the things you have invested in are making a difference, that can leave you frustrated, angry, disappointed. You might just walk away. Everybody is looking for a sense of confidence that they are actually making a big difference. We all want to know that what we are doing is yielding meaningful results."

12. Be proactive

If you find yourself considering a gift to a charity that called you on the phone, you've already lost most of the battle to do as much good as possible. Your efforts will go furthest if you set time aside, think about all your options, and then find the best charity for your values. If you wait for charities to come to you, you're just rewarding the ones that are most aggressive—not the ones that do the most good.

13. Accept gratitude

There's a debate about which kind of giving is more moral: giving anonymously, or letting your identity as the giver be known. Norton says that the happier giver is the one who lets his identity be known.

John Steinbeck eulogizes his recently deceased friend, Ed Ricketts: "I have tried to isolate and inspect the great talent that was in Ed Ricketts, that made him so loved and needed and makes him so missed now that he is dead. Certainly he was an interesting and charming man, but there was some other quality that far exceeded these. I have thought that it might be his ability to receive, to receive anything from anyone, to receive gracefully and thankfully, and to make the gift seem very fine. Because of this everyone felt good in giving to Ed—a present, a thought, anything."[3]

14. Recognize that it gets tough

When the very well-appointed Oprah Winfrey Leadership Academy for Girls was built in an impoverished region of South Africa, the school (whose bedrooms had high thread count sheets) was deemed too nice and extravagant, and people questioned whether the $40 million Winfrey spent might have benefitted a far greater number of students had it been spent with less emphasis on luxurious surroundings. She had the best of intentions, and all she wanted was to give girls an experience that they'd never had.

Another example of donors who got criticized for their deeds is the Salwen family of Atlanta, who funded a charity in Africa using the proceeds from the sale of their home. A common reproof is that their money should have gone to needy people within the United States, such as homeless Atlantans. But the Salwens are unapologetic. They decided unanimously that their money would go furthest in Africa and are pleased with their choice. Traveling with the Hunger Project's chief operating officer, John Coonrod, in Ghana, they saw for themselves the difference between Westerners arriving to dig wells, which often just encourages dependence on outsiders, and those who support long-term self-reliance. Their year of research exposed the many pitfalls of foreign aid, but they are optimistic their chosen project will do lasting good.

You too will most likely get criticized for doing something you never really had to do in the first place, particularly if you choose to support a cause that people don't regard as urgent, such as arts and culture or wildlife conservation. You too should be unapologetic about your giving.

Conclusion

"Will giving make you happier? You'll have to answer that for your-self. When I was in Africa with Bill and Melinda Gates, watching them talk to villagers whose lives they had improved, they seemed happy. When I saw young Brianne Schwantes risk more broken bones in her fragile body to help people in the Mississippi flood, she seemed happy. . . . When I met Oseola McCarty after she gave her life savings so that young people could have the education she never had, she seemed happy. When Carlos Slim looked at a crowd of ten thousand young people he'd sent to college, he seemed happy. When Barbra Streisand and Rupert Murdoch, two highly public figures who disagree on nearly everything politically, stood together to give the first contributions to my foundation's fight against climate change, they seemed happy. When Chris and Basil Stamos, Chris Hohn and Jamie Cooper-Hohn, Frank Giustra and Fred Eychaner, and all the others who fund my AIDS work look into the eyes of children who are alive because of them, they seem happy. Who's happier? The givers or the takers? I think you know the answer. There's a whole world out there that needs you, down the street or across the ocean. Give."[4]

—BILL CLINTON

THE KEY IS TO find the approach that fits you. When you do, then the more you give, the more you stand to get back—not in money but in other forms of value. Connection. Purpose. Meaning. Happiness. All the things that we look for but that are so hard to find. And you will radiate optimism, hope, and energy despite finding yourself in the most challenging circumstances. The challenges will not bring you down but will charge you up no matter how hard it gets. As Augie Nieto puts it, "Giving transforms the giver because the giver gets more than the recipient. If you truly give from an authentic place, you get more than you give."

If givers derive a greater sense of happiness from giving, then I hope these positive emotions will lead to more frequent and greater gifts. My wish is to see a world where we no longer need to be coerced, pressured, or frightened to make a difference, but where we intuitively understand that it is good to give. A world not where we give until it hurts, but where we give until it feels great.

ACKNOWLEDGMENTS

Feeling gratitude and not expressing it is like
wrapping a present and not giving it.

—WILLIAM ARTHUR WARD

This book was made possible by the love, support, time, creative energy, emotion, guidance, inspiration, and generosity of an incredible circle of friends old and new. Two years ago I followed the adage "Leap and a net will appear," and an amazing network of friends, creative colleagues, and unseen hands miraculously appeared exactly when I needed them, and became my safety net when I had no idea where to begin, had no experience writing anything longer than my college theses, and had absolutely no clue about the publishing industry. I cannot adequately express how grateful I am to everyone who had faith in me.

This book could not have been written without my dearest friend Steven Rowles. For months I had been talking about my plan to write a book, and it was Steven who decided it was time to lock me up in my apartment (and turn off the WiFi!) for an entire day to get me to just stop with the talking and actually get started writing. Steven was there every step of the way thereafter—spending many days poring through my outlines, drafts, and piles of research; listening to me think out loud; putting so much of his creative energy and talent into the project; and even coming up with the beautiful title of the book. I could only wish that when it's his turn to publish his writings I could be nearly as helpful.

To my friends—my chosen family—who shared my excitement over this project, and who cheered me on when it became so challenging. I would have given up without their support. I am grateful to Eddy Sariaatmadja, who taught me the meaning of giving, and who is truly the kindest person I have ever met. To Deepak Chopra, for helping create the perfect circumstances that set me off on my journey, and for saying yes to everything I ever asked for. To Simon Ou, who held me accountable to my promise to write a book. I was so lucky to have had Simon right next to me when the "flashing lightbulb moment" happened and I came upon the premise of this book, and Simon made me shake hands with him as a promise that I would actually write it. To Nadia Parvez Manzoor, for helping bring out my creativity during our many brainstorming sessions and road trips.

My deepest gratitude goes out to each one of the amazing, inspirational men and women who have shared with me their personal stories of giving, beginning with David Foster, who held fast to his promise to meet me for our interview in LA even after spending his morning in the emergency room. To Goldie Hawn, who not only eagerly participated in this project but also gave me the golden opportunity to be an advisor to her wonderful foundation. To Isabel Allende, Michael Bolton, Augie Nieto, Ray

Chambers, Djimon Hounsou, Philippe Cousteau, Kenneth Cole, Lily Cole, Mo Ibrahim, Klaus and Hilde Schwab, Petra Nemcova, Joshua Williams, Manny Pacquiao, Christy Turlington Burns, Muhammad Yunus, Ted Turner, Yang Lan, Natalia Vodianova, Ric O'Barry, Jill Robinson, Wendy Kopp, Liz Alderman, Kate Roberts, and to the late Richard Rockefeller, who all surprised me with their willingness to be in this book, and who all spoke so genuinely from the heart. Special thanks to Tom Freston for not only sharing his story but also helping me find a way to share everyone else's stories with a much broader audience than I had originally conceived of. Before I met Tom, my intention was just to write a little book that hopefully a bunch of friends would read, but it was Tom who said that I should aim higher and take this idea to New York.

I am grateful to all the brilliant scientists and researchers whose contributions added much substance to this book, especially Ashley Whillans, Lara Aknin, Elizabeth Dunn, Kat Rosqueta, and Michael Norton.

I am very deeply grateful and indebted to Adam Grant, who is such a giver. He not only gave so much of his input and time into this project, but also so generously introduced me to some of the most talented agents in the industry when I was almost a complete stranger to him. It was through Adam that I met the most wonderful Meg Thompson, whom I have had the incredible privilege to call my agent.

I am sincerely grateful to my magnificent team at Tarcher/ Penguin Random House: to my editor Sara Carder, who took a chance on me, and who has offered nothing but encouragement and constructive commentary; and to Brianna Yamashita, Brooke

Borneman, and Joanna Ng, who all made me feel that they really loved and believed in what this book is all about. And many others I never met but I know poured many hours into the production of this book.

Thank you to everyone who opened up doors, helped me frame my thoughts, and provided a wealth of ideas to spread word about *The Giving Way to Happiness*: Mary Beth O'Connor, Edward Wanandi, Carl Liederman, Robert Van Zwieten, Jane Wales, Vidar Jorgensen, Barbara Kardon, Kimberly McNatt, Shamir Shahi, Michiel Verhoeven, Corrin Varady, Karen Tse, Laura Bridgeman, Martin Halusa, Anthony Pangilinan, Sean Hinton, Drew Van Wyk, Phap Linh, Mark Johnson, Mahboob Mahmood, Justin Beavis, Genia Mineeva, Kathy Calvin, Zoran Svetlicic, Jason Fried, Brandt Goldstein, Tanya Farrell, and Elena Stokes. I also thank Pak Tahir for his confidence in my work.

I am deeply grateful to a stellar group of women in the literary world who believed in my idea when it was nothing but a book proposal. Their professional opinions made me have confidence in my ability as a writer. Thank you to Jennifer Rudolph Walsh, Claudia Ballard, Amber Qureshi, and Cheryl Robson. I appreciate the help of Joni Rodgers, Jerusha Rodgers, Anna Martin, Pia Macan-Umali, and Ng Yao Yee in assisting me in the mechanics of this big project. Special thanks to my friend Peter Galagy for reading the entire manuscript and giving valuable feedback.

For their encouragement over the years, I thank Agnes Alsua, Juerg Kaufmann, Christina Araneta-Tan, Frances Lim, Tin Briones, Malvinder Singh, Peter Kok, Chew Kwee San, Russel Caparas, Melissa Aseron, Elena Lachica, Christina Alfonso, Fred Sabio, Jayesh Parekh, Thomas Halusa, Morgan Smith, Regina Santi, Karla

Sigler, Jimmy JimBug, and Fernando Zobel. And to dear Coco: The life of a writer is solitary and isolating, and this little dog kept me company in my writing cave when humans would have been far too distracting.

I thank my parents for bringing me up in a way that helped me become a writer. My mom always helped me with my writing homework (thus convincing my teachers that I was a "very good" writer when I hardly deserved it), and my dad gifted me with Strunk & White's *The Elements of Style* and so many other useful writing manuals when I was just a little girl.

May I end this note of thanksgiving wishing that everyone who has given a part of themselves to *The Giving Way to Happiness*, especially you, Dear Reader, gain much more for everything you have given. I will always be grateful to each and every one of you, and thank you from the bottom of my heart.

NOTES

PREFACE

1   Bill Clinton, *Giving: How Each of Us Can Change the World* (New York: Alfred A. Knopf, 2007).

CHAPTER 1

1   Leslie Bennetts, "Petra's Story," *Vanity Fair*, May 2005.
2   A. Luks, "Helper's High: Volunteering Makes People Feel Good, Physically and Emotionally," *Psychology Today* 22, no. 10 (October 1988): 34–42.
3   Omotoyosi Fakologbon, "Voo Doo Death: The No Exit Syndrome and the Helpers High: Healing the Self by Helping Others," Academia.edu, http://www .academia.edu/3514892/VOO_DOO_DEATH_The_no_exit_syndrome _and_THE_HELPERS_HIGH_Healing_the_self_by_helping_others.
4   William T. Harbaugh, Ulrich Mayr, and Daniel R. Burghart, "Neural Responses to Taxation and Voluntary Giving Reveal Motives for Charitable Donations," *Science* 316, no. 5831 (June 2007): 1622–25.
5   Prosocial behavior is defined as "voluntary behavior intended to benefit another," which consists of actions that "benefit other people or society as a whole, such as helping, sharing, donating, cooperating, and volunteering." Nancy Eisenberg, Richard A. Fabes, and Tracy L. Spinrad, "Prosocial Development: Social, Emotional, and Personality Development," in *Handbook of Child Psychology* (New York: John Wiley & Sons, 2006), doi:10.1002/9780470147658.chpsy0311.ISBN 0-470-14765-2.
6   Amanda Enayati, "For Kids, It's Better to Give Than Receive," CNN .com, September 17, 2012, http://www.cnn.com/2012/09/17/living/giving-makes -children-happy/.

7 Elizabeth Dunn and Michael Norton, *Happy Money: The Science of Smarter Spending* (New York: Simon & Schuster, 2013).

8 Professor David Chan, Lee Kuan Yew Fellow, Professor of Psychology, Director of the Behavioural Sciences Institute at Singapore Management University; National Volunteer & Philanthropy Centre (NVPC). Individual Giving Survey 2012.

9 Lise Vesterlund, "Why Do People Give?" in *The Non-Profit Sector: A Research Handbook*, 2nd ed., ed. Walter W. Powell and Richard Steinberg (New Haven, CT: Yale University Press, 2006), 568–87.

10 Stephanie L. Brown, Randolph M. Nesse, Amiram D. Vinokur, et al., "Providing Social Support May Be More Beneficial Than Receiving It: Results from a Prospective Study of Mortality," *Psychological Science* 14, no. 4 (2003): 320–27.

11 Ibid.

12 S. L. Brown, D. M. Smith, R. Schulz, et al., "Caregiving Behavior Is Associated with Decreased Mortality Risk," *Psychological Science* 20, no. 4 (2009): 488–94.

13 Stephen G. Post, "Altruism, Happiness, and Health: It's Good to Be Good," *International Journal of Behavioral Medicine* 12, no. 2 (2005): 66–77.

14 Sarah Konrath, Andrea Fuhrel-Forbis, Alina Lou, et al., "Motives for Volunteering Are Associated with Mortality Risk in Older Adults," *Health Psychology* 31, no. 1 (2012): 87–96.

15 Hannah M. C. Schreier, Kimberly A. Schonert-Reichl, and Edith Chen, "Effect of Volunteering on Risk Factors for Cardiovascular Disease in Adolescents: A Randomized Controlled Trial," *JAMA Pediatrics* 167, no. 4 (2013): 327–32.

16 Other studies: Longitudinal research shows that volunteer work and well-being are reciprocally related over time. Y. Li and K. F. Ferraro, "Volunteering and Depression in Later Life: Social Benefit or Selection Processes," *Journal of Health and Social Behavior* 46, no. 1 (2005), 68–84; Y. Li and K. F. Ferraro, "Volunteering in Middle and Later Life: Is Health a Benefit, Barrier, or Both?" *Social Forces* 85, no. 1 (2006): 497–519; P. A. Thoits and L. N. Hewitt, "Volunteer Work and Well-being," *Journal of Health and Social Behavior* 42, no. 2 (2001): 115–31.

The more volunteer hours worked at one point in time, the better one's mental and physical health at a subsequent point, and individuals in better physical and mental health at one time point invest more hours in volunteer work in a future period. M. van Willigen, "Differential Benefits of Volunteering Across the Life Course," *Journals of Gerontology*. Series B, *Psychological Sciences and Social Sciences* 55, no. 5 (2000): S308–S318.

Recent studies indicate that people who participate in these activities live longer than those who do not. Volunteers had a 60 percent lower mortality rate compared with nonvolunteers. D. Oman, C. E. Thoresen, and K. McMahon, "Volunteerism and Mortality Among the Community Dwelling Elderly," *Journal of Health Psychology* 4, no. 3 (1999): 301–16.

Providers of social support had a 50 percent lower mortality rate than those who neither received nor provided social support. Brown, Nesse, Vinokur, et al., "Providing Social Support."

17 Stephen Post, "It's Good to Be Good: Dr. Stephen Post on the Scientific Evidence," December 21, 2011, press release, Stony Brook University.

18 Ibid.

19 K. C. Berridge, "The Debate over Dopamine's Role in Reward: The Case for Incentive Salience," *Psychopharmacology* 191, no. 3 (2007): 391–431.

20 Post, "Altruism, Happiness, and Health."

21 Barbara L. Fredrickson, Karen M. Grewen, Kimberly A. Coffey, et al., "A Functional Genomic Perspective on Human Well-being," *Proceedings of the National Academy of Sciences* 110, no. 33 (2013): 13684–89.

22 Cassie Mogilner, Zoë Chance, and Michael I. Norton, "Giving Time Gives You Time," *Psychological Science* 23, no. 10 (2012): 1233–38.

23 Post, "Altruism, Happiness, and Health."

CHAPTER 2

1 Steve Taylor, "The Power of Purpose," *Psychology Today*, July 21, 2013, https://www.psychologytoday.com/blog/out-the-darkness/201307/the-power-purpose.

2 Patrick E. McKnight and Todd B. Kashdan, "Purpose in Life as a System That Creates and Sustains Health and Well-being: An Integrative, Testable Theory," *Review of General Psychology* 13, no. 3 (2009): 242–51.

3 D. L. Debats, "Meaning in Life: Clinical Relevance and Predictive Power," *British Journal of Clinical Psychology* 35 (1996): 503–16; Sheryl Zika and Kerry Chamberlain. "On the Relation Between Meaning in Life and Psychological Well-being," *British Journal of Clinical Psychology* 83, no. 1 (1992): 133–45; Ann Elisabeth Auhagen, "On the Psychology of Meaning of Life," *Swiss Journal of Psychology* 59, no. 1 (2000): 34–48; V. E. Frankl, *Man's Search for Meaning* (New York: Washington Square Press, 1959/1985); A. A. Sappington, J. Bryant, and C. Oden, "An Experimental Investigation of Viktor Frankl's Theory of Meaningfulness in Life," *The International Forum for Logotherapy* 13 (1990): 125–30; Gary T. Reker, Edward J. Peacock, and Paul T. P. Wong, "Meaning and Purpose in Life and Well-being: A Life-span Perspective," *Journal of Gerontology* 42, no. 1 (1987): 44–49; Carol D. Ryff, "Beyond Ponce de Leon and Life Satisfaction: New Directions in Quest of Successful Ageing, *International*

Journal of Behavioral Development 12, no. 1 (March 1989): 35–55; Zika and Chamberlain, "Relation of Hassles and Personality to Subjective Well-being," *Journal of Personality and Social Psychology* 53, no. 1 (1987): 155–62.

4 Reker, Peacock, and Wong, "Meaning and Purpose"; Zika and Chamberlain, "Meaning in Life and Psychological Well-being." While acknowledging the limitations of correlational research in demonstrating causation, in 1992 Zika and Chamberlain said that "theory would suggest that meaning has a broad and pervasive influence on well-being."

5 Laura A. King and Christie K. Napa, "What Makes a Life Good?" *Journal of Personality and Social Psychology* 75, no. 1 (1998): 156–65. Christie N. Scollon and Laura A. King, "Is the Good Life the Easy Life?" *Social Indicators Research* 68, no. 2 (2004): 127–62.

6 R. R. Hutzell, "A Review of the Purpose in Life Test," *The International Forum for Logotherapy* 11 (1988): 89–101.

7 Taylor, "The Power of Purpose."

8 Viktor E. Frankl, "Jugendberatung," in *Enzyklopädisches Handbuch der Jugend-fürsorge* (1930).

9 Frankl, *Man's Search for Meaning.*

10 G. T. Reker and P. T. P. Wong, "Aging as an Individual Process: Toward a Theory of Personal Meaning," in *Emergent Theories of Aging*, ed. J. E. Birren and V. L. Bengston (New York, NY: Springer, 1988), 214–46; P. T. P. Wong, "Implicit Theories of Meaningful Life and the Development of the Personal Meaning Profile (PMP)," in *The Human Quest for Meaning: A Handbook of Psychological Research and Clinical Applications*, ed. P. T. P. Wong and P. S. Fry (Mahwah, NJ: Lawrence Erlbaum, 1998), 111–40.

11 James C. Crumbaugh, "Frankl's Logotherapy: A New Orientation in Counseling," *Journal of Religion and Health* 10, no. 4 (1971): 373–86; A. Marsh, L. Smith, J. Piek, et al., "The Purpose in Life Scale: Psychometric Properties for Social Drinkers and Drinkers in Alcohol Treatment," *Educational and Psychological Measurement* 63, no. 5 (2003): 859–71; J. Nicholson and A. Blanch, "Rehabilitation for Parenting Roles for People with Serious Mental Illness," *Psychosocial Rehabilitation* 18 (1994): 109–19.

12 Joseph Richman, *Preventing Elderly Suicide: Overcoming Personal Despair, Professional Neglect, and Social Bias* (New York: Springer, 1993); G. Ruckenbauer, F. Yazdani, and G. Ravaglia, "Suicide in Old Age: Illness or Autonomous Decision of the Will," *Archives of Gerontology and Geriatrics* 44, no. 1 (2007): 355–58.

13 McKnight and Kashdan, "Purpose in Life."

CHAPTER 3

1 Name changed.

2 Aaron Hurst, "Being 'Good' Isn't the Only Way to Go," *New York Times*, April 20, 2014.

3 Arthur C. Brooks, "A Formula for Happiness," *New York Times*, December 14, 2013, http://www.nytimes.com/2013/12/15/opinion/sunday/a-formula-for-happiness.html.

4 Alice Mills and Jeremy Smith, "How to Be Happy by Calling for Change: Constructs of Happiness and Meaningfulness Amongst Social Movement Activists," *Qualitative Report* 13, no. 3 (2008): 432–55.

5 Name changed.

6 "Prevention of Professional Burn-out with Care Workers: Self-Care and Organizational Care," in *Work For Care: A Trainer's Manual on Sexual and Domestic Violence During and After War* (Utrecht, Netherlands: Admira Foundation, 2005); Andrew Goliszek, *60 Second Stress Management* (New York: Bantam, 1993).

7 B. H. Stamm, "Measuring Compassion Satisfaction as Well as Fatigue," in *Treating Compassion Fatigue*, ed. C. R. Figley (New York: Brunner-Routledge, 2002).

8 C. R. Figley, ed. *Treating Compassion Fatigue* (New York: Brunner-Routledge, 2002); K. W. Saakvitneand and L. A. Pearlman, *Transforming the Pain: A Workbook on Vicarious Traumatization* (London: W. W. Norton, 1996); Stamm, "Measuring Compassion Satisfaction."

CHAPTER 4

1 R. C. Kessler, A. Sonnega, E. Bromet, et al., "Posttraumatic Stress Disorder in the National Comorbidity Survey," *Archives of General Psychiatry* 52, no. 12 (1995): 1048–60.

2 Terence Monmaney, "For Most Trauma Victims, Life Is More Meaningful," *Los Angeles Times*, October 7, 2001.

3 Liz refers to the first large-scale epidemiological study of Cambodian refugees confined to the Thailand-Cambodian border in the 1980s and 1990s. The results of the study suggest the extraordinary capacity of refugees to protect themselves against mental illness despite horrific life experiences. The recommendation emerges for refugee policy makers to create programs that support work, indigenous religious practices, and culture-based altruistic behavior among refugees.

4 Pete Sigmund, "Crews Assist Rescuers in Massive WTC Search," *Construction Equipment Guide*.

5 L. A. Morland, L. D. Butler, and G. A. Leskin, "Resilience and Thriving in a Time of Terrorism," in *Trauma, Recovery, and Growth: Positive Psychological Perspectives on Posttraumatic Stress*, ed. S. Joseph and P. A. Linley (Hoboken, NJ: John Wiley & Sons, 2008), doi: 10.1002/9781118269718.ch3.

6 Audrey Washington, "26 Acts of Kindness Continue," NBC Connecticut, December 14, 2013, http://www.nbcconnecticut.com/news/local/Newtown -Sandy-Hook-26-Acts-of-Kindness-Continue-On-235602891.html.

7 Harold K. Bush, "Grief Work: After a Child Dies," *Christian Century*, December 11, 2007.

8 "Foundation Helps Many in Memory of a Beloved Son," *Wiltshire Gazette and Herald*, January 4, 2014, http://www.thisiswiltshire.co.uk/news/10910222 .Foundation_helps_many_in_memory_of_a_beloved_son/?ref=rss.

9 S. L. Brown and R. M. Brown, "Selective Investment Theory: Recasting the Functional Significance of Close Relationships," *Psychological Inquiry* 17, no. 1 (2006): 1–29.

10 Stephen Joseph and P. Alex Linley, eds., *Trauma, Recovery, and Growth: Positive Psychological Perspectives on Posttraumatic Stress* (Hoboken, NJ: John Wiley & Sons, 2008).

11 S. J. Merchant, E. M. Yoshida, T. K. Lee, et al., "Exploring the Psychological Effects of Deceased Organ Donation on the Families of the Organ Donors," *Clinical Transplantation* 22, no. 3 (2008): 341–47.

CHAPTER 5

1 *UBS-INSEAD Study on Family Philanthropy in Asia* (Zurich: UBS, 2011).

2 *2013 U.S. Trust Insights on Wealth and Worth: Annual Survey of High Net Worth and Ultra High Net Worth Americans* (Charlotte, NC: Bank of America Corporation, 2013).

3 http://www.weforum.org/world-economic-forum.

4 http://www.schwabfound.org/content/about-us-0.

5 Emily Hohler, "The Power of Half: How Hannah Salwen and Her Family Gave Half Their Home Away," *The Telegraph*, March 26, 2010.

CHAPTER 6

1 A. H. Maslow, "A Theory of Human Motivation," *Psychological Review* 50, no. 4 (July 1943): 370–96.

2 As of March 2014.

3 In 2001, Marcus retired to focus on philanthropy. Through the Marcus Foundation, he pledged $250 million to open the Georgia Aquarium, the world's
   largest, with more than 10 million gallons of water in its exhibits. In 2013, he
   donated $2.5 million to the City of Hope, a medical research center for brain
   tumor and lymphoma treatment. In 2008 he founded the Marcus Autism Center in Atlanta. His foundation makes $40 million in donations annually.

4 Rod Dreher, "The Wealth of Generosity," *Templeton Report*, March 24, 2011,
   http://www.templeton.org/templeton_report/20110324/index.html.

5 Clinton, *Giving*.

6 Elizabeth Kolbert, "Everybody Have Fun," *New Yorker*, March 22, 2010.

7 Graeme Wood, "Secret Fears of the Super-Rich," *Atlantic*, April 2011.

8 Dunn and Norton, *Happy Money*.

9 Steven Bertoni, "Chuck Feeney: The Billionaire Who Is Trying to Go Broke,"
   Forbes, September 18, 2012, http://www.forbes.com/sites/stevenbertoni/2012/
   09/18/chuck-feeney-the-billionaire-who-is-trying-to-go-broke.

10 "The Secret Givers," *Bloomberg Business*, November 30, 2003, http://www
   .businessweek.com/stories/2003-11-30/the-secret-givers.

11 Lara B. Aknin, Elizabeth W. Dunn, Gillian M. Sandstrom, et al., "Does Social
   Connection Turn Good Deeds into Good Feelings? On the Value of Putting the
   'Social' in Prosocial Spending," *International Journal of Happiness and Develop-
   ment* 1, no. 2 (2013): 155–71.

12 A. Zahavi and A. Zahavi, *The Handicap Principle: A Missing Piece of Darwin's
   Puzzle*. (Oxford: Oxford University Press, 1997).

13 Douglas Cole and Ira Chaikin, *An Iron Hand upon the People: The Law Against
   the Potlatch on the Northwest Coast* (Vancouver: Douglas & McIntyre; Seattle:
   University of Washington Press, 1990).

14 R. S. Lockhart and B. B. Murdock, "Memory and the Theory of Signal Detection," *Psychological Bulletin* 74, no. 2 (1970): 100.

15 Eric Alden Smith and Rebecca L. Bliege Bird, "Turtle Hunting and Tombstone
   Opening: Public Generosity as Costly Signaling," *Evolution and Human Behav-
   ior* 21, no. 4 (2000): 245–61; E. A. Smith and R. B. Bird, "Costly Signaling and
   Cooperative Behavior," in *Moral Sentiments and Material Interests: On the Foun-
   dations of Cooperation in Economic Life*, ed. H. Gintis, S. Bowles, R. Boyd, and
   E. Fehr (Cambridge, MA: MIT Press, 2005).

16 James L. Boone, "The Evolution of Magnanimity: When Is It Better to Give
   than to Receive?" *Human Nature* 9, no. 1 (1998): 1–21; "Status Signaling,
   Social Power, and Lineage Survival," in *Hierarchies in Action: Cui Bono?*
   ed. Michael W. Diehl (Carbondale: Southern Illinois University Press, 2000),
   84–110; V. Griskevicius, J. M. Tybur, J. M. Sundie, et al., "Blatant Benevolence

and Conspicuous Consumption: When Romantic Motives Elicit Strategic Costly Signals," *Journal of Personality and Social Psychology* 93, no. 1 (2007): 85–102.

17 M. Gurven, W. Allen-Arave, K. Hill, et al., "It's a Wonderful Life: Signaling Generosity Among the Ache of Paraguay," *Evolution and Human Behavior* 21, no. 4 (2000): 263–82; C. L. Hardy and M. Van Vugt, "Nice Guys Finish First: The Competitive Altruism Hypothesis," *Personality and Social Psychology Bulletin* 32, no. 10 (2006): 1402–13; M. Milinski, D. Semmann, H-J. Krambeck, et al., "Stabilizing the Earth's Climate Is Not a Losing Game: Supporting Evidence from Public Goods Experiments," *Proceedings of the National Academy of Sciences of the USA* 103, no. 11 (2006): 3994–98.

18 *UBS-INSEAD Study on Family Philanthropy in Asia*. Note that "to pursue happiness/find fulfillment" was not among the options given to survey respondents and interviewees.

19 Caroline Graham, "This Is Not the Way I'd Imagined Bill Gates . . . A Rare and Remarkable Interview with the World's Second Richest Man," *Daily Mail* Online, June 9, 2011, http://www.dailymail.co.uk/home/moslive/article-2001697/Microsofts-Bill-Gates-A-rare-remarkable-interview-worlds-second-richest-man.html#ixzz3BtAFoYHm.

20 Joe Hagan, "Tom Steyer: An Inconvenient Billionaire," *Men's Journal*, March 2014, http://www.mensjournal.com/magazine/tom-steyer-an-inconvenient-billionaire-20140218.

21 Renée Frojo, "Lorry Lokey: 'Unstoppable' Donor," *San Francisco Business Times*, October 25, 2013, http://www.bizjournals.com/sanfrancisco/print-edition/2013/10/25/lorry-lokey-unstoppable-donor.html?page=all.

CHAPTER 7

1 Christopher Bergland, *The Athlete's Way: Sweat and the Biology of Bliss* (New York: St. Martin's Press, 2007).

2 Michael Seeber, "Christy Turlington: Beauty and Balance," *Psychology Today*, July 1, 2001, http://www.psychologytoday.com/articles/200107/christy-turlington-beauty-and-balance.

3 John Steinbeck, *The Log from the Sea of Cortez* (New York: Penguin Books, 1951), 272–73.

4 Clinton, *Giving*.

CONTACT DETAILS OF SELECTED FEATURED ORGANIZATIONS

PERSON	ORGANIZATION	WEBSITE
Alderman Family	Peter C. Alderman Foundation	www.petercaldermanfoundation.org/
Augie Nieto	Augie's Quest	http://augiesquest.org/
Christy Turlington Burns	Every Mother Counts	www.everymothercounts.org/
David Foster	David Foster Foundation	http://davidfosterfoundation.com/
Deepak Chopra	The Chopra Foundation	www.choprafoundation.org/
Djimon Hounsou	Oxfam America	www.oxfamamerica.org/people/djimon-hounsou/
Goldie Hawn	The Hawn Foundation	http://thehawnfoundation.org/
Isabel Allende	Isabel Allende Foundation	www.isabelallendefoundation.org/
Jill Robinson	Animals Asia	www.animalsasia.org/us/
Joshua Williams	Joshua's Heart Foundation	http://joshuasheart.org/
Kenneth Cole	Kenneth Cole Foundation	http://forgood.kennethcole.com/
Klaus and Hilde Schwab	The World Economic Forum	www.weforum.org/
Klaus and Hilde Schwab	The Schwab Foundation	www.schwabfound.org/
Michael Bolton	The Michael Bolton Charities	www.michaelboltoncharities.com/
Mo Ibrahim	Mo Ibrahim Foundation	www.moibrahimfoundation.org/

PERSON	ORGANIZATION	WEBSITE
Muhammad Yunus	Grameen Foundation	www.grameenfoundation.org/
Natalia Vodianova	Naked Heart Foundation	www.nakedheart.org/en/
Petra Nemcova	Happy Hearts Fund	http://happyheartsfund.org/
Philippe Cousteau	Earth Echo International	http://earthecho.org/
Ray Chambers	Office of the U.N. Special Envoy for Financing the Health Millennium Development Goals and For Malaria	www.mdghealthenvoy.org/
Ric O'Barry	The Dolphin Project	http://dolphinproject.org/
Richard Rockefeller	Rockefeller Brothers Fund	www.rbf.org/post/ fund-mourns-loss-richard-rockefeller
Richard Rockefeller	Médecins Sans Frontières (Doctors Without Borders)	www.msf.org/
Ted Turner	United Nations Foundation	www.unfoundation.org/
Tom Freston	ONE	www.one.org/
Wendy Kopp	Teach for America	www.teachforamerica.org/
Yang Lan	Sun Culture Foundation	www.sunculturefoundation.com/

INDEX

Note: Page numbers in *italics* indicate photographs and illustrations.

disaster relief *(cont.)*
  and Hurricane Katrina, 165
  Indian Ocean tsunami, 2–3
  and the Schwab Foundation, 68
  and September 11 attacks, 143
  and the "wounded healer" principle, 28–29
Doctors Without Borders (Médecins Sans
    Frontières [MSF]), 74, 208–12, 216, 314
documentaries, 58, 72, 80–81, 85, 89
dog meat trade, 61
The Dolphin Project, 89, 314
dolphins, 80–89, 314
Dongier, Philippe, 64
donor fatigue, 264–66
Door County YMCA, 266
dopamine, 25
Drayton, Bill, 69
Dunn, Elizabeth, xix, 11, 12–14
Duty Free Shoppers, 246
dynastic wealth, 208

Earle, Sylvia, 92
Earnshaw, David, 280–81
Earth Day, 83
Earth Echo International, 58, 314
Earth Island Institute, 89
education philanthropies, 109–15, 116, 271
efficacy of philanthropy, 26–27, 213
Eliot, George, 267
empathy, 49, 138
"encore careers," 67–68
environmental protection
  and activism, 71–72, 74
  and Earth Day, 83
  and family volunteerism, 200
  and pursuit of one's calling, 56–59
  and rewards of philanthropy, 225
  and tips for successful family
    philanthropy, 198
  and Turner, 168
epidemiological studies, 309n3
Erskine, K. H., 16
eudaimonia, xviii
euphoria, xviii–xix
European Management Symposium, 182
Every Mother Counts, 280, 313
existential crises, 42
Eychaner, Fred, 297

family philanthropies
  and celebrations, 202–4
  and couples, 201–2
  and effective planning, 194–98
  effect on volunteering on families, 199–201
  and the Giving Pledge, 176–79
  and in-house philanthropy advising, xv
  motivations for family philanthropy,
    169–76
  personal values and connections, 179–81
  potential pitfalls, 191–93
  and reciprocity, 204–15, 216
  Salwen family example, 189–91
  Turner family example, 167–69
  and voluntourism, 201
  and the World Economic Forum, 182–89
Feeney, Chuck, 245
feminism, 150
financial apartheid, 120–21
flexibility in giving, 196
Flipper (television), 82, 86
food allergies, 157
Forbes, Steve, 117
Forbes 400 Lifetime Achievement Award
    for Social Entrepreneurship, 117
Forum of Young Global Leaders, 186
Fossey, Dian, 61–62
Foster, David
  and anonymous giving, 249–51
  on inherited wealth, 172–73
  and motivations for philanthropy, 259
  philanthropy information, 313
  and rewards of philanthropy, 236–39
  and voluntourism, 201
founder's syndrome, 101–2
Fox, Michael J., 161–62
France, 125, 130
Francis of Assisi, 4
Frankl, Viktor, 36, 38, 39, 40
Franklin, Benjamin, 258
Fredrickson, Barbara, 25
Freston, Tom, xxiii, 66, 253, 276
Freud, Sigmund, 39, 155
Fulbright scholarships, 120
functional magnetic resonance imaging
    (fMRI), 6–7, 10
fund-raising
  and anonymous giving, 248